AIRCRAFT OF WORLD WAR I
1914–1918

**THE ESSENTIAL
AIRCRAFT IDENTIFICATION GUIDE**

AIRCRAFT OF WORLD WAR I
1914–1918

JACK HERRIS
AND BOB PEARSON

amber
BOOKS

First published in 2010 by
Amber Books Ltd
74–77 White Lion Street
London N1 9PF
United Kingdom
www.amberbooks.co.uk

A catalogue record for this book is available from the British Library.

ISBN: 978-1-906626-65-5

Distributed in the UK by
Casemate Ltd

17 Cheap Street
Newbury
RG14 5DD
www.casematepublishing.co.uk

Project Editor: James Bennett
Design: Hawes Design
Picture Research: Terry Forshaw

Printed in China

SPECIFICATIONS
The specifications in this book have been derived from many sources. In some cases original sources do not agree and the most generally known or well-accepted values are given. Unfortunately, in many cases certain performance specifications either were never measured or have not survived. Aircraft performance specifications are also subject to measurement errors and, frequently, lack of correction to standard atmospheric conditions. Furthermore, for WWI aircraft, which did not have superchargers, maximum speed normally decreased with altitude, and the maximum speed for different aircraft as recorded in the specifications sometimes was measured at different altitudes. In these cases the highest recorded speed is given.

PERFORMANCE VARIATIONS
The actual performance of individual aircraft in operational service was often lower than the performance of aircraft prototypes under test. Under factory test conditions the aircraft were normally fitted with well-maintained engines using good quality fuel and tuned and maintained by excellent mechanics for maximum performance. Furthermore, prototypes were flown by experienced test pilots who were usually more skilled than typical front-line pilots and could achieve better performance from the aircraft. Finally, aircraft at the Front deteriorated over time due to normal wear and tear. Additionally, wood airframes could absorb water, increasing weight and sometimes warping the airframe, both of which reduced performance. For all these reasons, the speed and climb rate of WWI aircraft in combat cannot be known with precision and is only approximated by the specifications in this book.

Contents

European Military Strengths 1914

Central Powers
Allied
Neutral

ICELAND

Norwegian Sea

Faeroe Islands

Finland

Helsingfors
St. Petersburg

Christiana
Stockholm

R U S S I A N

Riga

E M P I R E

Vitebsk

Minsk

Königsberg

North Sea

DENMARK

2,900,000
232
12

3,115,000
244
14

Glasgow
Edinburgh

U N I T E D
K I N G D O M

400,000
113
6

Hamburg
Berlin

Warsaw

P o l a n d

Dublin
Liverpool
Hull

Birmingham
Amsterdam

Bristol
London

450,000
29
0

NETHERLANDS

BELGIUM
Brussels

G E R M A N   E M P I R E

Frankfurt
Prague

Krakow

Lemberg

1,950,000
79
3

Calais

L

Paris

Munich

Vienna

Budapest

2,100,000
162
6

Orléans

F R A N C E

Bern
SWITZERLAND

A U S T R O - H U N G A R I A N   E M P I R E

ATLANTIC
OCEAN

Brest

Lyon
Milan

Trieste

ROMANIA

Bucharest

Bordeaux

Venice

Belgrade

A Coruña

Genoa

SERBIA

BULGARIA

SAN MARINO

MONACO

Adriatic Sea

Sarajevo

MONTE NEGRO

Sofia

Marseille

ANDORRA

ALBANIA

Corsica

Rome

I T A L Y

Naples

1,500,000
0
0

Barcelona

Madrid

S P A I N

Balearic Is.

Sardinia

1,200,000
220
9

Smyr

PORTUGAL

Alicante

Athens

Lisbon

Cádiz
Almería

GREECE

Tangier
Gibraltar
to Great Britain

M e d i t e r r a n e a n

Tunis

Crete

Algeria
to France

Tunisia
to France

S e a

Chapter 1

Opening Moves

The potential of the airplane for reconnaissance and bombing was obvious to most military leaders. The key question was, could this immature and hazardous new technology actually deliver practical results?

Once combat was joined, airplanes quickly proved themselves to be vital reconnaissance platforms and, after trench warfare had eliminated the cavalry's reconnaissance ability on the Western Front, aerial reconnaissance proved absolutely essential.

◀ **European Military Strengths, 1914**

The major combatants are shown at left with the number of army troops, aircraft and airships they had on their entry into the war at the beginning of August 1914. The Ottoman Empire joined the Central Powers on 29 October 1914, Italy joined the Allies on 23 May 1915, Bulgaria joined the Central Powers in October 1915, and in April 1916 Romania joined the Allies. America joined the Allies as a belligerent on 6 April 1917. The Treaty of Brest-Litovsk was negotiated in December 1917 ending Russia's participation in the war. On 11 November 1918 the Armistice was signed, ending the war with Germany's defeat.

Expectations and concerns
1910–1914

Although the airplane was still unproven in war at this time, no combatant nation could afford to ignore the new technology.

BALLOONS AND AIRSHIPS were the first craft to carry people aloft and, as early as the American Civil War in 1862, tethered balloons were used for military observation. Though early airplanes were largely experimental curiosities, military leaders quickly saw their potential for more practical use. The first flight of a heavier-than-air craft by the American Wright brothers on 17 December 1903 was quickly followed by flights of airplanes in other countries.

Great military potential – and skepticism

While some saw the airplane's military potential for reconnaissance and bombing there was a great deal of skepticism about whether the early airplanes would prove reliable and able to perform in combat conditions. Before the war debate raged over the practical value of airplanes.

Despite this disagreement, all the major combatant powers had small air services when war broke out, and the adjacent table gives the strengths of the various air arms. Perhaps surprisingly, the Imperial

AVIATION STRENGTH AT THE START OF WWI		
Country	Airplanes	Airships
Austria-Hungary	79	3
Germany	232	12
Subtotal Central Powers	**311**	**15**
France	162	6
Russia	244	14
United Kingdom	113	6
Subtotal Entente	**519**	**26**

Russian Air Service was larger than that of any other power. Once combat attrition set in, however, Russia was unable to replace her losses nearly as quickly as the other powers due to her small aviation industry.

Early reconnaissance airplanes were generally two-seaters with a pilot and observer to provide visual reconnaissance. Visibility from the cockpit was a key concern, and high stability was generally thought to be important to successful reconnaissance.

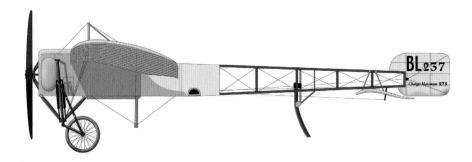

▲ **Blériot XI**

Escadrille BL 10 / Belfort Aerodrome, France / December 1913

A 1910 design, the Blériot XI was in reconnaissance service with France, Britain, Russia and Italy at the start of the war. Possessing modest performance and reliability, it was replaced by newer, more effective types as soon as practical. This example was flown by pilot Zarapoff from Belfort in December 1913. There are no unit or individual markings on the plane, just a serial number.

Specifications

Crew: 1

Powerplant: 1 x 37kW (50hp) or 60kW (80hp)
Gnome rotary engine

Maximum speed: 120km/h (75mph)

Endurance: 3 hours 30 mins

Service ceiling: 2000m (6560ft)

Dimensions: span 8.9m (29ft 3.5in);
length 7.65m (25ft 1in); height 2.5m (8ft 2in)

Weight: 800kg (1764lb) loaded

Armament: None

Early reconnaissance successes
AUGUST–NOVEMBER 1914

Aerial reconnaissance was decisive in the early battles of Tannenberg and the Battle of France, immediately proving the military value of the airplane.

DESPITE LIMITED PERFORMANCE and reliability, the fledgling air forces gave crucial service in visual reconnaissance, fully vindicating the hopes of their supporters. Compared to cavalry, airplanes were much faster, could easily overfly obstacles like rivers and enemy troop concentrations, and enjoyed a much broader view from above ground level. However, airplanes were fragile and grounded by bad weather.

Tannenberg
Within weeks of the start of the conflict, aerial reconnaissance was crucial to the fighting on both fronts. The first important victory enabled by aerial reconnaissance was the German defeat of the Russian army at Tannenberg in East Prussia. With the bulk of her army on the decisive Western Front, Germany was threatened by the huge Russian army on the Eastern Front. On 23 August the German airship *Z.V* detected Russian advances that enabled the out-numbered German army to get in position in time to surprise and defeat them. On 29 August a second

Russian thrust in the area was detected by airplanes, again enabling Germany to position their army in time to defeat the Russian attack. As a result, the Russian Second Army surrendered on 31 August.

Schlieffen Plan shattered
The next crucial victory made possible by aerial reconnaissance was in France, and possibly saved the Entente (at this time France, Britain, and Russia, also called the Allies) from early defeat. The key objective of the German Schlieffen Plan was to quickly capture Paris, thereby defeating France before her allies could effectively intervene. Holding on their left and center, a strengthened German right flank attacked through Belgium and northern France toward the French capital. German troops had to march several hundred miles against strong French resistance to succeed, making the plan problematic militarily. However, the plan's fatal flaw was diplomatic; by violating Belgian neutrality, Britain was brought into the war against Germany, which eventually proved decisive.

▲ Rumpler Taube
Unknown unit / Eastern Front / c.1914–15

Taube designs were inherently stable and safe, winning them popularity in prewar Germany. However, they were also slow with poor manoeuvrability and downward visibility, and were soon replaced by faster, more manoeuvrable biplanes. The only markings are national insignia.

Specifications

Crew: 2	Dimensions: span 14m (45ft);
Powerplant: 1 x 74.6kW (100hp) Mercedes D.I engine	length 10.2m (33ft 6in); height 3.2m (10ft 5in)
Maximum speed: n/a	Weight: 971kg (2142lb) max take-off
Range: n/a	Armament: None
Service ceiling: n/a	

Specifications

Crew: 2

Powerplant: 1 X 74.5kW (100hp) Mercedes
 D.I engine

Maximum speed: 90km/h (55.9mph)

Endurance: Unknown

Service ceiling: About 2500m (8200ft)

Dimensions: 14.5m (47ft 7in);
 length 9.0m (29ft 6in); height unknown

Weight: 1132kg (2496lb) max take-off

Armament: Light bombs

▲ LVG B.I

Unknown Feld Flieger Abteilung / c.1915

The LVG B.I was the most numerous German reconnaissance biplane at the start of the war because of its reliability, stability, and good handling characteristics. Like most B.Is, this example is in plain finish with no unit or personal markings.

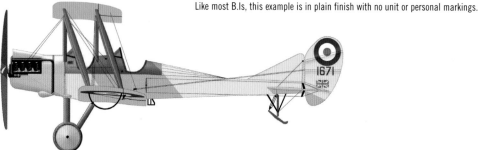

▲ Royal Aircraft Factory BE.2C

No. 6 Squadron, RFC / France / April 1915

In the early war years the BE.2 was the most widely used British reconnaissance airplane. It was designed before the war, when great stability was thought to be very important for reconnaissance. This characteristic made the BE.2 a safe airplane to fly, but also made it especially vulnerable to fighter attack from the Autumn of 1915. The aircraft is shown as of April 1915; the rudder displays an early style of insignia and there are no unit markings.

Specifications

Crew: 2	Dimensions: span 12.42m (40ft 9in); length
Powerplant: 1 x 67kW (90hp) RAF 1a inline	8.31m (27ft 3in); height 3.66m (12ft)
engine	Weight: 971kg (2142lb) max take-off
Maximum speed: 120km/h (75mph)	Armament: 1 x 7.62mm (0.303in) Vickers MG
Endurance: 3 hours 15 minutes	in front cockpit
Service ceiling: 3048m (10,000ft)	

▲ Albatros B.I

Feld Flieger Abteilung 2 / Western Front / late 1914–early 1915

The Albatros B.I was a mainstay of the early German reconnaissance units because of its robust reliability and good handling characteristics. This example, named for the hero of Tannenburg, was flown by Wunderlich and *Oblt.* Schulz. There are no unit markings.

Specifications

Crew: 2	Dimensions: span 14.48m (47ft 6in);
Powerplant: 1 X 74.6kW (100hp) Mercedes D.I	length 8m (26ft 3in); height 3.15m
engine	(10ft 4in)
Maximum speed: 100km/h (62.1mph)	Weight: 1197kg (2639lb) max take-off
Endurance: 4 hours	Armament: None
Service ceiling: 3000m (9842ft)	

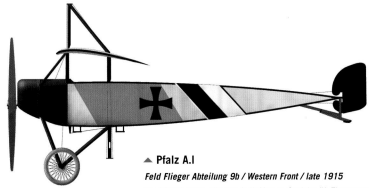

Specifications

Crew: 2

Powerplant: 1 X 60kW (80hp) Oberursel U.O
engine

Maximum speed: 135km/h (83.4mph)

Endurance: 4 hours

Service ceiling: 3000m (9842ft)

Dimensions: span 11.2m (36ft 9in);
length 6.9m (22ft 7in); height 3.4m
(11ft 2in)

Weight: 593kg (1309lb) max take-off

Armament: None

▲ Pfalz A.I

Feld Flieger Abteilung 9b / Western Front / late 1915

The Pfalz A.I was a license-built Morane-Saulnier 'L'. They were used in small
numbers, primarily by Bavarian units because the Pfalz company was located in
Bavaria. The black and white stripes are the unit markings.

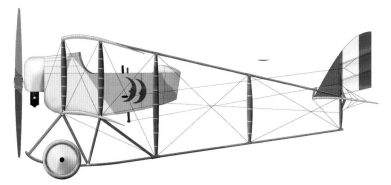

▲ Caudron G.3

Unknown Training Unit / Juvisy Aerodrome, France / 1916

Despite being a tractor biplane, the Caudron G.3 used the high-drag pusher
configuration, giving it a very modest performance. The G.3 was widely used as a
reconnaissance plane and trainer by France and Italy and in smaller numbers by
Russia and Britain. The moon marking is an individual insignia.

Specifications

Crew: 2

Powerplant: Various rotary engines of
52–74.6kW (70–100hp)

Maximum speed: 105km/h (65mph)

Endurance: 3hours 30 mins

Service ceiling: 3050m (10,000ft)

Dimensions: span 13.26m (43ft 6in);
length 6.89m (22ft 7in); height 2.59m
(8ft 4in)

Weight: 710kg (1565lb)

Armament: Various combinations of rifles
and pistols

▼ Caudron G.4

Escadrille C 66 / France 1917

The Caudron G.4 was a twin-engine development of the earlier G.3. The additional
power gave the G.4 better speed, climb rate, and ceiling and enabled it to carry
two machine guns. Unfortunately, it retained the high-drag pusher
configuration, which limited its performance. The checks are an
individual identification marking.

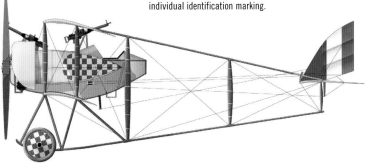

Specifications

Crew: 2

Powerplant: 2 x 60kW (80hp) Le Rhone
rotary engines

Maximum speed: 130km/h (80mph)

Endurance: 5 hours

Service ceiling: 4300m (14,107ft)

Dimensions: span 13.26m (43ft 6in);
length 7.16m (23ft 6in);
height 2.55m (8ft 6in)

Weight: 1232kg (2716lb) max take-off

Armament: 1–2 x 7.7mm (0.303in) MGs

GERMAN CLASS A UNARMED, SINGLE-ENGINE MONOPLANES AT THE FRONT

Manufacturer and Type	1914			1915						1916		
	31 Aug	31 Oct	31 Dec	28 Feb	30 Apr	30 Jun	31 Aug	31 Oct	31 Dec	28 Feb	30 Apr	30 Jun
Albatros												
A/13	5	–	1	–	–	2	–	–	–	–	–	–
A/14	–	–	1	–	1	8	–	–	–	–	–	–
A.	–	2	5	7	8	–	–	–	–	–	–	–
A.I	2	–	–	–	–	–	2	2	–	–	–	–
A.II	–	–	–	–	–	–	2	–	–	–	–	–
Fokker												
A/14	–	–	2	–	–	–	1	–	2	1	–	–
A.	–	5	1	15	–	–	–	–	–	–	–	–
A.I	–	–	6	8	7	10	2	3	2	1	1	–
A.II	–	–	–	–	13	4	4	4	4	3	2	–
A.III	–	–	–	–	1	3	1	2	–	2	2	–
Gotha												
A/13	13	3	6	2	15	–	–	–	–	–	–	–
A/14	3	5	14	4	2	4	–	2	2	2	2	1
A.I	–	5	4	–	–	1	–	2	–	–	–	–
Halberstadt												
A.II	–	–	2	5	5	3	–	–	–	–	–	–
Hirth												
A.	1	–	–	–	–	–	–	–	–	–	–	–
Jeannin												
A/13	6	–	–	–	–	–	–	–	–	–	–	–
A/14	3	9	7	16	3	1	–	–	–	–	–	–
Kondor												
A/13	–	–	1	–	–	–	–	–	–	–	–	–
A/14	–	1	3	6	1	–	–	–	–	–	–	–
LVG												
A.	1	–	–	–	–	–	–	–	–	–	–	–
A/14	–	–	–	–	–	1	–	–	–	–	–	–
Otto												
A.	–	2	–	–	–	–	–	–	–	–	–	–
Parasol												
A.	–	1	2	–	–	–	–	–	–	–	–	–
A.I	–	–	–	–	–	–	1	–	–	–	–	–
Pfalz												
A.I	–	–	–	–	–	–	–	3	–	–	–	–
A.II	–	–	–	–	–	–	–	–	–	–	–	1
A/15	–	–	–	–	–	–	–	–	1	1	–	–
Rumpler												
A/13	2	–	–	–	–	–	–	–	–	–	–	–
A/14	8	3	–	–	–	–	–	–	–	–	–	–
Total	44	36	55	63	56	37	13	18	11	10	7	2

Regardless, the German army advanced on Paris, but as they neared the city a gap developed between two German armies. French aerial reconnaissance spotted the gap and on 6 September the Allies attacked it, starting the Battle of the Marne. Thanks to aerial reconnaissance, the German advance was halted, Paris was saved, and the Allies avoided quick defeat.

Both sides dug in, and by mid November the Western Front had settled into the bloody stalemate of trench warfare.

Trench warfare
DECEMBER 1914

When trench warfare eliminated the cavalry's ability to carry out reconnaissance, aviation remained the sole means, making it indispensable in combat.

THE MAJOR IMPACT of trench warfare on aviation was to immediately increase its importance. At a stroke cavalry, the army's traditional reconnaissance arm, was unable to function in that role. Only aircraft could fly over the trenches to observe what the enemy was doing. Cavalry still had a role to play on the more open Eastern Front, but the more critical Western Front, where both sides knew the war would be decided, had set the precedent for aircraft being the essential reconnaissance tool.

Specifications

Crew: 2
Powerplant: 1 x 74.6kW (100hp) Mercedes
  D.I engine
Maximum speed: 100km/h (62mph)
Endurance: 4 hours
Service ceiling: 3000m (9842.5ft)
Dimensions: span 14.48m (47ft 6in);
  length 8m (26ft 3in); height 3.15m
  (10ft 4in)
Weight: 1197kg (2639lb) max take-off
Armament: None

▲ **Albatros B.I**

Feld Flieger Abteilung 2 / Western Front / late 1914–early 1915

The reliable Albatros B.I saw widespread service on both Eastern and Western Fronts. This example is named in honor of Otto Weddigen, the captain of *U-9* that sank the Royal Navy cruisers *Cressy*, *Aboukir* and *Hogue* in a single action on 22 September 1914. There are no unit markings.

▲ **Aviatik B.I**

Feld Flieger Abteilung 34 / Cunel Aerodrome, France / 1915

The Aviatik B.I represented one of the three main families of early German reconnaissance airplanes, the others being Albatros and LVG. A reliable if not brilliant performer, this example was assigned to *Hptm* Hugo Geyer and flew from Cunel Aerodrome. The only distinguishing marking is its military serial number.

Specifications

Crew: 2
Powerplant: 1 x 75kW (100hp) Mercedes D.I
  inline engine
Maximum speed: 100km/h (62mph)
Endurance: 4 hours
Service ceiling: n/a

Dimensions: span 12.40m (40ft 8in);
  length 8m (26ft 3in); height 3.3m (10ft 10in)
Weight: 1090kg (2403lb) loaded
Armament: Generally none. Sometimes the
  observer carried a carbine or a pistol

Specifications

Crew: 2

Powerplant: 1 x 52kW (70hp) Renault 8-
cylinder Vee piston engine

Maximum speed: 116km/h (72mph)

Endurance: 3 hours 45 mins

Service ceiling: 3800m (12,470ft)

Dimensions: span 15.77m (51ft 9in);
length 9.30m (30ft 5in); height 3.15m
(10ft 4in)

Weight: 928kg (2045lb) max take-off

Armament: initially none, some had rifles and
revolvers and later a 7.7mm (.303) Lewis MG

▲ **Farman MF.11**

No.16 Squadron, RFC / Western Front / Summer 1915

The Maurice Farman series was widely used by France for reconnaissance and occasional light bombing and air combat early in the war. In addition, Maurice Farmans were also widely exported to Allied air services. They were slow and, like all pushers, vulnerable to fighter attack. The significance of the black lines on the nacelle is unknown; they may have been for decoration.

GERMAN MISCELLANEOUS VISUAL RECONNAISSANCE AIRPLANES AT THE FRONT

Manufacturer and Type	1914			1915						1916		
	31 Aug	31 Oct	31 Dec	28 Feb	30 Apr	30 Jun	31 Aug	31 Oct	31 Dec	28 Feb	30 Apr	30 Jun
Brandenburg		3										
DFW Mars	1	2		5								
Farman		1										
Parasol			1	1	5	17	18	15	2	1	–	–
TOTAL	1	6	1	6	5	17	18	15	2	1		

The beginning of air combat
AUGUST 1914–MARCH 1915

Primitive early warplanes were soon replaced by more robust, powerful airplanes able to carry weapons, leading to frequent air combat.

THE FIRST RECONNAISSANCE planes were generally unarmed. The crews often carried a pistol, and on the Eastern Front it was common to carry a rifle to hunt game for survival if the crew came down and had to make their way back to base on foot. Of course, it was not long before crewmen were using these weapons to take shots at one another as they passed on their reconnaissance duties. In addition, crewmen sometimes took grenades, darts or even bricks to drop on the enemy during their reconnaissance missions. While dangerous to individuals, these efforts were ineffective in a wider sense.

Manufacturer and Type	1914 31 Aug	31 Oct	31 Dec	1915 28 Feb	30 Apr	30 Jun	31 Aug	31 Oct	31 Dec	1916 28 Feb	30 Apr	30 Jun	31 Aug	31 Oct	31 Dec	1917 28 Feb	30 Apr	30 Jun	31 Aug	31 Oct	31 Dec
AEG																					
B.I	3	2	3	8	1	2	–	1	2	–	–	–	–	–	–	–	1	–	–	–	–
B.II	–	–	–	–	8	8	9	–	–	–	–	–	–	–	–	–	–	–	–	–	–
Albatros																					
B/12	1	–	–	–	–	–	–	–	–	–	–	–	–	–	–	–	–	–	–	–	–
B/13	6	3	7	3	–	100	2	–	–	–	–	–	–	–	–	–	–	–	–	–	–
B.	–	2	3	41	55	–	–	–	–	–	–	–	–	–	–	–	–	–	–	–	–
B.I	18	27	55	87	157	145	116	90	42	26	7	3	3	5	1	–	–	–	1	1	2
B.II	5	9	7	14	27	30	149	212	185	92	49	30	5	6	12	3	5	4	3	3	2
B.IIa	–	–	–	–	–	–	–	–	–	–	–	–	–	–	–	–	–	–	–	–	–
B.Lf	–	–	–	–	–	–	–	–	–	–	–	–	–	–	–	–	1	1	–	–	–
Aviatik																					
B/12	1	–	–	–	–	–	–	–	–	–	–	–	–	–	–	–	–	–	–	–	–
B/13	34	24	13	4	4	2	1	1	–	–	1	1	–	–	–	–	–	1	–	–	v
B.	–	–	–	17	23	–	–	–	–	–	–	–	–	–	–	–	–	–	–	–	–
B.I	12	43	51	28	53	48	35	20	11	–	5	–	–	–	–	–	–	–	–	–	–
B.II	–	–	–	–	–	1	29	38	32	18	7	2	–	–	1	–	–	–	–	–	–
B.III	–	–	–	–	–	–	–	–	–	2	–	–	–	–	–	–	–	–	–	–	–
Brandenburg																					
B.I	–	–	2	1	–	–	–	–	–	–	–	–	–	–	–	–	–	–	–	–	–
B.II	–	–	–	1	–	–	–	–	–	–	–	–	–	–	–	–	–	–	–	–	–
DFW																					
B.I	2	17	12	2	–	–	–	1	–	–	–	–	–	–	–	–	–	–	–	–	–

GERMAN CLASS B UNARMED, SINGLE-ENGINE BIPLANES AT THE FRONT (table continued on page 17)

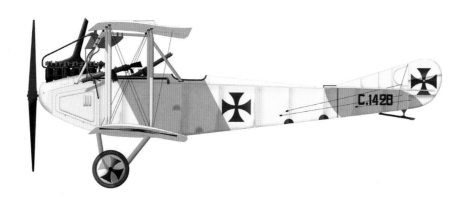

▲ Aviatik C.I

Flieger Abteilung (A) 206 / Western Front / c.1916

The Aviatik C.I was an armed, more powerful replacement for the earlier, unarmed B-types. Unlike other German two-seaters, the Aviatiks retained the older seating arrangement with the observer in front. Armament was two machine guns, one mounted to a rail on each side of the cockpit.

Specifications

Crew: 2

Powerplant: 1 x 112kW (150hp) Benz Bz.III inline engine

Maximum speed: 120km/h (75mph)

Endurance: 3 hours

Service ceiling: 3500m (11,485ft)

Dimensions: span 12.5m (40ft); length 7.93m (26ft); height 2.95m (9ft 8in)

Weight: 1245kg (2744lb) max take-off

Armament: 2 x 7.92mm (0.312in) flexible MG

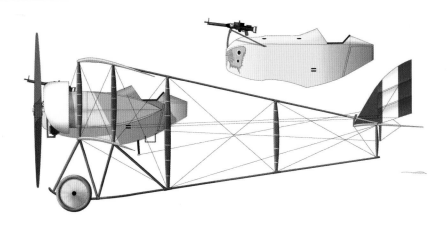

▲ **Caudron G.4**

Franco-Belgian Escadrille C 74 / Western Front / 1915

The G.4 retained the outdated pusher configuration, which made it vulnerable to fighter attack from the rear, yet it was widely used by France and Italy and in smaller numbers by Russia and Britain.

Specifications

Crew: 2

Powerplant: 2 x 60kW (80hp) Le Rhone rotary
  engines

Maximum speed: 130km/h (80mph)

Endurance: 5 hours

Service ceiling: 4300m (14,107ft)

Dimensions: span 13.26m (43ft 6in);
  length 7.16m (23ft 6in);
  height 2.55m (8ft 6in)

Weight: 1232kg (2716lb) max take-off

Armament: 1–2 x 7.7mm (0.303in) MGs

▲ **Albatros C.I**

Unknown Unit / Eastern Front / 1916

The Albatros C.I was a more powerful, armed development of the earlier Albatros B-type reconnaissance airplanes. It inherited the robust reliability and good handling characteristics of its predecessors and served widely on both the Eastern and Western Fronts. This example has no unit or personal markings.

Specifications

Crew: 2

Powerplant: 1 x 112kW (150hp) Benz Bz.III
  inline piston engine or 1 x 119kW (160hp)
  Mercedes D.III inline piston engine

Maximum speed: 132km/h (82mph)

Endurance: 2 hours 30 mins

Service ceiling: 3000m (9845ft)

Dimensions: span 13.8m (45ft 4in);
  length 7.85m (25ft 9in); height 2.96m
  (9ft 9in)

Weight: 1350kg (2976lb) loaded

Armament: 1 x 7.92mm (0.313in) LMG 14
  Parabellum trainable rearward-firing
  MG

The first air victory of the war occurred on 25 August 1914 when three RFC aircraft of No. 2 Squadron forced down a German Taube (Dove). Not long after, on 30 August, Ltn von Hiddessen in an Aviatik bombed Paris. Two days later an RFC airplane dropped two bombs on German cavalry, the first such RFC mission. The first example of true air combat between a pair of enemy airplanes armed with machine guns occurred on 5 October, and the French airplane downed a German Aviatik for the world's first true air-to-air victory. These first encounters were primitive in nature and tactics consisted mainly of manoeuvring to give the gunner a good field of fire while denying the enemy observer

The vibrant butterfly on the nose of this Franco-Belgian Caudron G.4 was a personal insignia, not a unit marking. The side view is shown at left.

a similar opportunity. In reality, aircrew were in more peril from engine failures and accidents than from enemy action.

Bombing begins

Bombing quickly gained popularity as a military tactic. The RFC made its first raid into Germany on 22 September, and on 8 October two RNAS Sopwith Tabloids bombed Düsseldorf, destroying Zeppelin

Z.IX in its shed. On 21 November three RNAS Avro 504 aircraft bombed the Zeppelin sheds at Lake Constance, destroying another airship. Two days later the French formed G.B.1 (Groupe de Bombardement 1) for the purpose of bombing Germany.

The aerial arms race was now on. Airplanes that went to war at this time lacked the power and payload capacity to carry many bombs or machine guns, but were quickly followed by more robust and powerful types designed to carry such weapons. Aviation technology was still in its infancy, but the intention for using it aggressively was clearly demonstrated in the first weeks of the war. Aviation's impact was to grow with its technical development.

GERMAN CLASS B UNARMED, SINGLE-ENGINE BIPLANES AT THE FRONT (continued)

Manufacturer and Type	1914 31 Aug	31 Oct	31 Dec	1915 28 Feb	30 Apr	30 Jun	31 Aug	31 Oct	31 Dec	1916 28 Feb	30 Apr	30 Jun	31 Aug	31 Oct	31 Dec	1917 28 Feb	30 Apr	30 Jun
Euler B/13	2	–	–	–	–	–	–	–	–	–	–	–	–	–	–	–	–	–
B.I	3	1	2	–	–	–	3	–	–	1	1	–	–	–	–	–	–	–
B.II	–	–	–	–	–	–	5	–	–	–	–	–	–	–	–	–	–	–
Fokker B/13	1	–	–	–	–	–	–	–	–	–	–	–	–	–	–	–	–	–
B.I	–	–	–	1	3	12	4	4	–	1	35	–	–	–	–	–	–	–
Gotha B.I	–	1	–	–	–	1	–	–	5	–	3	–	–	–	–	–	–	–
Halberstadt B.I	–	–	–	–	–	2	3	4	2	1	–	–	–	–	–	–	–	1
B.II	–	–	–	–	–	–	3	3	8	2	5	3	–	–	–	–	–	–
B.III	–	–	–	–	–	–	–	5	6	2	5	3	–	–	–	–	–	–
B.	–	–	–	–	–	–	–	–	–	–	–	–	–	–	–	1	1	–
LVG B.	22	17	22	62	65	15	–	–	–	–	–	–	–	–	–	–	–	–
B/13	30	14	13	1	3	9	7	2	–	2	–	–	–	–	–	–	–	–
B.I	32	42	60	61	106	124	94	37	14	7	6	4	–	–	4	–	–	–
B.II	–	–	12	16	31	52	95	165	77	40	16	10	5	3	2	–	–	–
B.III	–	–	–	–	–	–	–	–	6	–	–	–	–	–	–	–	–	–
Otto B/14	–	–	–	–	1	–	–	–	–	–	–	–	–	–	–	–	–	–
B.I	–	1	–	–	–	–	8	–	–	–	–	–	–	–	–	–	–	–
B.	–	–	–	–	3	–	–	–	–	–	–	–	–	–	–	–	–	–
Roland B.I	–	–	–	–	–	–	–	–	–	–	32	–	–	–	–	4	1	–
Rumpler B.I	1	6	21	32	41	38	17	14	6	5	4	2	–	8	–	–	–	–
Unidentified	–	–	–	–	–	–	–	–	–	–	–	–	–	–	–	1	–	–

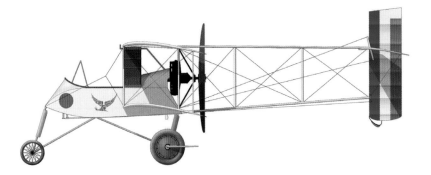

▲ **Voisin LA**

Escadrille V 210 / Rosnay Aerodrome / France 1916

The Voisin was an early French pusher series that served widely with Allied air services. Most were used for reconnaissance, but others were armed with a 37mm cannon for attacking other airplanes, However, the Voisins were too slow to catch them and the single-shot cannon was ineffective against moving targets, so they were primarily used for ground attack. The winged snail, in red, white, or black, was used as the unit marking in tribute to the type's low speed. The red circle was a personal marking.

Specifications

Crew: 2

Powerplant: 1 x 89kW (120hp) Salmson M9 radial engine

Maximum speed: 98km/h (61mph)

Range: 200km (124 miles)

Service ceiling: 4000m (13,120ft)

Dimensions: span 14.74m (48ft 4in); length 9.5m (31ft 2in); height 2.95m (9ft 8in)

Weight: 1350kg (2976lb) loaded

Armament: 1 x 8mm (0.31in) Hotchkiss MG

Observation balloons
1914–1918

Observation balloons were important for local reconnaissance and were even used to spot artillery fire. They were a valuable tool and were rapidly targeted by enemy aviators.

OBSERVATION BALLOONS HAD first been used in the American Civil War, and by 1914 all the combatants had them and continued to use them throughout the war. Ground tethers held observation balloons in position, and the observers used binoculars to scout enemy positions. Balloons became more important and more numerous on the Western Front when the fighting transitioned from a war of movement to static trench warfare. In addition to visual observation, these aerial observation posts were used to direct artillery fire; the observer normally had a telephone line to the ground and could direct the fall of shot.

Unarmed, airborne and dangerous

The balloons became a critical link directing artillery in addition to their basic observation role, even though they remained unarmed. As combat aircraft developed, the balloons became important targets to destroy. Even if a balloon was not as evasive a target as another airplane, attacking one still took a great deal of courage and tenacity. A ring of anti-aircraft guns defended each balloon and, when practical, defending fighters were positioned overhead to shield against air attack. Filled with highly flammable hydrogen gas, the balloons were vulnerable to being ignited. However, the attacker had to run a gauntlet of anti-aircraft fire and defending fighters to reach the balloon, and then avoid being burned up by the flaming balloon itself. Balloon observers had large, bulky parachutes to use for escaping under attack. Upon sighting an attacking fighter, a balloon could be pulled to the ground by a powered winch while the observer took to his parachute.

Balloon designs evolved to improve stability in windy conditions. Hydrogen was either brought to the site and stored in cylinders, or was generated on site by a cumbersome mobile chemical plant.

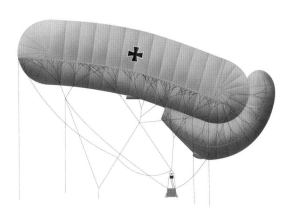

▲ **Drachen observation balloon**

Unknown Unit

The *Drachen* (sausage) balloon served with both sides;
this is a German example.

▼ **Caquot observation balloon**

Unknown Unit

The Caquot design was an improvement on the *Drachen*; it was more stable in
windy conditions than the *Drachen* and gradually replaced it.

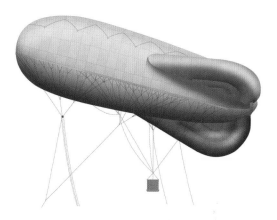

Specifications

Crew: 1–2	Dimensions: diameter 9.75m (32ft);
Powerplant: None	length 19.8m (65ft); height n/a
Maximum speed: n/a	Capacity: 911.8 cubic metres
Observation range: 10km (6.5 miles)	(32,000 cubic feet)
Service ceiling: 1219m (4000ft)	Armament: None

Specifications

Crew: 1–2	Dimensions: diameter 8m (27ft);
Powerplant: None	length 28m (92ft); height n/a
Maximum speed: n/a	Capacity: 930 cubic metres
Observation range: 10km (6.5 miles)	(32,840 cubic feet)
Service ceiling: 1219m (4000ft)	Armament: None

Airships
1914–1918

Airships had greater range, payload and endurance than early airplanes, making them the initial choice for long-range reconnaissance and bombing.

AT THE BEGINNING of the war, airships competed with airplanes for the leading role in military and naval aviation. Airships had a number of advantages over the early airplanes: they were more reliable; had longer range and greater endurance; and greater payload. But they were big, slow, more vulnerable to hostile gunfire, and costly. Early actions over the battlefronts highlighted their vulnerability as bombers and reconnaissance craft, so they were gradually relegated to naval reconnaissance where their strengths were most important and their vulnerability to ground fire was minimized. Furthermore, airplane performance evolved much faster than that of airships, making the airships increasingly vulnerable to interception by airplanes.

Zeppelins in the lead

Airship technology, especially the large Zeppelins, was one area where Germany lead the world until the end of the war. While Zeppelins were the weapon of choice in the world's first strategic bombing campaign, they were most effective for naval reconnaissance. Allied airships were more useful in anti-submarine warfare than any other role, and numerous smaller airships were in service in this capacity until the Armistice.

Chapter 2

Air Combat Turns Deadly

Aerial reconnaissance and bombing became
more valuable as technology evolved and aircrews gained
operational experience. It became even more important to
stop airplanes from flying over enemy lines, and so air
combat developed. Both sides experimented with multiseat
airplanes with flexible guns, but the synchronized machine
gun fitted to a fast, agile single-seat airplane proved its
worth. Development of fighter tactics soon followed,
and some pilots became expert at downing
other airplanes. As the grim death toll of trench warfare
grew, governments publicized successful fighter pilots in
order to encourage their populations despite the terrible
news from the Front. The fighter ace was born and became
a fixture in the public imagination.

◀ **Royal Aircraft Factory FE.2d**
The gunner of an FE.2d demonstrates how to fire at attacking fighters. The gunner has two flexible Lewis machine guns, while a third Lewis is fixed in place for the pilot. The camera is on the side of the nacelle. The FE.2d was powered by a 186Kw (250hp) Rolls Royce engine. Despite its prewar, pusher design, the FE.2 series was operational at the Front longer than any other design of either side.

The synchronized machine gun
1915–April 1917

There was general agreement that the machine gun was the most practical weapon for air combat, but what was the most effective way to use it?

BEFORE WORLD WAR I MANY people were thinking about air-to-air combat and what might be effective. Machine guns were generally viewed as the weapon of choice but the next question was how to mount them. Should guns be moveable or fixed to fire along the axis of the airplane? If the gun were fixed and the engine was in front, this would involve firing the gun through the propeller arc, an arrangement that would inevitably damage the propeller blades with potentially catastrophic results. The solution would prove to be mechanical synchronizing gear that allowed the bullets to pass between the propeller blades when the gun was fired. Interestingly, Franz Schneider, a Swiss engineer working with Germany's LVG company, patented a synchronizing device in 1912. France's Robert Esnault-Pelterie also patented a machine-gun synchronizing device before the war. Surprisingly, given the interest in such a capability, neither invention was taken up before the war.

Even as World War I was under way, it was still not clear how air combat would be conducted. If most participants thought the machine gun was the most practical weapon, how it should be mounted and employed was a matter of dispute. Following the naval practice of guns mounted in turrets, a number of different aircraft were designed with two crewmembers, a pilot to fly the craft and a gunner to shoot at enemy airplanes. In the Spring of 1915 the Vickers F.B.5, a prewar concept known as the Gunbus, was one of the first such types to see combat, and others followed. To avoid the problem of synchronizing the machine gun, the F.B.5 was designed as a pusher, with the propeller behind the fuselage nacelle, the pilot in the middle, and the gunner in front, where he had the maximum field of fire. The Gunbus was reasonably effective against the slow, unarmed two-seat observation airplanes it met over the Front, but the main difficulty it had was catching them because the F.B.5 was so slow.

Germany had started developing multi-seat, twin-engine battle planes before the war. The *Kampfflugzeug* was conceived as an armoured, twin-engine biplane intended for 'low altitude work amidst enemy fire'. Specifications were submitted to manufacturers in July 1914 and in January 1915 the first AEG *Kampfflugzeug* flew. AEG soon modified

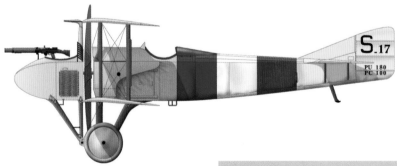

▲ **SPAD A.2**

Unknown Escadrille / France / early 1916

'Pulpit' SPADs such as this type were failures on operations, but their robust structure lead to the excellent SPAD VII and all subsequent SPAD designs to see operational service in the war. The gunner was seated in a nacelle ahead of the propeller and was clearly at risk in case of a crash. This one served in an unknown French escadrille. The fuselage stripes were an individual marking.

Specifications

Crew: 2	Dimensions: span 9.56m (31ft); length 7.30m
Powerplant: 1 x 82kW (110hp) Le Rhône 9J	(23ft 11in) height 2.60m (8ft 6in)
engine	Weight: 735kg (1620lb) max take-off
Maximum speed: 154km/h (95mph)	Armament: 1 x 7.7mm (.303in) Lewis MG
Endurance: 2hrs 30 mins	
Service ceiling: 4297m (14,100ft)	

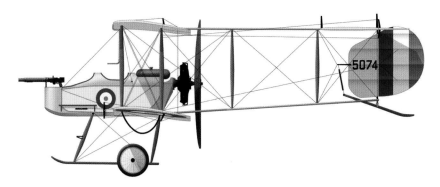

Specifications

Crew: 2	Dimensions: span 11.12m (36ft 6in); length
Powerplant: 1 x 82kW (110hp) Gnôme engine	8.28m (27ft 2in) height 2.60m (8ft 6in)
Maximum speed: 112.65km/h (70mph)	Weight: 930kg (2050lb) max take-off
Endurance: 4hrs 30 mins	Armament: 1 x 7.7mm (.303in) Lewis MG
Service ceiling: 2743m (9000ft)	

▲ **Vickers FB.5**

No.11 Squadron, RFC / Bertangles Aerodrome, France November 1915
The Vickers F.B.5 was based on a prewar concept and served reliably on the Western Front from 1915–16. It was too slow to be very effective intercepting German reconnaissance airplanes but scored some victories and chased many intruders back behind their own lines. Lt G. S. M. Insall was awarded the Victoria Cross for an action in this Gunbus on 7 November 1915.

the design to feature three crewmen, a pilot in the middle and gunners fore and aft. The slow machine was much more effective when used for bombing than for interception, and became the forerunner of German bombers.

Garros and the armoured propeller

While the aviation establishment struggled to come to grips with air combat, a renowned prewar French pioneer pilot, Roland Garros, took the initiative to solve the problem. Garros, who had gained fame in 1913 for being the first person to fly across the Mediterranean, volunteered to fly and was assigned to *Escadrille* M.S. 23. In December 1914 Garros was in Paris and visited Raymond Saulnier, co-owner of Morane-Saulnier, manufacturer of the airplanes Garros was flying. Saulnier had been working with early synchronizers and found that even if the synchronizer was working, sometimes the gun fired late because defects and variations in the bullets made some fire later than others. Sometimes the result was a bullet-hole through the propeller, which could cause the propeller blade to break off, causing severe vibration that could tear the engine out of the airplane, which was clearly a catastrophic situation. Saulnier had experimented with fitting metal bullet deflectors on the propeller to protect it from this potential disaster.

Meanwhile, Garros had become exasperated with the difficulties of trying to manoeuvre his airplane

into position so his observer could get a good shot with a rifle. Garros asked permission to test Saulnier's invention in flight. Many French authorities had strong misgivings about the practicality of precisely manoeuvring an airplane in flight so as to aim the entire airplane at an enemy airplane, but Garros soon received permission. When Garros and his mechanic, Jules Hue, examined Saulnier's deflectors in more detail, Hue determined that the deflectors were too weak and designed a stronger device attached to the propeller and its shaft, then fitted the modified propeller and a Hotchkiss machine gun to a standard Morane-Saulnier L parasol monoplane.

Poor flying weather delayed a combat test until 1 April 1915. Spotting an unsuspecting German two-seat reconnaissance plane, Garros swung in behind it. The German crew was shocked as Garros opened fire and, after a chase with the German plane desperately trying to escape, it fell in flames. Two weeks later Garros scored again, and on 18 April a third fell; the fixed machine gun had proved itself. Later that day, while attacking a train behind the lines, Garros was downed by ground fire that severed the fuel line of his airplane. Garros tried to burn the airplane and escape, but he was soon captured and the partially burned airplane, complete with its armoured propeller and machine gun, was shipped back to Germany for technical analysis.

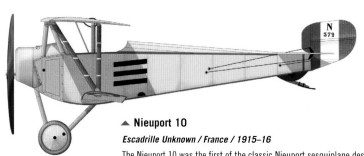

▲ **Nieuport 10**

Escadrille Unknown / France / 1915–16

The Nieuport 10 was the first of the classic Nieuport sesquiplane designs and was used as a two-seat reconnaissance airplane and a single-seat fighter. The lines on the fuselage may identify this airplane within its unknown unit.

Specifications

Crew: 2

Powerplant: 1 x 60kW (80hp) Le Rhône 9C
  9-cylinder rotary engine

Maximum speed: 91km/h (57mph)

Endurance: 3 hours

Service ceiling: 4000m (13,123ft)

Dimensions: span 7.90m (25ft 11in); length
  7m (22ft 12in); height 2.70m (8ft 10in)

Weight: 1452kg (3201lb) max take-off

Armament: None

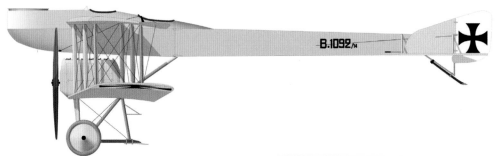

▲ **Gotha G.I**

Flieger Ersatz Abteilung 3 / Darmstadt Aerodrome, Germany / early 1915

Designed as a '*Kampfflugzeug*' or battle plane, the unusual G.I arrived at the Front in June 1915 and, like similar designs, proved too slow to catch enemy airplanes. The high-mounted fuselage gave the two gunners clear fields of fire but proved problematic during landing accidents. This airplane, known as the Friedel-Ursinius, was built at FEA 3 and served as the prototype G.I.

Specifications

Crew: 3

Powerplant: 2 x 112kW (150hp) Benz Bz.III
  engines

Maximum speed: 130km/h (80.78mph)

Endurance: n/a

Service ceiling: About 2500m (8,202ft)

Dimensions: 20.30m (66ft 7in); length 12m
  (39ft 4.4in) height 3.9m (12ft 9.5in)

Weight: 2966kg (6538lb) max take-off

Armament: 2 x 7.92mm (0.313in) MGs

▲ **Breguet Br.V**

No. 3 Wing, RNAS / Luxeuil-Les-Bains Aerodrome, France / October 1916

Like similar designs, the Breguet Br.V was not fast enough to succeed as a battle plane or escort fighter. French built, it was used by France and Britain. This one flew from Luxeuil-les-bains Aerodrome on the costly Obendorf raid of 12 October 1916.

Specifications (Breguet Br. V Ca.2)

Crew: 2

Powerplant: 1 x 168kW (225hp) Renault 12Fb
  Vee engine or 1 x 186kW (250hp) Rolls-Royce

Maximum speed: 130km/h (83mph)

Endurance: 3 hours 30 mins

Service ceiling: 3700m (12,139ft)

Dimensions: span 17.5m (57ft 7.8in);
length 9.90m (32ft 9.8in); height 3.90m (12ft
9.3in)

Weight: 1890kg (4167lb) max take-off

Armament: 1 x 7.7mm (.303in) Lewis MG, 20 x
  102mm (5in) bombs

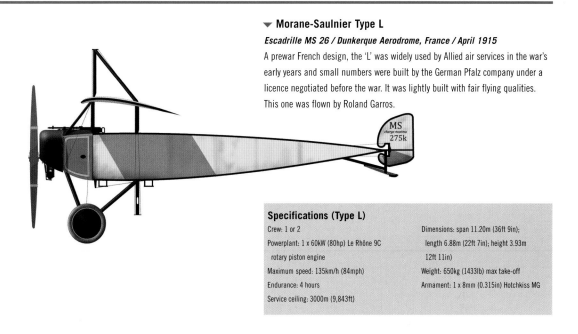

MS
charge maxima
275k

Specifications (Type L)

Crew: 1 or 2	Dimensions: span 11.20m (36ft 9in);
Powerplant: 1 x 60kW (80hp) Le Rhône 9C	length 6.88m (22ft 7in); height 3.93m
rotary piston engine	12ft 11in)
Maximum speed: 135km/h (84mph)	Weight: 650kg (1433lb) max take-off
Endurance: 4 hours	Armament: 1 x 8mm (0.315in) Hotchkiss MG
Service ceiling: 3000m (9,843ft)	

Fokker and the first fighter planes
SUMMER 1915

After examining Garros's armoured propeller, a team lead by Fokker quickly developed an effective machine-gun synchronizing gear and used it to create the first fighter airplane.

WHAT HAPPENED NEXT is the subject of several conflicting accounts. It is known that the German military had studied the problem, and despite Schneider's prewar patent (which had been published two months after the war began by *Flugsport*, a German aviation magazine), decided to copy the armoured propeller. However, the German machine guns, with higher muzzle velocity and steel-jacketed bullets, tore the propeller apart. At that point, the authorities turned to Anthony Fokker. The details are not known, but it would seem that Fokker and his engineering team had already been working on a synchronizer, probably with the knowledge of the German authorities, before Garros's device was shown to him, and this prior work was probably why Fokker was brought in. Fokker and his team quickly developed a successful, cam-operated synchronizer.

Fokker adapted the new synchronizer to his M 5K monoplane, which was similar in configuration to the

Morane-Saulnier H; the airplane was given the military serial E.1/15. The German authorities demanded that Fokker, a citizen of neutral Holland, shoot down an enemy airplane as a final proof of concept and an unwilling Fokker soon found himself at the Front in uniform with documentation to

FRENCH AVIATION MILIAIRE, 15 AUGUST 1915	
Type	**Front-Line Units**
M.F.7 & 11	193
Nieuport 10 & 11	42
M.-S. L & LA	57
Caudron G.3 & G.4	64
Voisin 3 & 4	129
Breguet 4 & 5	2
Vendôme	1
Total	488

▲ Morane-Saulnier Type N

No. 60 Squadron, RFC / Le Hameau Aerodrome, France / August 1916

The single-seat Type 'N' was faster and more manoeuvrable than the 'L', making it a better fighter. This example flown by the RFC features an unsynchronized machine gun; the armoured bullet deflectors are shown on the propeller. The nose was painted red to distinguish it from similar Pfalz monoplanes with black noses.

Specifications (Type N)

Crew: 1

Powerplant: 1 x 60kW (80hp) Le Rhône 9C
rotary piston engine

Maximum speed: 144km/h (89mph)

Endurance: 1hr 30 mins

Service ceiling: n/a

Dimensions: span 8.15m (26ft 9in);
length 5.83m (19ft 2in); height 2.25m
7ft 5in)

Weight: 444kg (979lb) max take-off

Armament: 1 x 7.7mm (.303in) Lewis MG

prevent him being shot as a spy if he came down in Allied hands. After a week of flights, Fokker finally found a French Farman reconnaissance airplane and approached it, but could not bring himself to shoot it down, an act Fokker later described as simple murder. The airmen did not share his reluctance, and soon *Ltn* Kurt Wintgens shot down a Morane-Saulnier over French lines to prove the concept worked. The nature of air warfare had changed forever.

Fodder for Fokkers

Two of the Fokker *Eindeckers* (monoplanes), as they were known, were assigned to *Ltns* Max Immelmann and Oswald Boelcke. On 1 August they attacked a formation of British airplanes that had just bombed their airfield at Douai. A severe gun jam forced Boelcke to land to repair it, but Immelmann attacked. After several jams he was able to clear, Immelmann succeeded in downing the British airplane. This combat, four months to the day after Garros's first victory, started the so-called Fokker Scourge, when the Fokker fighters maintained air superiority over Allied airmen, many of whom came to feel like 'Fokker fodder'.

Immelmann and Boelcke are two names that live on in history. Boelcke became known as the father of German fighter aviation and mentor of the Red Baron, and Immelmann became known for the

invention of the aerial manoeuvre that still bears his name to this day.

The Allies soon recognized the peril they were in. By September the air situation became critical, and the commander of the RFC's Third Wing ordered that reconnaissance aircraft be escorted by Vickers Gunbus fighters. The Fokkers were faster and more manoeuvrable than the Gunbus, but the Vickers, with its flexible gun, was surprisingly successful in combat with them. From then on German pilots tended to describe all Allied pusher fighters as 'Vickers'. The Fokker itself was not a wonder plane; for the time it had good speed, climb, and manoeuvrability, but its main attribute as a fighter was its synchronized machine gun. Indeed, both the Morane-Saulnier N and the Bristol Scout had better performance than the Fokker, but neither had a synchronized gun. The Morane relied on deflector plates as had Garros, and the Bristol Scout had a variety of gun mounts that aimed the gun to miss the propeller. The non-synchronized gun mount that most crew preferred, and continued in use to the end of the war, was mounting the gun above the top wing to fire over the propeller arc. The drawback was that the gun was out of convenient reach if a jam occurred, which gave pilots many awkward moments during air combat.

The Allies did not deploy a fighter with a synchronized gun until the Summer of 1916, when

▲ Fokker E.II

Feld Flieger Abteilung 53 / France / October 1915

The E.II was very similar to the E.III and is difficult to distinguish in photographs. Both types used the same engine and had similar dimensions. This E.II was flown by *Ltn* Kurt Freiherr von Crailsheim, who scored his sole victory in this aircraft. The fuselage bands are his personal markings.

Specifications

Crew: 1	Service ceiling: 3500m (11,500ft)
Powerplant: 1 x 75kW (100hp)	Dimensions: span 10.05m (32ft 12in); length
Oberursel U.I rotary engine	7.20m (23ft 7in) height 2.49m (8ft 2in)
Maximum speed: 140km/h (87mph)	Weight: 498kg (1098lb)
Endurance: 1hr 30 mins	Armament: 1 x 7.92mm (0.313in) MG

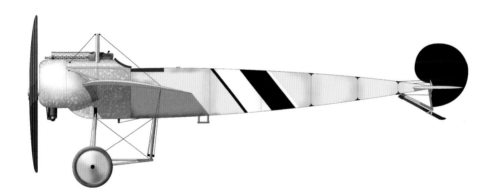

▲ Fokker E.III

Feld Flieger Abteilung 9b / France / Summer 1916

The Fokker E.I, E.II and E.III are difficult to distinguish from one another. This E.III was flown by *Vzfw* Eduard Böhme; the black and white fuselage stripes and black rudder are the unit markings. Sharing its basic configuration with the Morane-Saulnier 'L', the Fokker was faster and much more manoeuvrable.

Specifications

Crew: 1	Service ceiling: 3505m (11,500ft)
Powerplant: 1 x 75kW (100hp) Oberusel U.I	Dimensions: span 9.50m (31ft 2in); length
rotary engine	7.20m (23ft 7in); height 2.39m (7ft 10in)
Maximum speed: 140km/h (87mph)	Weight: 609kg (1342lb)
Endurance: 1hr 30 mins	Armament: 1 x 7.92mm (0.313in) Spandau MG

several types appeared. Until then, the Allies had to rely on pusher fighters and those, like the Nieuport, with an over-wing gun.

Development of fighter tactics

The Fokker pilots developed tactics that, in elaborated form, are still used today. A Fokker pilot would cruise over the Front and, on spotting an Allied airplane, would attempt to position himself above it and between the sun and the target, which would make him invisible to the crew. Waiting for the right time, the Fokker pilot would then dive down from behind the enemy airplane to fire a devastating burst from close range. If the enemy plane did not fall immediately, the Fokker pilot would continue his dive, zoom back to altitude and repeat the attack. If the enemy was an armed two-seater, the Fokker would initially dive beneath it to

FRENCH AVIATION MILIAIRE, FEB 1916	
Plane	Number
Breguet 4	22
Breguet 5	11
Caproni (R.E.P.-built)	7
Caudron G.3	141
Caudron G.4	167
Caudron R.4	1
Maurice-Farman 7	71
Maurice-Farman 11	101
Nieuport 10	120
Nieuport 11	90
Morane-Saulnier L/LA	18
Ponnier N	5
SPAD A.2	4
Voisin 4	20
Voisin 3/5	159
Total	937

avoid the observer's defensive fire, using the fuselage of the enemy plane to block visibility and return fire, then zoom up underneath it to fire a burst from close range into its belly. These were two variations of the 'Fokker bounce'. If the Fokker did not have an altitude advantage, the pilot might stalk the enemy airplane from behind and below so its crew would not see him approach. Of course, the Allies adopted the same tactics when they fielded fighters with fixed, forward-firing guns.

Importantly, the Germans were allocating the Fokkers in singles and pairs to reconnaissance units instead of grouping them into squadrons. They continued to win victories and had air superiority, but operating individually and in small numbers limited their effectiveness. Certainly production could have been increased, and the fact that it was not, together with failure to group the Fokkers into squadrons, gave the Allies the opportunity to continue their reconnaissance behind German lines despite increasing losses. The RFC responded by arming all reconnaissance planes with defensive machine guns and escorting them with one or two airplanes. But Hugh Trenchard, the commander of the RFC in France, avoided large changes in tactics that he feared might make the Germans respond with better tactics of their own, such as grouping their

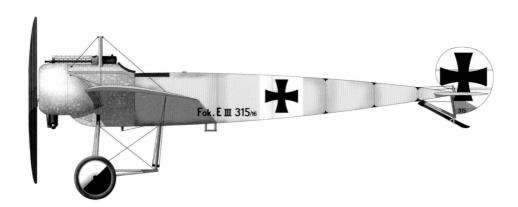

▲ **Fokker E.III**

KEK Avilliers / Avillers Aerodrome, France / 1916

Originally Fokkers were assigned alone or in pairs to reconnaissance units. Later they were sometimes assigned to KEKs (*Kampfeinsitzer Kommando*, a single-seat fighter detachment) before creation of fighter squadrons. This example was flown by *Oblt* Hans Berr, an early ace and recipient of the Pour le Mérite. Berr scored 10 victories before being killed 6 April 1917 in a midair collision during combat.

Specifications

Crew: 1

Powerplant: 1 x 75kW (100hp) Oberusel U.I rotary engine

Maximum speed: 140km/h (87mph)

Endurance: 1hr 30 mins

Service ceiling: 3505m (11,500ft)

Dimensions: span 9.50m (31ft 2in); length 7.20m (23ft 7in); height 2.39m (7ft 10in)

Weight: 609kg (1342lb)

Armament: 1 x 7.92mm (0.313in) Spandau MG

fighters into squadrons. Trenchard realized the RFC would incur more losses, but he wanted to continue offensive operations while waiting for improved British fighters.

Nevertheless, at its peak in January 1916, the Fokker Scourge had severely limited RFC operations by forcing the RFC to escort each reconnaissance airplane with at least three other armed airplanes. This meant it took many more airplanes to fly each reconnaissance mission, stretching RFC resources.

Verdun

On 21 February 1916 a bombardment by 850 German guns on the French fortress city of Verdun marked the beginning of a ten-month battle that ended in a bloody stalemate costly to both sides. But if the ground battle was indecisive, the evolving aerial battle strongly influenced both sides.

Unlike the Germans, the French had already started grouping their fighters into units that fought together. Only one fighter escadrille was in position near Verdun when the battle started, but within a week six fighter and eight reconnaissance escadrilles were on hand. These were opposed by a mixed force of 168 German aircraft and even four Zeppelins. While not as committed to the offensive in principle

as Trenchard and the RFC, the French decided to adopt an offensive strategy of sending groups of three to six fighters to patrol behind German lines, and they asked for, and received, much equipment from the RFC in support. Of equal importance, the French fighter escadrilles now flew the Nieuport 11, a diminutive biplane with an over-wing Lewis machine gun. The Nieuport had a narrow lower wing for good downward visibility and was faster and more manoeuvrable than the Fokker *Eindeckers*. The Fokkers represented the first generation of fighter technology and the Nieuport was one of the second generation fighters.

In contrast, the Germans adopted an air blockade defensive strategy known as *Luftsperre*, which was ineffective and wasteful of resources. This strategy, combined with the new French technical superiority, gave air supremacy back to the French, who ruled the skies over Verdun by the middle of April. Known as the *Groupe des Cigognes* (Stork Group), the French fighter pilots included many stars who became famous aces, such as Jean Navarre, Georges Guynemer and Charles Nungesser.

From this time the Germans, realizing they would always be outnumbered by Allied airplanes, stayed on the strategic defensive, and intercepted Allied aircraft

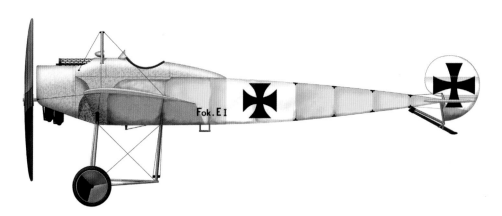

▲ **Fokker E.IV**

Flieger Abtielung 62 / Douai Aerodrome, France / January–March 1916

The E.IV was fitted with a more powerful engine and two machine guns to improve the performance and fire-power of the *Eindeckers*. Unfortunately, the engine was unreliable and the extra weight reduced manoeuvrability. The basic design had reached the end of its development potential; entirely new designs were needed. The white fuselage band indicated this one was flown by the great ace *Hptm* Oswald Boelcke, who won the Pour le Mérite and downed 40 opponents.

Specifications	
Crew: 1	Service ceiling: 4500m (14,764ft)
Powerplant: 1 x 119kW (160hp)	Dimensions: span 10m (32ft 10in); length
Oberursel U.III rotary engine	7.50m (24ft 7in) height 2.77m (9ft 1in)
Maximum speed: 170km/h (106mph)	Weight: 724kg (1596lb) max take-off
Endurance: 1hr 30 mins	Armament: 2 x 7.92mm (0.313in) MGs

over their own lines to conserve their strength. Allied pilots downed behind German lines became PoWs lost to their air service; German pilots went back to their units. The prevailing westerly winds aided the Germans, usually blowing airplanes towards German lines, which could be crucial during air combat.

The air battle over Verdun provided some hard lessons. First, the success of the offensive strategy convinced the Allies that was the most effective employment of airplanes, and they pursued the aerial offensive from then until the Armistice. Second, Germany realized the ineffectiveness of the air blockade and abandoned it. Third, the effectiveness of specialized fighter units operating in strength was clear, and the fighter emerged as a full-fledged partner to the reconnaissance airplane and bomber. Finally,

increased cooperation between the British and French air services was maintained from that time onwards.

Battle of the Somme

The British had long planned their offensive on the Somme, but by the time they actually launched it on 1 July 1916, much of its intention was to take pressure off the French at Verdun. On the first day, the British sustained 60,000 casualities for little change in the front lines. The Battle of the Somme ground on until November with massive casualties on both sides but no real change in the ground situation.

The Allied situation was much better in the air. The French Nieuport 11 entered British service in January 1916, soon followed by the British DH.2 and FE.2b. Both these second-generation types were

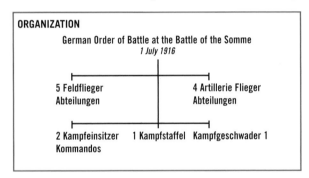

ORGANIZATION

German Order of Battle at the Battle of the Somme
1 July 1916

5 Feldflieger Abteilungen

4 Artillerie Flieger Abteilungen

2 Kampfeinsitzer Kommandos

1 Kampfstaffel

Kampfgeschwader 1

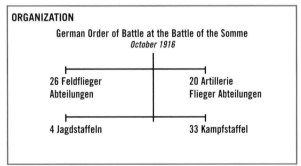

ORGANIZATION

German Order of Battle at the Battle of the Somme
October 1916

26 Feldflieger Abteilungen

20 Artillerie Flieger Abteilungen

4 Jagdstaffeln

33 Kampfstaffel

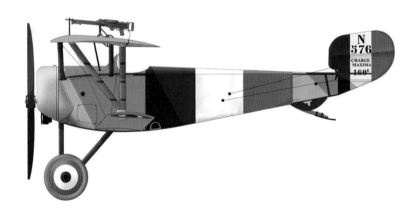

▲ **Nieuport 11**

Escadrille N 67 // Verdun sector, France / Spring 1916

Flying this distinctively marked Nieuport 11, French ace Jean Navarre became famous as 'The Sentinel of Verdun' for flying in constant patrols over that battlefield. Navarre scored 12 victories before being severely wounded in aerial combat on 17 June 1916, which ended his wartime flying.

Specifications

Crew: 1

Powerplant: 1 x 60kW (80hp) Le Rhône 9C rotary engine

Maximum speed: 167km/h (104mph)

Endurance: 2 hours

Service ceiling: 5000m (16,404ft)

Dimensions: span 7.90m (25ft 11in); length 5.50m (18ft 1in); height 2.40m (7ft 10in)

Weight: 480kg (1058lb)

Armament: 1 x 7.7mm (.303in) Lewis MG

pushers designed as fighters. The FE.2b was a two-seater with the gunner in front of the pilot with two flexible guns, one firing forwards and one back over the upper wing. Fairly manoeuvrable for a large airplane, the FE.2b was a well armed and dangerous opponent for the Fokkers. The DH.2 was a single-seat fighter that was superior to the Fokker in every performance respect. These fighters quickly established air superiority over the Fokker in the British area of the Front and finally dispelled the 'Fokker Scourge' mentality of the RFC, which had given the Fokker a fiercer reputation than it deserved.

Sopwith 1½ Strutter

Mention should also be made of the Sopwith 1½ Strutter, so-called because of its unusual W-shaped interplane struts. The Strutter was a handsome, two-seat fighter with its engine and propeller in front. The gunner had a flexible machine gun and the pilot had a fixed, synchronized gun, making the Strutter the first two-seat fighter with this configuration to appear. In addition to its effective armament, the Strutter had good performance; it was faster and had better climb and ceiling than its contemporary, the FE.2b. The Strutter had good handling characteristics and,

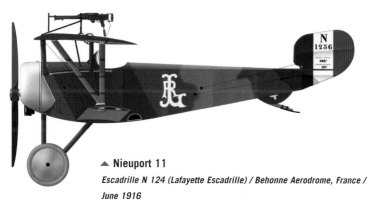

▲ **Nieuport 11**

Escadrille N 124 (Lafayette Escadrille) / Behonne Aerodrome, France / June 1916

This Nieuport 11 was flown by Raoul Lufberry, the leading ace of N 124, the Lafayette Escadrille, who eventually achieved 16 victories before being killed in action on 19 May 1918 in his Nieuport 28 while commanding the 94th Aero Squadron, USAS. The intials on the fuselage were Lufberry's personal marking.

Specifications
Crew: 1
Powerplant: 1 x 60kW (80hp)
  Le Rhône 9C rotary engine
Maximum speed: 167km/h (104mph)
Endurance: 2 hours
Service ceiling: 5000m (16,404ft)
Dimensions: span 7.90m (25ft 11in); length
  5.50m (18ft 1in); height 2.40m (7ft 10in)
Weight: 480kg (1058lb)
Armament: 1 x 7.7mm (.303in) Lewis MG

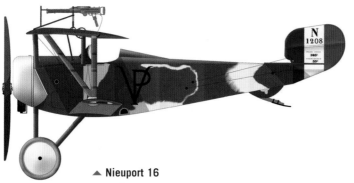

▲ **Nieuport 16**

Escadrille N 124 (Lafayette Escadrille) / Behonne Aerodrome, France / August 1916

The Nieuport 16 was created from the Nieuport 11 by fitting a more powerful engine, but the larger engine made the type somewhat nose heavy. Nonetheless, the type was used by France, Britain and Russia. This camouflaged example was flown by Sgt Paul Pavelka and has his personal marking on the fuselage.

Specifications
Crew: 1
Powerplant: 1 x 82kW (110hp)
  Le Rhône 9J rotary engine
Maximum speed: 165km/h (102.5mph)
Endurance: 2 hours
Service ceiling: 4800m (15,748ft)
Dimensions: 7.52m (24ft 8in); length 5.64m
  (18ft 6in) height 2.40m (7ft 10.4in)
Weight: 550kg (1212.5lb)
Armament: 1 x 7.7mm (.303in) Lewis MG

together with its pusher contemporaries, contributed to the end of the 'Fokker Scourge'. The Strutter was a flexible design used as a single-seat bomber and night fighter in addition to its roles as a two-seat fighter and reconnaissance airplane. It was also built in large quantities in France, but delays in licence production meant that it arrived in quantity a year later than its British predecessor, resulting in greatly reduced combat effectiveness.

While literally holding their ground on land, the Germans were facing defeat in the air. German losses rose significantly as the Allies gained air superiority all along the Western Front. Even Immelmann fell in combat with FE.2bs, although it is unclear whether it was structural failure or British gunfire that caused his demise. He had 15 confirmed victories and scored two more the day he died, for a total of 17. With the loss of Immelmann the Fokker *Eindecker* era was over.

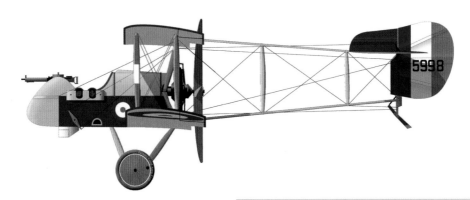

▲ DeHavilland DH.2

No. 24 Squadron, RFC / Bertangles Aerodrome, France / Summer 1916

Arriving at the Front early in 1916, the DH.2, together with the Nieuport 11, ended the 'Fokker Scourge'. The DH.2 was faster, more manoeuvrable, and had a better rate of climb than the Fokker *Eindeckers*. However, its pusher configuration severely limited its development potential.

Specifications

Crew: 1

Powerplant: 1 x 75kW (100hp) Gnome Monosoupape, 82kW (110hp) Le Rhône 9Z or 82kW (110hp) Clerget rotary engine

Maximum speed: 148km/h (92mph)

Endurance: 3 hours

Service ceiling: 4267m (14,000ft)

Dimensions: span 8.60m (28ft 3in); length 7.68m (25ft 2in); height 2.91m (9ft 6in)

Weight: 702kg (1547lb)

Armament: 1 x 7.7mm (.303in) Lewis MG

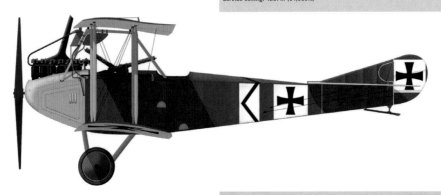

▲ Aviatik C.I

Schutzstaffel 16 or 26 / Western Front / 1916

When the Aviatik C.I was designed there was no operational experience to determine for certain which seating arrangement (observer in front or in back), was more effective. So the Aviatik was specified to have the observer up front while competing Albatros and LVG types had the observer in the back, which quickly proved to be more effective in air combat.

Specifications

Crew: 2

Powerplant: 1 x 112kW (150hp) Mercedes Bz.III inline engine

Maximum speed: 120km/h (75mph)

Endurance: 3 hours

Service ceiling: 3500m (11,485ft)

Dimensions: span 12.5m (41ft); length 7.91m (25ft 11in); height 2.95m (9ft 8in)

Weight: 1245kg (2745lb) max take-off

Armament: 1-2 flexible 7.92mm (0.312in) MG

Heroes of the skies

Shocked by Immelmann's death, the Kaiser ordered Boelcke, then with 18 victories, away from the front to keep him safely out of combat. By this time Immelmann and Boelcke were famous throughout Germany as heroes of the air. Guynemer and Nungesser were similarly famous in France. In a time of senseless mass slaughter, the home fronts needed heroes, and the fighter aces filled that need. Their individual courage and exploits could be celebrated as a ray of hope and knightly courage and prowess as the war ground on with countless soldiers dying anonymously in the horror of trench warfare.

The bloody Somme stalemate had further implications. For one, the last hope for a negotiated peace died with the tens of thousands of casualties. In addition, Germany recognized that Britain was a more serious threat than France, and the bulk of the fighting shifted to the British sector. This was particularly true in the air, where Trenchard's relentless offensive strategy resulted in Germany having to fight far more air combats with Britain than with France. This is hardly to suggest that air combat with French airplanes was easy or unimportant; it is just that French aviation was not consistently on the offensive like the RFC and RNAS.

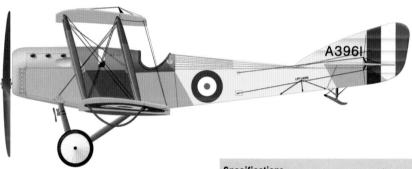

▲ Martinsyde Elephant
Unknown RFC Squadron / Western Front / 1916

The handsome Elephant was a single-seat bomber; the pilot had a flexible machine gun mounted behind his left shoulder for self-defence. Inadequate engine power precluded a heavier, more conventional two-seat design.

Specifications

Crew: 1	Dimensions: span 11.58m (38ft);
Powerplant: 1 x 119kW (160hp) Beardmore	length 8.08m (26ft 6in); height 2.95m
inline piston engine	(9ft 8in)
Maximum speed: 167km/h (102mph)	Weight: 1115kg (2458lb) max take-off
Endurance: 4 hours 30 minutes	Armament: 1 or 2 x 7.7mm (.303in) Lewis MGs
Service ceiling: 4875m (16,000ft)	plus max bomb load of 152kg (336lb)

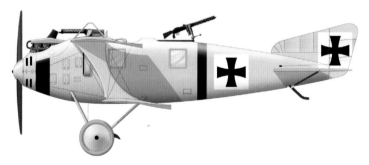

▲ LFG Roland C.II
Unknown Unit / Western Front / c.1916

Despite being produced in relatively small numbers, the Roland C.II made a big impression. For some time it was the best German warplane thanks to its speed and armament. Its fuselage was made of thin wooden strips wrapped around a mould and glued together, making it strong and streamlined. After the Pfalz company produced the smaller Roland D.II fighter under licence, this innovative structure was later used by Pfalz for all their fighters, starting with the famous Pfalz D.III.

Specifications

Crew: 2
Powerplant: 1 x 119kW (160hp) Mercedes
  D.III inline piston engine
Maximum speed: 165km/h (103mph)
Endurance: 4 hours
Service ceiling: 4000m (13,120ft)
Dimensions: span 10.30m (33ft 10in);
  length 7.70m (25ft 3in); height 2.90m
  (9ft 6in)
Weight: 1309kg (2886lb) max take-off
Armament: 1 x 7.92mm (.312in) Spandau
  MG for pilot and 1 x 7.92mm (.312in)
  Parabellum MG for observer

Specifications

Crew: 2

Powerplant: 1 x 119kW (160hp) Mercedes
D.III inline

Maximum speed: 152km/h (94mph)

Endurance: 4 hours

Service ceiling:5000m (16,200ft)

Dimensions: span 12.15m (39ft 10in);
length 7.85m (25ft 9in); height 3.05m
(10ft)

Weight: 1333kg (2939lb) max take-off

Armament: 1 x 7.92mm (.312in) fixed
Spandau MG and 1 x 7.92mm (.312in)
Parabellum MG

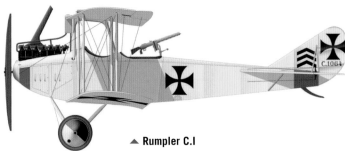

▲ **Rumpler C.I**

Unknown Unit / 1916

The first Rumpler C-type was an excellent design for its time. Robust, reliable,
and manoeuvrable, it served long and widely in German two-seater units. The
chevrons on the fin are an individual marking.

Specifications

Crew: 2

Powerplant: 1 x 112kW (150hp) Benz Bz.III
or 119kW (160hp) Mercedes D.III inline
piston engine

Maximum speed: 150km/h (93mph)

Endurance: 4 hours

Service ceiling: 3350m (11,000ft)

Dimensions: span 11.70m (38ft 5in);
length 7.95m (26ft 1in); height 3.07m
(10ft);

Weight: 1271kg (2802lb)

Armament: 1 x 7.92mm (.312in) fixed
Spandau MG and 1 x 7.92mm (.312in)
flexible Parabellum MG. 200lbs of bombs

▲ **Albatros C.III**

Kagohl IV, Staffel 20 / Western Front / 1916

The Albatros C.III was a robust, reliable two-seater of good performance that
served in large numbers. The number '20' is the *Staffel* number, and individual
machines had black and white fuselage bands in different patterns.

Specifications

Crew: 2

Powerplant: 1 x 139kW (175hp) Hispano-
Suiza 8Aa V8 engine

Maximum speed: 138km/h (85.7mph)

Endurance: 3 hours

Service ceiling: 3500m (11,483ft)

Dimensions: span 11.90m (39ft 1in); length
7.90m (25ft 11in); height 2.65m
(8ft 8in)

Weight: 1030kg (2270.8lb) max take-off

Armament: 1 x 7.7mm (.303in) Lewis MG, 4
x 120mm (4.72in) bombs

This Gallic rooster was the first of several variations
used as the escadrille symbol of N 62 and also
appeared on Nieuport 16s of this unit.

▲ **Nieuport 14**

Escadrille N 62 / Cachy Aerodrome, France / Summer 1916

The Nieuport company is almost synonymous with rotary-engine sesquiplanes, but here is an example of the rare Nieuport
14 reconnaissance bomber with Hispano-Suiza V-8 power. Few were built; the type was not a great success and the
engines were badly needed for SPAD fighters.

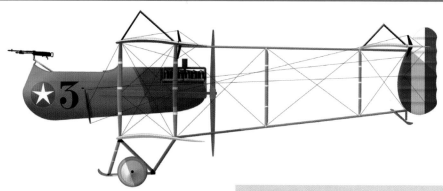

▲ **Farman F.40**

Escadrille F.24 / Morlancourt Aerodrome, France / September 1916

Farman used the obsolete pusher configuration long after it should have been replaced. The F.40 superseded earlier Farmans in production and was widely used by France, Italy and Belgium despite its archaic design, and a few found their way to Russia. Primarily a reconnaissance plane, it was also used for light bombing and training. The star was the escadrille insignia.

Specifications

Crew: 2	Dimensions: span 17.6m (57ft 9in); length
Powerplant: 1 x 101kW (135hp) Renault 12-	9.25m (30ft 4in); height 3.9m (12ft 9in)
cylinder Vee piston engine	Weight: 1120kg (2469lb) max take-off
Maximum speed: 135km/h (84mph)	Armament: 1–2 x 7.7mm (0.303in) Lewis guns
Endurance: 2 hours 20 mins	on flexible mounts in nose, plus light bombs
Service ceiling: 4000m (13,125ft)	

German Reorganization & First *Jastas*
AUGUST–OCTOBER 1916

Their loss of air superiority at Verdun forced the Germans to develop new airplanes, new tactics and a new organization to regain the initiative.

THEIR LOSS OF AIR SUPERIORITY at Verdun forced the Germans out of their lethargy and they started searching for solutions. An effective response had to be both technological and tactical, because the Allies were superior in both areas. Even as the Fokkers were being driven from the sky over Verdun, new German fighters were being designed and tested. Fokker delivered a new family of biplane fighters, the D.I/D.II/D.III which, while superior to his monoplanes, were still not as good as the Nieuport. The Halberstadt company delivered an excellent new series of biplane fighters that were strong, manoeuvrable and a pleasure to fly. The Halberstadt fighters brought the Germans to technical parity with the Allies, but more needed to be done.

That advance was delivered by the powerful Albatros firm, the largest airplane manufacturer in Germany. The sleek new Albatros D.I and D.II combined good streamlining with a powerful 120kW (160hp) Mercedes six-cylinder engine, giving them

enough power to carry two synchronized machine guns. The result was a fighter that was faster and more heavily armed than the Nieuports and DH.2s of the Allies. Hedging their bets, the German authorities also decided to copy the French Nieuport, which clearly had more development potential than the pusher DH.2. Passing some captured Nieuports around key manufacturers resulted in the Siemens-Schukert D.I, essentially a copy of the Nieuport powered by an innovative Siemens counter-rotary engine. It was used in small numbers at the Front, but by the time it reached combat newer designs had outclassed it.

Come fly with me

With the technology advantage once more on their side thanks to the Albatros fighters, the Germans needed to close the tactical and organizational gaps. Finally they decided they must emulate the fighter squadrons of the Allies, and Boelcke was re-called to the Front to form one of the first *Jagdstaffeln* (literally

FIGHTER TACTICS – BOELCKE'S DICTA

Number	Tactic
1	Try to secure the upper hand before attacking. If possible, keep the sun behind you.
2	Always follow through an attack once you have started it.
3	Fire only at close range, and only when your opponent is properly in your sights.
4	Always keep your eye on your opponent, and never let yourself be deceived by ruses.
5	In any form of attack it is essential to assail your opponent from behind.
6	If your opponent dives on you, do not try to evade his onslaught, but fly to meet it.
7	When over enemy lines, never forget your line of retreat.
8	For the *Staffel*: Attack in groups of four or six. When the fight breaks up into a series of single combats, take care that several do not go for one opponent.

hunting squadron), abbreviated as *Jasta*. During his travels Boelcke met many German airmen, and while on the Russian Front before returning home, met a number of eager young pilots and told them he was returning to the Western Front to form a *Jasta* with pilots he chose. The pilots quickly realized he was

evaluating them. The next morning he appeared at the hut of two of them and asked "Want to come to the Somme with me?" *Ltn* Erwin Böhme and *UlanenLeutnant* Manfred von Richthofen enthusiastically accepted.

Boelcke returned to the Western Front in late August and formally established *Jagdstaffel* 2 (also called *Jasta* 2) by the end of the month. The first fighters, an Albatros D.I and two Fokker D.IIIs, arrived on 1 September. In early September Boelcke trained his pilots thoroughly in combat flying. He developed a set of eight rules, known as Boelcke's Dicta, for successful fighter combat. These rules (see left) still apply today. As well as training his new pilots Boelcke also flew missions by himself, scoring more victories. On 17 September came the graduation exercise. Boelcke led five of his pupils on patrol and they soon spotted a British formation of BE.2cs and FE.2bs below them. The British dropped their bombs just before the Albatros fighters attacked. The Germans caught the British by surprise and a violent dogfight erupted. When it was over, four FE.2bs and two BE.2cs had fallen; the six Albatros fighters of *Jasta 2* returned home without loss.

The next month the Germans re-organized their entire air service. As early as March 1916 *Oblt* Hermann von der Lieth-Thomsen, the dynamic German *Feldflugchef* (Chief of Field Aviation), had

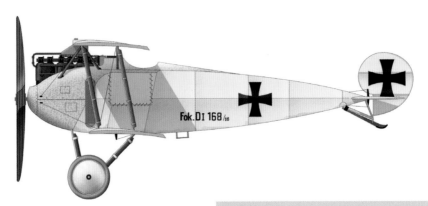

▲ **Fokker D.I**

Jasta 2 / Velu Aerodrome, France / September 1916

This Fokker biplane fighter was flown briefly by by *Hptm* Oswald Boelcke, 40-victory ace, before Albatros fighters were delivered to *Jasta 2*. The early Fokker biplane fighters could not match competing Albatros and Halberstadt fighters; not until the superlative Fokker D.VII did Fokker produce a successful biplane fighter.

Specifications

Crew: 1

Powerplant: 119kW (160hp) Mercedes D.III inline piston engine

Maximum speed: 150km/h (93mph)

Endurance: 1hr 30 mins

Service ceiling: 3500m (11,500ft)

Dimensions: span 9.05m (29ft 8in); length 5.7m 18ft 8in) height 2.25m (7ft 5in)

Weight: 671kg (1479lb)

Armament: 1 x 7.92mm (.313in) Spandau MG

▲ Fokker D.II

KEK Ensisheim / Ensisheim Aerodrome, France / October 1916

The rotary-powered Fokker D.II was obviously developed from the earlier Fokker Eindeckers. Although superior to them, the D.II was in turn over-shadowed by the competing Albatros and Halberstadt fighters. This example was flown by *Ltn.* Otto Dessloch, OC of *KEK Ensisheim*, who scored one victory before force-landing in Switzerland.

Specifications

Crew: 1

Powerplant: 1 x 75kW (100hp) Oberursel U.I rotary engine

Maximum speed: 150km/h (93mph)

Endurance: 1hr 30 mins

Service ceiling: About 4500m (14,764ft)

Dimensions: span 8.75m (28ft 8.5in); length 6.40m (21ft) height 2.55m (8ft 4in)

Weight: 576kg (1270lb) max take-off

Armament: 1 x 7.92mm (.313in) Spandau MG

Specifications

Crew: 1

Powerplant: 1 x 75kW (100hp) Oberursel U.I rotary engine

Maximum speed: 150km/h (93mph)

Endurance: 1hr 30 mins

Service ceiling: About 4500m (14,764ft)

Dimensions: span 8.75m (28ft 8.5in); length 6.40m (21ft) height 2.55m (8ft 4in)

Weight: 576kg (1270lb) max take-off

Armament: 1 x 7.92mm (.313in) Spandau MG

▲ Fokker D.II

Kest 4b / Freiburg Aerodrome, Germany / 1916

Engine exhaust has damaged the finish on this D.II of home defence unit *Kest 4b* based at the time at the Freiburg Aerodrome. The streaked camouflage finish would later appear on the Fokker Triplane and early Fokker D.VIIs.

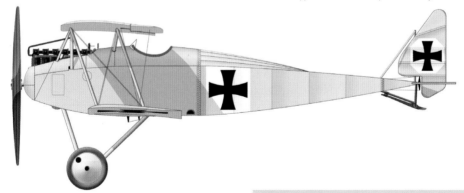

▲ Halberstadt D.II

Unknown Unit / Western Front / 1916

The Halberstadt was the first German biplane fighter to reach the Front. It was a very strong airplane with delightful handling and manoeuvrability and was far superior to the *Eindeckers* it replaced. Continued development lead to the famous Halberstadt CL.II two-seat fighter.

Specifications

Crew: 1

Powerplant: 1 x 90kW (120hp) Mercedes D.II inline engine

Maximum speed: 150km/h (93mph)

Range: 250km (155 miles)

Service ceiling: 5791m (19,000ft)

Dimensions: span 8.80m (28ft 10in); length 7.30m (23ft 11in); height 2.67m (8ft 9in)

Weight: 771kg (1700lb) max take-off

Armament: 1 x 7.92mm (.313in) Spandau MG

proposed that all German aviation organizations should be combined under one central authority. While the German navy did not like this idea, the initial failure of German aviation at the Somme eliminated doubts, and on 8 October the Kaiser issued a decree placing all army aviation units under the authority of the commanding officer of the air services. *Generalleutnant* Ernst von Hoeppener, a professional cavalry officer, was appointed to this position, *Kommandierenden General der Luftstreitkräfte (Kogenluft)*, General in command of the German Army Air Service. Thomsen was appointed as his chief of staff, and Major Siegert remained at *Idflieg* (*Inspektion der Fliegertruppen* – Inspectorate of Aviation Troops). These three men ran the *Luftstreitkräfte* (the Imperial German Air Service) until the end of the war. Like the RFC, the *Luftstreitkräfte* was part of the army, not a fully independent air service. In von Hoeppner's words, the Germans now realized 'numbers, leadership, fighting spirit and the technical excellence of fighter airplanes themselves would increasingly determine the outcome of the struggle for air superiority'.

The Germans had learned their lessons; they had combined the latest tactics, training, and organization with the best available technology. The result was German air superiority until the late spring of 1917, when new Allied fighters arrived. The German fighter pilots became significantly more aggressive and started scoring heavily against Allied airmen. The improved training instigated by Boelcke and adopted by other *Jasta* leaders also came at a time when British training standards had reached a low point. In September the RFC lost 170 airmen in combat, more than two-thirds in the last half of the month following introduction of the new *Jasta* tactics. British casualties continued to rise in October, and the life expectancy of a new RFC pilot at the Front dropped to three weeks.

Tragically, although he played a key role in resurrecting German air superiority, Boelcke was not to enjoy it for long. On 28 October 1916, with his victory score standing at 40, the first ace on either side to reach this number, Boelcke was killed as the result of a mid-air collision during combat. Taking off with Böhme, his closest friend, von Richthofen, and three other pilots to intercept British airplanes that had just crossed the lines, they came upon two DH.2s of No. 24 Squadron, RFC. During the attack

that followed, Böhme and Boelcke both closed on the same DH.2 when another flew across their path. Böhme and Boelcke manoeuvred abruptly to avoid a collision, and in doing so lost sight of each other because their wings blocked their view. As they recovered from this manoeuvre, Boelcke's upper left wing lightly touched Böhme's undercarriage, breaking it. Böhme quickly recovered and watched in growing concern as Boelcke's Albatros glided down in an ever steepening dive, crashing near a German artillery battery. Unrestrained by a safety harness, Boelcke was killed in a crash that he likely would have otherwise survived.

'Our brave and chivalrous foe'

Boelcke's death shocked the German fighter community and the nation. An RFC airplane flew over Boelcke's elaborate funeral and dropped a laurel wreath with the inscription 'To the memory of Captain Boelcke, our brave and chivalrous foe. From the British Royal Flying Corps'. By imperial decree the Kaiser renamed *Jasta* 2 as *Jasta Boelcke*, with Boelcke's life to serve as a model for all aspiring fighter pilots. More than just a great fighter pilot, Boelcke was the first great fighter tactician, and his Dicta became the official tactical air doctrine of the German fighter forces. He also set an unprecedented example by intensely training his pilots before combat. And he was one of the uncommon examples of chivalry in an air war that has been romanticized, perhaps partly in comparison to the ghastly horror on the ground. Early in his flying career Boelcke rescued a drowning French boy and the villagers wrote the French government requesting he be given a medal for his heroic action. Not surprisingly, no French medal was forthcoming, although he did receive a German lifesaving medal for his deed.

On 23 November von Richthofen avenged Boelcke's death by shooting down Major Lanoe Hawker, VC, who was CO of No. 24 Squadron, which had figured in Boelcke's death. Hawker was an excellent pilot and early ace who was awarded the first Victoria Cross awarded for air combat between airplanes after shooting down two German aircraft while flying the Bristol Scout with its obliquely firing armament. In September 1915 Hawker was posted to command newly formed No. 24 Squadron, destined to be the RFC's first fighter squadron. After forming up and receiving its DH.2s, the squadron flew to

St Omer in France on 8 February 1916. Hawker's combat tactics were simpler than Boelcke's; a board was erected in the squadron area that said: 'Tactical Orders by O.C. No. 24 Squadron, Royal Flying Corps: Attack everything'. It was signed by Hawker. On the fateful day, Hawker, now with 12 victories, ended up in single combat with von Richthofen in his Albatros D.II. The DH.2 was easier to manoeuvre but the Albatros possessed every other advantage, and during the fight lasting some minutes, Richthofen had the initiative and Hawker was on the defensive. In the course of the fight the prevailing westerly wind was pushing the two combatants further into German lines. Finally, Hawker had to break off combat and run for British lines; Richthofen shot him down and Hawker was killed. Both pilots were experienced aces, and Richthofen owed this victory, his 11th out of an eventual 80 that made him the leading ace of the war, to the superiority of the Albatros.

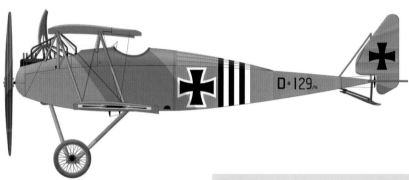

▲ Halberstadt D.III

Unknown Unit / Western Front / 1916

The Halberstadt D.III differed from the earlier D.II only in its use of an Argus engine in place of a Mercedes. It retained the strength and excellent handling and manoeuvrability of the D.II.

Specifications

Crew: 1	Service ceiling: 4500m (14,764ft)
Powerplant: 1 x 890kW (120hp) Argus As.II inline engine	Dimensions: span 8.80m (28ft 10.4in); length 7.30m (23ft 11.4in) height 2.66m (8ft 8.8in)
Maximum speed: 160km/h (99.4mph)	Weight: 771kg (1770lb) max take-off
Endurance: 2 hours	Armament: 1 x 7.92mm (.313in) Spandau MG

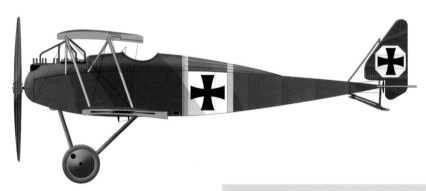

▲ Halberstadt D.V

Jasta 4 / Western Front / 1916

The D.V featured redesigned bracing struts to improve the pilot's field of view. This Halberstadt D.V was flown by *Oblt*. Hans-Joachim Buddecke, *Staffelführer* of *Jasta 4*. The third ace to win the Pour le Mérite, Buddecke scored 13 confirmed victories in France and the Middle East before being KIA 10 March 1918.

Specifications

Crew: 1	Service ceiling: 4500m (14,764ft)
Powerplant: 1 x 90kW (120hp) Argus As.II engine	Dimensions: span 8.80m (28ft 10.4in); length 7.30m (23ft 11.4in) height 2.66m (8ft 8.8in)
Maximum speed: 160km/h (99mph)	Weight: 812kg (1790lb) max take-off
Endurance: 2 hours	Armament: 1 x 7.92mm (.313in) Spandau MG

New Allied Fighters

While the Germans introduced the superior Albatros and other new biplane fighters, the Allies also continued developing new fighters. The 60kW (80hp) Nieuport 11 was given a more powerful 82kW (110hp) engine to create the nose-heavy Nieuport 16; an enlarged, more balanced airframe resulted in the Nieuport 17 that arrived in June. In most Nieuport 17 fighters a synchronized gun replaced the over-wing gun.

The French SPAD company's first fighter series was the unusual SA series of 'pulpit' two-seat fighters. The SA series were tractor biplanes with a gunner's nacelle mounted in front of the engine and propeller to give a wide field of fire. As well as its additional weight, the nacelle limited propeller efficiency and impeded the flow of cooling air to the engine, limiting the power of the engine that could be fitted. The concept was a failure and only about a hundred were built. Only one

▲ **Albatros D.I**

Jasta Boelcke (Honor Name for Jasta 2) / Lagnicourt Aerodrome, France / November 1916

The Albatros D.I was the fastest, most powerful fighter at the Front when it first arrived, and immediately established superiority over Allied fighters. This is the D.I of *Ltn* Karl-Heinrich Büttner of *Jasta Boelcke*, who was downed 16 November 1916 by Capt Parker and Lt Harvey of No. 8 Sqdn. RFC in a BE.2C.

Specifications

Crew: 1	Dimensions: span 8.50m (27ft 10in);
Powerplant: 1 x 119kW (160hp) Mercedes D.III	length 7.40m (24ft 3in); height 2.95m
inline piston engine	(9ft 8in)
Maximum speed: 175km/h (109mph)	Weight: 922kg (1980lb) max take-off
Endurance: 1hr 30 mins	Armament: 2 x 7.92mm (.313in) Spandau MG
Service ceiling: 5182m (17,000ft)	

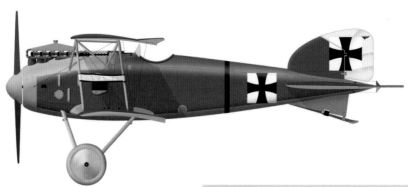

▲ **Albatros D.II**

Jasta Boelcke (Honor Name for Jasta 2) / Lagnicourt Aerodrome, France / late 1916

The Albatros D.II differed from the earlier D.I by its upper-wing position, which was lowered to improve the pilot's field of view. This D.II was flown by *Oblt* Stephan Kirmaier, *Staffelführer* of *Jasta 2* after Boelcke's death, who achieved 11 victories before being KIA 22 November 1916.

Specifications

Crew: 1	Dimensions: span 8.50m (27ft 10in);
Powerplant: 1 x 119kW (160hp)	length 7.40m (24ft 3in); height 2.65m
Mercedes D.III inline piston engine	(8ft 8in)
Maximum speed: 175km/h (109.4mph)	Weight: 898kg (1980lb) max take-off
Endurance: 1hr 30 mins	Armament: 2 x 7.92mm (.313in) Spandau MGs
Service ceiling: 5182m (17,000ft)	

French SPAD SA succeeded in downing a German airplane, although a few more victories were scored by the SA in Russian service. The story could have ended there with failure. However, the SA series, while flawed in concept, had a robust airframe, and in one of the great aviation success stories of the war, the failed SA series was developed into the highly successful SPAD VII that was one of the best fighters of the war. By eliminating the troublesome gunner's nacelle, installing a synchronized machine gun, and replacing the underpowered rotary engine with the innovative 112kW (150hp) Hispano-Suiza V-8, SPAD transformed the SA failure into the SPAD VII success. All subsequent wartime SPAD aircraft were developed from the SPAD VII, and SPAD fighters were supplied to Britain, Italy, Belgium, Russia and the USA.

The SPAD VII was a very strong airplane and its 112kW (150hp) Hispano-Suiza engine, later boosted to 134kW (180hp), gave it excellent performance. Arriving at the Front the same month as the

▲ Albatros D.II LVG

Jasta 22 / Vauz Aerodrome, Western Front / March 1917

Late production D.IIs had an airfoil radiator instead of the ear radiator shown here. The airfoil radiator reduced drag and retained water in the engine in event of a leak, enabling the engine to run longer. This D.II was flown by *Ltn* Josef Jacobs in March 1917. Jacobs went on to score 48 victories and was awarded the Pour le Mérite. Jacobs survived the war; 'Kobes' was his personal marking.

Specifications

Crew: 1

Powerplant: 1 x 119kW (160hp) Mercedes
    D.III inline engine

Maximum speed: 175km/h (109.4mph)

Endurance: 1hr 30 mins

Service ceiling: 5180m (17,000ft)

Dimensions: span 8.50m (27ft 10in); length
    7.40m (24ft 3in) height 2.65m (8ft 8in)

Weight: 937kg (2068lb) max take-off

Armament: 2 x 7.92mm (0.313in) Spandau
    MGs

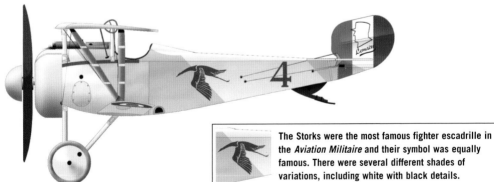

The Storks were the most famous fighter escadrille in the *Aviation Militaire* and their symbol was equally famous. There were several different shades of variations, including white with black details.

▲ Nieuport 17

Escadrille N 3 (the Storks) / Cachy Aerodrome, France / 1916

The Nieuport 17 combined the engine of the Nieuport 16 with a slightly enlarged airframe for better manoeuvrability and flying characteristics. It was used widely by France, Belgium, Italy, Russia and Britain. This example was flown by *Adj* Lemaire. The red stork was the unit insignia, the silhouette on the rudder was personal. The *'cone de penetration'* was fixed and did not rotate with the propeller.

Specifications

Crew: 1

Powerplant: 1 x 82kW (110hp) Le Rhône 9J
    rotary piston engine

Maximum speed: 170km/h (106mph)

Range: 250km (155 miles)

Service ceiling: 1980m (6500ft)

Dimensions: span 8.2m (26ft 11in); length
    5.96m (19ft 7in); height 2.44m (8ft)

Weight: 560kg (1235lb) max take-off

Armament: 1 x 7.7mm (0.303in) fixed forward-
    firing Vickers MG

Albatros, its main shortcoming was its single machine gun compared to the two guns of the Albatros. But the SPAD also had teething problems with its engine and radiator and initially this limited its combat effectiveness and, for a time, slowed the numbers that reached service; eventually it was produced in great quantity. While French industry was focusing on Nieuports and the new SPAD VII, the British developed the Sopwith 'Pup' fighter, so called because it looked like a smaller version of the earlier Strutter. The Pup was enjoyable to fly and a good match for the Albatros in a dogfight, but its 60kW (80hp) engine only enabled it to carry a single synchronized machine gun. The first of a long line of successful Sopwith fighters, the Pup was superior to the DH.2 pusher in all respects.

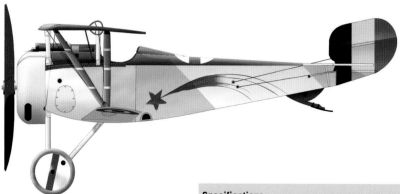

▲ **Nieuport 23**

5eme Escadrille Belge / De Moeren Aerodrome, Belgium / 1917

This Nieuport 23 was flown by Adj Edmond Thieffry, Belgium's third-ranking ace who scored 10 victories before being shot down by a two-seater and being taken prisoner. The Nieuport 23 differed from the Nieuport 17 in minor details like the synchronizing gear and served alongside the Nieuport 17 in fighter units.

Specifications

Crew: 1	Dimensions: span 8.20m (26ft 11in);
Powerplant: 1 x 90kW (120hp)	length 6.40m (21ft 0in); height 2.40m
Le Rhône 9Jb engine	(7ft 11in)
Maximum speed: 168km/h (105mph)	Weight: 574kg (1263lb) loaded
Endurance: 1hr 7 mins	Armament: 1 x 7.7mm (0.303in) fixed forward-
Service ceiling: 6500m (21,000ft)	firing Vickers MG

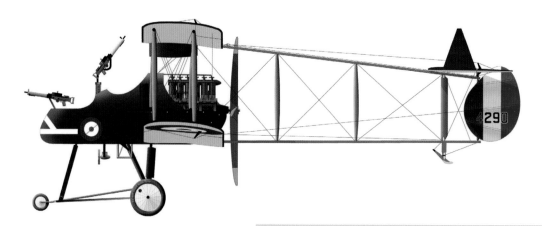

▲ **RAF FE.2B**

No.11 Squadron, RFC / France / September 1916

The FE.2 series arrived at the Front in January 1916 and served to war's end, establishing the longest record of combat service of any World War I airplane despite its pusher configuration. Lt E. Burton and 2/Lt F.W. Griffith were downed and taken prisoner in this example on 2 September 1916. The white triangle on the nose was an unofficial squadron marking.

Specifications

Crew: 2	Service ceiling: 2745m (9000ft)
Powerplant: 1 x 89kW (120hp) Beardmore or 1	Dimensions: span 14.55m (47ft 9in); length
x 119kW (160hp) Beardmore inline piston	9.83m (32ft 3in); height 3.85m (12ft 7in)
engine	Weight: 1347kg (2970lb) max take-off
Maximum speed: 129km/h (80mph)	Armament: 1–2 x 7.62mm (0.303in) Lewis
Endurance: 3 hours	MGs, plus up to 159kg (350lb) of bombs

Bloody April
APRIL 1917

New German airplanes, tactics, training and organization resulted in a period of growing air superiority culminating in the Allied disaster of 'Bloody April' 1917.

DESPITE THE NEWER Allied fighters being introduced, momentum remained with the German *Jastas*. In late 1916, the powerful, two-gun Albatros was the best fighter at the Front, and the new *Jastas* made the most of it. And this time, the Germans did not rest on their technology laurels; with the Albatros D.II superior to Allied fighters and strength building rapidly, the Germans introduced the Albatros D.III with even better performance. The D.III adapted the Nieuport sesquiplane (one and a half wing) wing cellule to the basic Albatros design, improving its downard visibility, speed and climb rate. However, the single-spar lower wing of the Nieuport was not robust, a weakness exacerbated by the greater weight and speed of the Albatros D.III, which subjected the wing to greater stresses. This would lead to problems.

Meanwhile, Trenchard was alarmed about the appearance of superior German fighters, their use of better tactics, and their growing numbers. He communicated his concern as early as September, and in December visited London to urge that his fighter strength be increased dramatically and soon. The only effective way this could be done was to introduce a signficant number of new fighter types with better performance. Unfortunately, production and training difficulties delayed delivery of most of these better airplanes until late spring 1917.

In January 1917 von Richthofen was finally awarded the Pour le Mérite, known familiarly as the Blue Max, Germany's highest award, after his 16th victory and given command of *Jasta 11*. Until Richthofen arrived, *Jasta 11* had not claimed a single victory. Richthofen immediately solved that problem; the day he arrived at *Jasta 11* he shot down an FE.8

At this time there was no squadron marking but the flight letter, in this case 'C', was marked on the nose and the aircraft tactical number in the flight, in this case '6', was painted on either side.

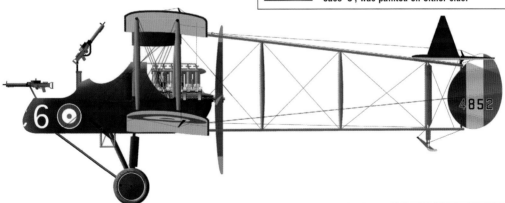

▲ **RAF FE.2B**

No. 23 Squadron, RFC / France / September 1916

The FE.2 served as a day fighter, reconnaissance plane, day bomber and night bomber during its long career. When flown in formation the FE.2s were dangerous opponents; the Red Baron was severely wounded in combat with an FE.2. While flying this aircraft on 17 September 1916, Lt F.G. Thiery and Lt Buck were downed by *Hptm* Zander of *KG 1* and made prisoners of war.

Specifications

Crew: 2

Powerplant: 1 x 89kW (120hp) Beardmore or 1 x 119kW (160hp) Beardmore inline piston engine

Maximum speed: 129km/h (80mph)

Endurance: 3 hours

Service ceiling: 2745m (9000ft)

Dimensions: span 14.55m (47ft 9in); length 9.83m (32ft 3in); height 3.85m (12ft 7in)

Weight: 1347kg (2970lb) max take-off

Armament: 1–2 x 7.62mm (0.303in) Lewis MGs, plus up to 159kg (350lb) of bombs

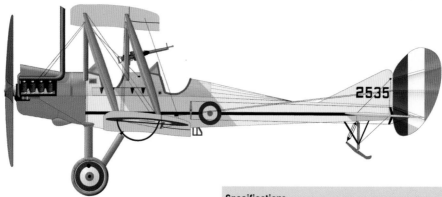

▲ Royal Aircraft Factory BE.2c

No.13 Squadron, RFC / France / 1916

The reliable but vulnerable BE.2 series remained at the Front long after it was obsolete, suffering heavy losses to German fighters. Only their crews' courage enabled them to carry on.

Specifications

Crew: 2

Powerplant: 1 x 52kW (70hp) Renault V-8 and 1
x 67kW (90hp) RAF 1a V-8

Maximum speed: 121km/h (75mph)

Endurance: 3 hours 15 mins

Service ceiling: 3048m (10,000ft)

Dimensions: span 12.42m (40ft 9in); length
8.31m (27ft 3in); height 3.66m (12ft)

Weight: 972kg (2142lb) max take-off

Armament: 1 x 7.7mm (.303in) Lewis MG for
observer in front cockpit

Specifications

Crew: 1

Powerplant: 1 x 60kW (80hp) Le Rhône 9C,
1 x 60kW (80hp) Clerget 7Z, 1 x 60kW
(80hp) Gnome Lambda, 1 x 75kW (100hp)
Gnome Monosoupape B-2, 82kW (110hp)
LeRhone 9J, 45kW (60hp) LeRhone 7B
rotary

Maximum speed: 169km/h (105mph)

Endurance: 3 hours

Service ceiling: 5334m (17,500ft)

Dimensions: span 8.08m (26ft 6in); length
5.89m (19ft 4in); height 3.30m (8ft 11in)

Weight: 556kg (1225lb) max take-off

Armament: 1 x 7.7mm (.303in) Vickers MG

▲ Sopwith Pup

No. 66 Squadron, RFC / Estree Blanche Aerodrome, France / September 1917

The Sopwith Pup was a delightful airplane beloved by its pilots. Despite having half the engine power and firepower of the Albatros, it could hold its own in a dogfight. This example was flown by Lt. P.G. Taylor from Estree Blanche Aerodrome in September 1917.

Specifications

Crew: 1

Powerplant: 1 x 60kW (80hp) Le Rhône 9C,
1 x 60kW (80hp), 1 x 60kW (80hp) Clerget
7Z, 1 x 60kW (80hp) Gnome Lambda, 1 x
75kW (100hp) Gnome Monosoupape B-2,
82kW (110hp) LeRhone 9J, 45kW (60hp)
LeRhone 7B rotary

Maximum speed: 169km/h (105mph)

Endurance: 3 hours

Service ceiling: 5334m (17,500ft)

Dimensions: span 8.08m (26ft 6in); length
5.89m (19ft 4in); height 3.30m (8ft 11in)

Weight: 556kg (1225lb) max take-off

Armament: 1 x 7.7mm (.303in) Vickers MG

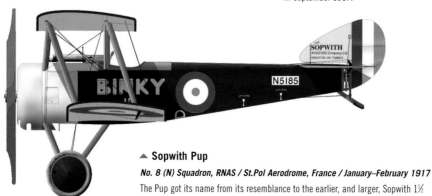

▲ Sopwith Pup

No. 8 (N) Squadron, RNAS / St.Pol Aerodrome, France / January–February 1917

The Pup got its name from its resemblance to the earlier, and larger, Sopwith 1½ Strutter. *Binky II* was probably flown by FSL G.G. Simpson, who flew the similarly marked Sopwith Triplane *Binky III*.

Specifications

Crew: 2

Powerplant: 1 x 142kW (190hp) Rolls-Royce
  Falcon I V-12

Maximum speed: 171km/h (106mph)

Endurance: 3 hours 15 mins

Service ceiling: 5029m (16,500ft)

Dimensions: span 11.86m (39ft 3in);
  length 7.85m (25ft 9in); height 2.95m
  (9ft 9in)

Weight: 1210kg (2667lb) loaded

Armament: 1 x 7.7mm (.303in) fixed Vickers
  MG and 1 x 7.7mm (.303in) flexible
  Lewis MG

▲ Bristol F.2A

No. 48 Squadron, RFC / La Bellevue Aerodrome, France / April 1917

The Bristol F.2A and F.2B was one of the great warplanes of WWI but initially was
misused, being flown as a typical two-seater with painful losses. This F.2A flown
by Pike and Griffiths was one of the two survivors of the disastrous first combat
with *Jasta 11* when four of the six Bristols were downed. When flown as a two-
seat fighter the Bristol excelled.

▲ Albatros D.III

*Jasta Boelcke (Honor Name for Jasta 2) / Pronville Aerodrome, France /
Spring–Summer 1917*

Albatros D.III of *Ltn.* Werner Voss of *Jasta Boelcke.* Voss scored 48 victories before being killed in action on 23 September
1917 while flying a prototype Fokker Triplane in single-handed combat with a flight from 56 Sqdn, RFC, in one of the most
famous dogfights of the war. He was 20 and already a holder of the Pour le Mérite. The heart and swastika with wreath
were Voss's personal markings; the white tail was the unit marking at this time.

Specifications

Crew: 1

Powerplant: 1 x 119kW (160hp)
  Mercedes D.III inline piston engine

Maximum speed: 164km/h (102mph)

Endurance: 2 hours

Service ceiling: 5486m (18,000ft)

Dimensions: span 8.99m (29ft 6in);
  length 7.33m (24ft); height 2.90m (9ft 6in)

Weight: 908kg (2002lb) loaded

Armament: 2 x 7.92mm (.313in) Spandau
  MGs

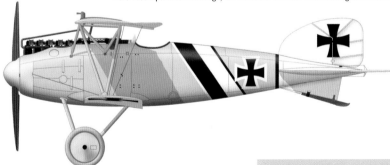

▲ Albatros D.III

*Jasta Boelcke (Honor Name for Jasta 2) / Pronville Aerodrome, France /
Spring–Summer 1917*

Albatros D.III of *Ltn.* Hermann Frommherz of *Jasta Boelcke.* Frommherz scored 32
victories and was nominated for the Pour le Mérite, but the Kaiser abdicated
before it could be awarded. The white tail was the unit marking at this time; the
stripes were Frommherz's personal marking.

Specifications

Crew: 1

Powerplant: 1 x 119kW (160hp)
  Mercedes D.III inline piston engine

Maximum speed: 164km/h (102mph)

Endurance: 2 hours

Service ceiling: 5486m (18,000ft)

Dimensions: span 8.99m (29ft 6in);
  length 7.33m (24ft); height 2.90m (9ft 6in)

Weight: 908kg (2002lb) loaded

Armament: 2 x 7.92mm (.313in) Spandau MGs

fighter, a pusher design much like the DH.2 and obsolete when it reached the Front. The next day he downed an FE.2b. Richthofen also instructed his pilots in Boelcke's Dicta and that, together with his dynamic leadership by example, transformed the unit.

Arras Offensive approaches

In March 1917 the weather improved significantly, enabling increased air activity. Air fighting became much more intense, and British losses rose to 120 aircraft, almost half over the British lines. Trenchard now faced a dilemma; his losses were high in the face of German technical superiority, but the imminent Arras offensive required extensive reconnaissance well behind German lines. British hours flown per casualty fell from 186 hours in October 1916 to a mere 101 hours in March 1917. At the same time, the demand for more and deeper reconnaissance missions increased as the date for the Arras offensive approached. Despite increasing casualties, Trenchard was compelled to order the essential reconnaissance flights.

March was a difficult month. On the 24th, No. 70 Squadron dispatched six Sopwith Strutters on a reconnaissance mission. A dozen Albatros fighters bounced them, shooting down two and riddling the rest, which barely made it home. The next day 70 Squadron attempted to complete the mission with another group of six Strutters. One survived because it turned back early with engine trouble; the other

five were shot down over the German lines by Albatros fighters of *Jastas* 5 and 6. In 11 months the Strutter had gone from triumph over the *Eindeckers* to obsolescence against the Albatros. So great were the casualties that the RFC had to recruit gunners from the infantry. Frank Courtney, a flight commander in 70 Squadron, related that a volunteer infantry gunner arrived at the squadron and during his briefing, asked why the squadron was known as the Suicide Club; he was posted missing the next day.

At this time the British had 754 aircraft along their front, including 385 fighters, arrayed against 264 German airplanes, 114 of which were fighters. Some of the British fighters were Nieuports, Sopwith Pups and SPADs, but most of them were the old DH.2 and FE.2b. Trenchard decided to go on the offensive on 4 April, five days before the Arras ground offensive was to begin. Things went badly. On 5 April a formation of six new Bristol F.2A two-seat fighters from No. 48 Squadron, the first of their kind at the Front, flew their first mission over the lines lead by Capt Leefe Robinson, VC. (Robinson had been awarded the VC for shooting down a German airship at night over Britain in 1916.) Unfortunately, Robinson had no experience in combat against other fighters, and he insisted on following defensive tactics whereby the pilot was supposed to manoeuvre the airplane to give the gunner the best opportunity for a shot. These tactics were appropriate for a typical

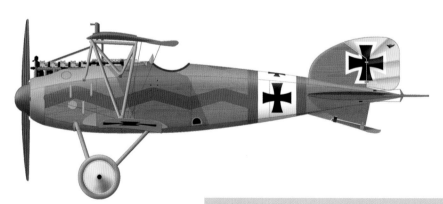

▲ **Albatros D.III**

Jasta 11 / Douai Aerodrome, France / Spring 1917

When the Red Baron reached *Jasta 11* as its commander in January 1917, the unit had not downed a single enemy airplane. Richthofen scored his first victory with *Jasta 11* the day he arrived, and through his personal leadership transformed it into a feared fighter unit. Red was the unit's color; the design was the personal marking of the unknown pilot.

Specifications

Crew: 1	Dimensions: span 8.99m (29ft 6in);
Powerplant: 1 x 119kW (160hp)	length 7.33m (24ft); height 2.90m (9ft 6in)
Mercedes D.III inline piston engine	Weight: 908kg (2002lb) loaded
Maximum speed: 164km/h (102mph)	Armament: 2 x 7.92mm (.313in) Spandau MGs
Endurance: 2 hours	
Service ceiling: 5486m (18,000ft)	

Specifications

Crew: 1

Powerplant: 1 x 119kW (160hp)
  Mercedes D.III inline piston engine

Maximum speed: 164km/h (102mph)

Endurance: 2 hours

Service ceiling: 5486m (18,000ft)

Dimensions: span 8.99m (29ft 6in);
  length 7.33m (24ft); height 2.90m (9ft
  6in)

Weight: 908kg (2002lb) loaded

Armament: 2 x 7.92mm (.313in) Spandau
  MGs

▲ Albatros D.III

Flieger Abteilung (A) 263 / Western Front / 1917

This Albatros was fitted with a camera for high-speed reconnaissance and flown
by *Ltn.* Rudolf Hohberg. The insignia on the fuselage was his personal marking.

▲ LVG C.II

Kagohl I, Staffel 6 / Western Front / 1916

The LVG C.II was a sturdy reconnaissance plane used on both Eastern and
Western Fronts. This C.II was flown by *Fähnrich* Jureck and *Ltn* Christensen
of *Staffel 6, Kagohl 1.*

Specifications

Crew: 2

Powerplant: 1 x 119kW (160hp) Mercedes D.III
  inline engine

Maximum speed: 130km/h (80.78mph))

Endurance: 4 hours

Service ceiling: 4000m (13,123ft)

Dimensions: span 12.85m (42ft 2in); length
  8.10m (26ft 7in) height 2.93m (9ft 7in)

Weight: 1405kg (3097lb) max take-off

Armament: 1 x 7.92mm (.313in) fixed Spandau
  MG and 1 x 7.92mm (.313in) flexible
  Parabellum MG

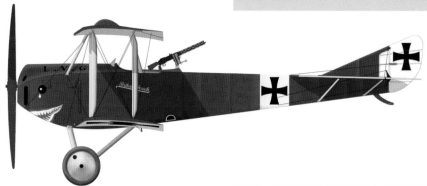

▲ LVG C.IV

Unknown Unit / Western Front / 1916

LVG C.IV *Britenschreck* (Briton's Terror) of an unknown unit sports one of the
earliest known shark-mouth schemes. The C.IV was powered by the Mercedes
D.IV straight-eight engine and was as fast as opposing fighters when it
reached the Front. On 28 November 1916 a lone C.IV was the first aircraft to
bomb London.

Specifications

Crew: 2

Powerplant: 1 x 164kW (220hp)
  Mercedes D.IV inline engine

Maximum speed: 172km/h (106.9mph)

Endurance: n/a

Service ceiling: About 4500m (14,764ft)

Dimensions: span 13.6m (44ft 7.3in); length
  8.51m (27ft 11in); height Unknown

Weight: 1600kg (3527lb) max take-off

Armament: 1 x 7.92mm (.313in) fixed Spandau
  MG and 1 x 7.92mm (.313in) flexible
  Parabellum MG

reconnaissance two-seater, but the new Bristol F.2A was designed as a fighter. As luck would have it, the six Bristol Fighters ran into five Albatros fighters from *Jasta* 11 lead by von Richthofen. The Bristols flew like any other group of two-seaters and *Jasta* 11 treated them that way. The Albatros fighters shot down four of the Bristols, including Robinson's, and

the other two returned riddled with bullets. Robinson survived as a prisoner of war, but died in the worldwide flu epidemic.

This disaster was a major setback to Trenchard's hopes for the new fighter. Fortunately, it was a case of inexperience and poor tactics overcoming excellent technology; this would be resolved as the RFC slowly

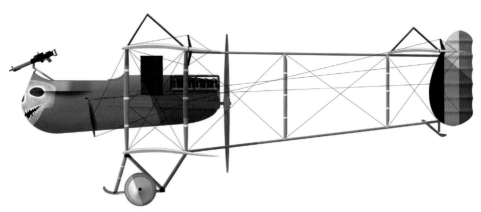

▲ Farman F.40bis Type 60

8eme Escadrille Belge / Coudekerke Aerodrome, France / July 1917

The Farman Type 60 was a Farman F.40bis with a 119kW (160hp) Renault 8c engine. In fact, it was one of many variations on the basic F.40; the extra power gave it a useful speed increase. This one was flown by Lt Jaumotte and *Sous-Lt* Wouters from Coudekerke Aerodrome in July 1917, long after it was obsolete in the face of contemporary fighers.

Specifications

Crew: 1	Dimensions: span 17.67m (57ft 9in); length
Powerplant: 1 x 119kW (160hp) Renault 8c	9.15m (30ft 4in); height 3.75m (12ft 9in)
Maximum speed: 150km/h (84mph)	Weight: 1200kg (2469lb) max take-off
Endurance: 2 hours 20 mins	Armament: 1–2 x 7.7mm (.303in) Lewis MGs
Service ceiling: 4000m (13,125ft)	on flexible mounts in nose, plus light bombs

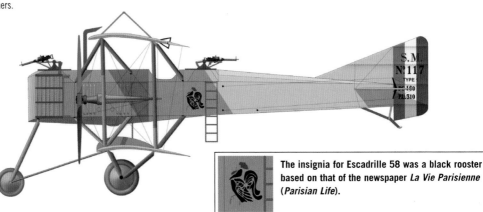

The insignia for Escadrille 58 was a black rooster based on that of the newspaper *La Vie Parisienne* (*Parisian Life*).

▲ Salmson-Moineau SM.1

Escadrille F 58 / France / 1917

The SM.1 was an unusual long-range reconnaissance plane. One engine drove two propellers via extension shafts and there were gunners fore and aft. It served in small numbers in a variety of units, but no unit was entirely equipped with it. The rooster on the side is the unit marking.

Specifications

Crew: 3	Service ceiling: Unknown
Powerplant: 1 x 179kW (240hp) Salmon 9A2c	Dimensions: span 17.48m (57ft 4in); length
engine	10m (32ft 9.7in) height 3.80m (12ft 5.7in)
Maximum speed: n/a	Weight: 2050kg (4519lb) max take-off
Endurance: 3 hours	Armament: 2–3 x 7.7mm (.303in) Lewis MGs

LEADING BELGIAN ACES	
Ace	Score
Lt Willy Coppens	37
Lt Andre Demeulemeester	11
SLt Edmond Thieffry	10
Cmdt Fernand Jacquet	7
Lt Jan Olieslagers	6

LEADING UNITED KINGDOM ACES	
Ace	Score
Lt Col William Bishop	73
Lt Col Raymond Collishaw	62
Major Edward Mannock †	61
Major James McCudden †	57
Captain Anthony Beauchamp Proctor	54
Major Donald MacLaren	54
Major William Barker	50
Captain Robert Little †	47
Captain George McElroy †	46
Captain Albert Ball †	44
Major Tom Hazell	43
Captain Philip Fullard	40

Note: † indicates killed in the war.

learned to exploit the Bristol's performance as a fighter. When properly used it became the best two-seat fighter of the war. The F.2A model was powered by a 141kW (190hp) Rolls Royce Falcon V-12, and the F.2B had a more powerful, 205kW (275hp) version of the Falcon that gave it even better speed and climb. With good manoeuvrability for its size, excellent performance, and good armament (a synchronized Vickers for the pilot and flexible Lewis for the gunner) it could be flown offensively like a single-seat fighter, but with the added protection of the rear gunner. Sadly, this learning curve took too long to avoid the heavy casualties of Bloody April.

Weapon of ruthless efficiency

The intense fighting that opened April continued without respite for the month. The twin-gunned Albatros wrecked havoc with the single-gunned Allied fighters and obsolescent reconnaissance planes.

Gordon Taylor, an RFC Pup pilot, had an opportunity to fly a captured Albatros D.II a few weeks after Bloody April; he thought the Albatros 'a war machine, a weapon of ruthless efficiency', whereas he viewed the Pup as suitable for sport flying after the war. While the Pup could outmanoeuvre the Albatros, the Albatros had twice the firepower and twice the engine power, and being faster and able to out-climb and out-dive the Pup, usually had the initiative. The Albatros could also break off combat at

▲ **DFW C.V**

1.Marine Feld Flieger Abteilung / Flanders / Summer 1917

Introduced in late 1916, the DFW C.V was the quintessential German two-seater. More DFW C.Vs were built than any other German warplane and it served with distinction until the end of the war. Tough, manoeuvrable, and with good handling characteristics, the DFW C.V was a dangerous opponent of even the best fighters.

Specifications

Crew: 2

Powerplant: 1 x 149kW (200hp) Benz Bz.IV
  inline engine

Maximum speed: 155km/h (96.3mph)

Endurance: 3 hours 30 mins

Service ceiling: 5000m (16,400ft)

Dimensions: span 13.27m (43ft 6in); length
  7.88m (25ft 10in) height 3.25m (10ft 8in)

Weight: 1430kg (3234lb) max take-off

Armament: 1 x 7.92mm (.313in) fixed Spandau
  MG and 1 x 7.92mm (.313in) flexible
  Parabellum MG

▲ DFW C.V

Flieger Abteilung (A) 48 / Western Front / 1916

This early-production DFW C.V sports the ear radiators that were later regulated out of production to protect the engine in case of radiator leaks. The robust, manoeuvrable DFW was a tough opponent of Allied fighters from its introduction until the end of the war.

Specifications

Crew: 2

Powerplant: 1 x 149kW (200hp) Benz Bz.IV inline

Maximum speed: 155km/h (96.3mph)

Endurance: 3 hours 30 mins

Service ceiling: 5000m (16,400ft)

Dimensions: span 13.27m (43ft 6in); length 7.88m (25ft 10in) height 3.25m (10ft 8in)

Weight: 1430kg (3234lb) max take-off

Armament: 1 x 7.92mm (.313in) fixed Spandau MG and 1 x 7.92mm (.313in) flexible Parabellum MG

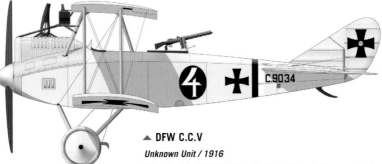

▲ DFW C.C.V

Unknown Unit / 1916

This Aviatik-built DFW C.V has the later style radiator mounted above the engine. Aviatik built 75 of their C.II type designed to the same requirement as the DFW C.V, then Aviatik were ordered to build the superior DFW under licence. The upper engine cowling panels were often removed in warm weather to improve cooling.

Specifications

Crew: 2

Powerplant: 1 x 149kW (200hp) Benz Bz.IV inline

Maximum speed: 155km/h (96.3mph)

Endurance: 3 hours 30 mins

Service ceiling: 5000m (16,400ft)

Dimensions: span 13.27m (43ft 6in); length 7.88m (25ft 10in) height 3.25m (10ft 8in)

Weight: 1430kg (3234lb) max take-off

Armament: 1 x 7.92mm (.313in) fixed Spandau MG and 1 x 7.92mm (.313in) flexible Parabellum MG

▲ Sopwith 1½ Strutter two-seater

No. 3 Wing, RNAS / Luxeuil-Les-Bains Aerodrome, France / October 1916

The Sopwith 1½ Strutter was the first two-seat fighter with a gun for both crewmen. This example from No. 3 Wing, RNAS was flown from Luxeuil-les-bains Aerodrome on the costly Oberndorf raid of 12 October 1916.

Specifications

Crew: 2

Powerplant: 1 x 97kW (130hp) Clerget 9B, 1 x 82kW (110hp) Clerget 9Z, 1 x 82kW (110hp) LeRhone rotary piston engine

Maximum speed: 164km/h (105mph)

Endurance: 3 hours 30 mins – 4 hours 30 mins

Service ceiling: 3960m (13,000ft)

Dimensions: span 10.21m (33ft 6in); length 7.70m (25ft 3in); height 3.12m (10ft 3in)

Weight: 2052kg (4524lb) max take-off

Armament: 1 x 7.7mm (.303in) fixed Vickers MG and 4 x 29kg (65lb) bombs, or similar weight of other sizes

LEADING FRENCH ACES	
Ace	Score
Captain René Fonck	75
Captain Georges Guynemer †	53
Lt Charles Nungesser	43
Captain Georges Madon	41
Lt Maurice Boyau †	35
Lt Michel Coiffard †	34
Lt Jean Bourjade	28
Captain Armand Pinsard	27
S-Lt René Dorme †	23
Lt Gabriel Guérin †	23
S-Lt Claude Haegelen	22
S-Lt Pierre Marinovitch	21
Captain Alfred Heurtaux	21
Captain Albert Deullin	20

Note: † indicates killed in the war.

LEADING GERMAN ACES	
Ace	Score
Rittm Manfred von Richthofen †	80
Oblt Ernst Udet	62
Oblt Eric Lowenhardt †	53
Lt Josef Jacobs	48
Lt Werner Voss †	48
Lt Fritz Rumey †	45
Hptm Rudolf Berthold	44
Lt Paul Baümer	43
Hptm Oswald Boelcke †	40
Lt Franz Büchner	40
Lt Lothar von Richthofen	40

Note: † indicates killed in the war.

will if a Pup got the tactical advantage. Among the RFC fighters the Nieuports took especially heavy losses; in two weeks 60 Squadron lost 13 pilots.

Within the first four days of the aerial offensive, the RFC lost 75 airplanes in combat and a further 56 airplanes in accidents. Squadron Commander Sholto Douglas recalled that his unit, 43 Squadron, took more than 100 percent casualties during April while flying the Strutter; 32 pilots and gunners were authorized the squadron and 35 were lost.

Replacements arrived just in time to be shot down, and six or seven of the original 32 squadron members survived April. So many escorts had to be provided, at least five for a reconnaissance plane, that the nominal RFC numerical superiority was nullified.

British losses were severe; 245 airplanes known lost directly as a result of combat, 211 aircrew killed, missing, or died of wounds, 108 taken prisoner and 116 wounded in action. In comparison, the RFC lost 499 aircrew in the four and a half months between 1 July and 22 November 1916, the period of the Somme. British aircrew never gave up, but by the end of April 1917 RFC morale was at its nadir.

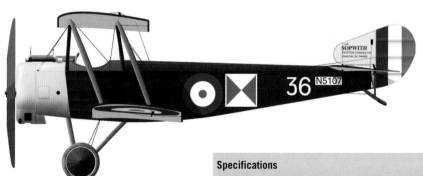

▲ **Sopwith 1½ Strutter single-seater**

No. 3 Wing, RNAS /Ochey Aerodrome, France / January 1917

The Sopwith 1½ Strutter was also flown as a single-seat bomber. This was because of the type's limited payload; with the weight of a gunner aboard it could not carry bombs. This example is from No. 3 Wing, RNAS, in January 1917. It was also built in large numbers in France to replace obsolete pusher designs.

Specifications

Crew: 1

Powerplant: 1 x 97kW (130hp) Clerget 9B, 1 x 82kW (110hp) Clerget 9Z, 1 x 82kW (110hp) LeRhone rotary piston engine

Maximum speed: 164km/h (102mph)

Endurance: 3 hours 30 mins – 4 hours 30 mins

Service ceiling: 3960m (13,000ft)

Dimensions: span 10.21m (33ft 6in); length 7.97m (25ft 3in); height 3.12m (10ft 3in)

Weight: 1062kg (2342lb) max take-off

Armament: 1 x 7.7mm (.303in) fixed Vickers MG and 1 x .7.7mm (.303in) flexible Lewis MG

▲ **Nieuport 20**

No. 45 Squadron, RFC / Ste Marie Cappel Aerodrome, France /
April–May 1917

The Nieuport 20 was essentially a development of the Nieuport 12 with a 82kW
(110hp) Le Rhône 9J engine, horseshoe cowling and other changes. Only 21 were
purchased for the RFC, its only user, as an emergency stopgap until the Sopwith
1½ Strutter became available in greater numbers.

Specifications

Crew: 2
Powerplant: 82kW (110hp) Le Rhône 9J
    rotary
Maximum speed: 157km/h (98mph)
Endurance: 3 hours
Service ceiling: 4000m (13,123ft)
Dimensions: span 9.0m (29ft 6in);
    length 7.0m (22ft 12in); height 2.7m (8ft
    10in)
Weight: 752kg (1658lb) loaded
Armament: 1 x 7.7mm (.303in) fixed Vickers
    MG and 1 x .7.7mm (.303in) flexible
    Lewis MG

Specifications

Crew: 1
Powerplant: 119kW (160hp) Mercedes D.III
    or 134kW (180hp) Mercedes D.IIIa inline
    piston engine
Maximum speed: 186km/h (116mph)
Endurance: About 2 hours
Service ceiling: 5700m (18,700ft)
Dimensions: span 9.05m (29ft 7in); length
    7.33m (24ft); height 2.70m (8ft 10in);
Weight: 937kg (2066lb) max take-off
Armament: 2 x 7.92mm (0.313in) LMG
    08/15 MGs

▲ **Albatros D.V**

Jasta 11 / Douai Aerodrome, France / June 1917

The more streamlined Albatros D.V reached the Front in May 1917, but there was
no noticable performance improvement over the D.III. This example was flown by
Manfred von Richthofen, the famous Red Baron, in June 1917. Red was the *Jasta
11* livery and Richthofen's airplane was all red. He scored 80 victories to make
him the war's leading ace before falling on 23 April 1918. Credit for shooting him
down was given both to RAF Capt A.R. Brown and Australian ground gunners.

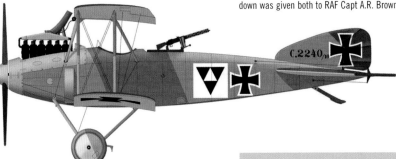

▲ **Albatros C.VII**

Unknown Unit / Western Front / 1916–17

The Albatros company was the largest airplane manufacturer in Germany during
the war and produced many different designs. The C.VII was a solid, reliable
reconnaissance plane that served in large numbers on both Eastern and Western
Fronts. This is a typical example of the type at the Front; the marking on the
fuselage identified this machine within its unit.

Specifications

Crew: 2
Powerplant: 1 x 149kW (200hp) Benz Bz.IV
    inline piston engine
Maximum speed: 170km/h (106mph)
Range: 3 hours 20 minutes
Service ceiling: 5000m (16,405ft)
Dimensions: span 12.78m (41ft 11in);
length 8.70m (28ft 6in); height 3.60m
    (11ft 9in)
Weight: 1550kg (3417lb) max take-off
Armament: 1 x 7.92mm (0.3in) LMG 08/15
    fixed forward-firing MG; 1 x 7.92mm
    (0.312in) LMG 14 Parabellum trainable
    rearward-firing MG

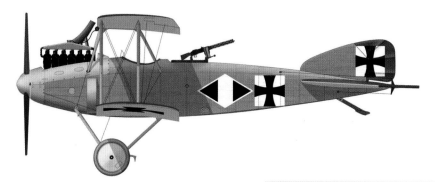

▲ Albatros C.VII

Unknown Unit / Western Front / 1916–17

The Albatros C.VII shared the robust, streamlined plywood fuselage of the Albatros fighters but retained the ear radiators that were later removed from production. Flamboyant markings were a rarity on the C.VII, but it was camouflaged on top of the wings and tailplane at the factory. The fuselage marking was an individual marking.

Specifications

Crew: 2

Powerplant: 1 x 149kW (200hp) Benz Bz.IV inline piston engine

Maximum speed: 170km/h (106mph)

Range: 3 hours 20 minutes

Service ceiling: 5000m (16,405ft)

Dimensions: span 12.78m (41ft 11in); length 8.70m (28ft 6in); height 3.60m (11ft 9in)

Weight: 1550kg (3417lb) max take-off

Armament: 1 x 7.92mm (0.3in) LMG 08/15 fixed forward-firing MG; 1 x 7.92mm (0.312in) LMG 14 Parabellum trainable rearward-firing MG

The striking Egyptian scarab emblem was the insignia of Escadrille C 56.

▲ Caudron G.6

Escadrille C 56 / Touljan Aerodrome, France / 1917

The Caudron G.6 replaced the G.4 in production and finally used a modern configuration that improved performance. The additional gunner in the nose together with the greater field of fire for the rear gunner greatly improved self-defence capability. This example was based at Touljan in 1917.

Specifications

Crew: 3

Powerplant: 2 x 89kW (120hp) Le Rhone rotary engines

Maximum speed: 163km/h (101mph)

Endurance: 3 hours

Service ceiling: 4400m (14,436ft)

Dimensions: span 17.22m (55ft 6in); length 8.6m (28ft 3in); height 2.5m (8ft 2in)

Weight: 1440kg (3175lb) max take-off

Armament: 4 x 7.7mm (0.303in) Lewis MG plus up to 100kg (220lb) of bombs

▲ **Dorand AR.1**

Escadrille AR 44 / France / 1917

Desperate to replace the obsolete and extremely vulnerable pusher designs used for reconnaissance, France introduced the AR.1 to the Front in early 1917. The boar marking is the escadrille insignia.

The black chimera holding a red shield with white Cross of Lorraine was the unit insignia of Escadrille 14. It replaced the earlier unit marking of a simple white Cross of Lorraine.

Specifications

Crew: 2	Dimensions: span 13.27m (43ft 6in);
Powerplant: 1 x 142kW (190hp) Renault 8Gd	length 9.3m (30ft 6in); height 3.3m (10ft 10in)
V-8 inline piston engine	Weight: 1250kg (2756lb) max take-off
Maximum speed: 152km/h (94mph)	Armament:1x 7.7mm (.303in) fixed Vickers MG;
Range: 375km	1 or 2 7.7mm (.303in) Lewis MGs, 4 x 120mm
Service ceiling: 5500m (18,045ft)	bombs

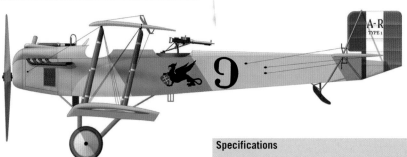

▲ **Dorand AR.1**

Escadrille AR 14 / France / 1917

The AR.1 was an inelegant design of mediocre performance. Nevertheless, even if its performance was little better than the Farman F.40 pusher, its configuration offered superior self-defence compared to the obsolete pushers used by the Allies for far too long. '9' was the tactical number within the escadrille.

Specifications

Crew: 2	Dimensions: span 13.27m (43ft 6in);
Powerplant: 1 x 142kW (190hp) Renault 8Gd V-	length 9.3m (30ft 6in); height 3.3m (10ft
8 inline piston engine	10in)
Maximum speed: 152km/h (94mph)	Weight: 1250kg (2756lb) max take-off
Range: 375km	Armament:1x 7.7mm (.303in) fixed Vickers MG;
Service ceiling: 5500m (18,045ft)	1 or 2 7.7mm (.303in) Lewis MGs, 4 x 120mm
	bombs

Who volunteered?
1914–1918

Despite the obvious dangers, the prestige of aviation and horrors of life in the trenches ensured there were always enough volunteers for aviation.

GIVEN THE ODDS, who would volunteer for such hazardous duty as flying in combat, especially at a time when flying was dangerous enough without someone shooting at you? While there was often a shortage of trained aircrew at the Front, there was seldom, if ever, a shortage of volunteers. A major factor was the romance and glory associated with combat flying in the minds of many. Others considered the alternative, the abomination of trench warfare, and decided that air combat, if not safer, would at least offer better living conditions until the inevitable. And unlike today, it was also a time of great patriotism and naiveté and limited cynicism.

At the time of World War I Britain still ruled over a huge empire and had a very large population to draw from. Of course, flying required basic skills that were not spread evenly throughout the Empire, but there were many aircrewmen from Canada,

Australia and New Zealand in the RFC. Flight schools were established in Canada and eventually Australia as well as Britain. Many Americans went to Canada before the United States entered the war to volunteer to fly for Britain. A few Americans even went to Germany to volunteer. However, Canada was much closer and more convenient, and not a few were primarily adventurers for whom getting into the action was perhaps more important than which side they found themselves fighting on.

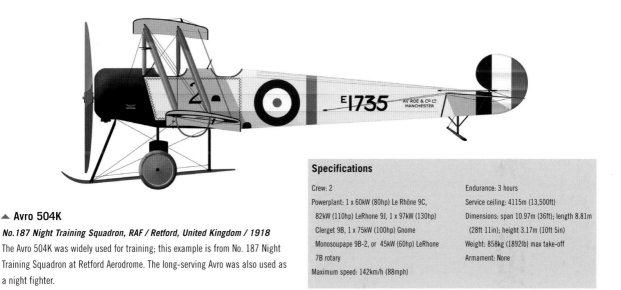

▲ **Avro 504K**

No.187 Night Training Squadron, RAF / Retford, United Kingdom / 1918

The Avro 504K was widely used for training; this example is from No. 187 Night Training Squadron at Retford Aerodrome. The long-serving Avro was also used as a night fighter.

Specifications

Crew: 2	Endurance: 3 hours
Powerplant: 1 x 60kW (80hp) Le Rhône 9C,	Service ceiling: 4115m (13,500ft)
82kW (110hp) LeRhone 9J, 1 x 97kW (130hp)	Dimensions: span 10.97m (36ft); length 8.81m
Clerget 9B, 1 x 75kW (100hp) Gnome	(28ft 11in); height 3.17m (10ft 5in)
Monosoupape 9B-2, or 45kW (60hp) LeRhone	Weight: 858kg (1892lb) max take-off
7B rotary	Armament: None
Maximum speed: 142km/h (88mph)	

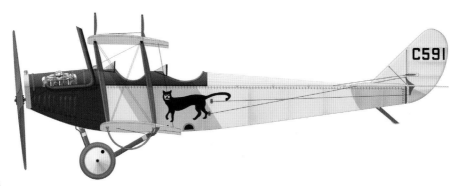

▲ **Curtiss JN4A**

No. 85 Canadian Replacement Squadron, RFC (Canada) / Rathbun Aerodrome, Canada / 1917

The Curtiss JN4 series were built under licence in Canada to train Canadians for the RFC. This example was based at Rathbun in Ontario; the black cat was the unit marking for No. 85 CRS. Many of No. 85's aircraft had tick marks on the tail of the cat to indicate the number of crashes that aircraft was involved in. This particular aircraft had a white-faced cat not seen on others in the squadron.

Specifications

Crew: 1	Dimensions: span 13.28m (43ft 7in);
Powerplant: 1 x 67kW (90hp) Curtiss OX-5	length 8.30m (27ft 3in); height 3.00m (9ft
inline piston engine	11in)
Maximum speed: 119km/h (74mph)	Weight: 875kg (1930lb) loaded
Range: 249km (155 miles)	Armament: None
Service ceiling: 3352m (11,000ft)	

France and Germany also had empires, although both were much smaller than the British Empire. In their cases, especially for Germany, which was immediately cut off from her colonies at the start of war, nearly every aviation volunteer came from the mother country.

Once war was under way, there was a continuous stream of volunteers for aviation from the armies and navies. The cavalry provided an especially fertile field for volunteers because after the Western Front trenches were extended from Switzerland to the sea, the cavalry was unable to perform their normal scouting function and was forced to fight as infantry. Many cavalrymen soon tired of this, and, with no end to it in sight, decided to volunteer for aviation. Manfred von Richthofen, the war's greatest ace, was one of many former cavalrymen who moved to aviation after trench warfare became the norm on the Western Front. Many infantrymen also wanted an honorable way out of the miseries of trench warfare and volunteered for aviation. Another source of aviation volunteers was recovered wounded. Many who were wounded in ground fighting wanted to continue serving their country but now lacked the physical strength and agility required of infantrymen. Often these men volunteered for flying. After all, while flying, a pilot was sitting down, an activity viewed as less strenuous than infantry fighting. It is interesting to compare that perspective with the attitude during and since World War II, where airmen must maintain the highest physical standards.

Early Allied aviation training

Aviation was in its infancy during the war as was flight training. Initially, the key prerequisite for being a flying instructor was being a pilot. There was little organization of the training syllabus and understanding was limited. As further experience was gained in flight, more rigorous standards for selecting flight instructors were used and a more comprehensive training syllabus was devised.

All pilot training involved instruction in flight with an instructor aboard the training airplane, but details differed. The French preferred a system that included students first learning to taxi a flightless airplane, or *rolleur* (often called a penguin), to master the controls and get a feel for handling an airplane before taking to the air the first time with an instructor. This approach was not used by the other major combatants and is now obsolete, having been replaced by sophisticated flight simulators. But only very primitive training aids were available during World War I. The British and American methods were more similar to what is used now, with ground school followed by dual flight instruction, then solo flight instruction, with no 'penguin' training.

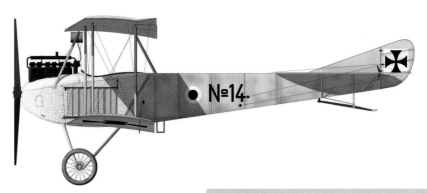

▲ **LVG B.I**

Herzog Karl Eduard Fliegerschule / Germany

When the sturdy, reliable LVG B.I was removed from the Front due to obsolescence, the survivors were sent to the training schools to give flight training to student pilots. Frequently they retained the markings from their front-line service. The black and white cockade was the insignia of the Herzog Karl Eduard Fliegerschule.

Specifications

Crew: 2

Powerplant: 1 x 75kW (100hp)

Maximum speed: 90km/h (56mph)

Range: n/a

Service ceiling: 2500m (8202ft)

Dimensions: span 14.5m (47ft 7in);
length 9m (29ft 7in); height n/a

Weight: 1132kg (2496lb) loaded

Armament: bomb load n/a

German aviation training

German flight instruction was similar in concept. However, whereas most Allied pilots had no previous flight experience before entering flight training, Germany preferred sending experienced observers to flight school to become pilots. These men already had a great deal of experience in the air and therefore had a much better idea of what to expect, something of significant practical value in the days before realistic flighty simulators. A German pilot's first operational posting was normally to a two-seater unit. After gaining experience as an operational pilot, posting back to a *fliegerschule* (pilot school) for transition to fighter airplanes would be the next step for those interested and considered qualified. Thus a typical new German fighter pilot would have significant operational experience as both an observer and pilot in two-seat airplanes before arriving at a *Jasta*, and von Richthofen was but one of many successful German fighter pilots to take this path. Of course, this was not always the case, and by the end of the war the pressure to train more pilots, coupled with the limited fuel available for training, significantly reduced the quality of training a German pilot received before posting to a *Jasta*.

Likewise, German observer training was very rigorous compared to Allied observer training, and included intensive tuition in map reading, map making and wireless telegraphy in addition to gunnery training. The observer was generally an

▲ **Nieuport Trainers**

Nieuport trainers lined up and awaiting students at a French training base.

officer with prior training with maps and infantry tactics, and the pilot was initially viewed merely as a chauffeur. From this viewpoint and the relative ranks, the observer was normally the airplane commander. When German two-seat fighters started to become numerous, many units had only one officer as commander, and all the other pilots and observers were enlisted. In this case the airplanes were tasked primarily with ground attack and visual observation, and the gunners did not normally receive the extensive training of observers in reconnaissance units.

The empirical and immature nature of flight training can be gauged from the fact that more than half of British aviation fatalities were in training. Though it is dismaying to contemplate, more pilots were killed during training than in combat.

▲ **Curtiss JN4**

C Flight, No. 78 Canadian Training Squadron, RFC (Canada) / Everman Field, Texas / Winter 1917–18

At least the USA was capable of building a useful training airplane; the Curtiss JN4 was delivered in quantity and served for years postwar. This example flew from Everman Field, Texas, training Canadians for the RFC during the winter of 1917–1918. Winter weather in Texas was more conducive to flying than that in Canada.

Specifications

Crew: 2

Powerplant: 1 x 67kW (90hp) Curtiss OX-5 inline piston engine

Maximum speed: 121km/h (75mph)

Range: n/a

Service ceiling: 1980m (6500ft)

Dimensions: span 13.3m (43ft 8in); length 8.33m (27ft 4in); height 3.01m (9ft 10in); Weight: 871kg (1920lb) max take-off

Armament: None

Chapter 3

Strategic Bombing

Strategic bombing is generally considered to be the bombing of targets well behind the front lines that are not specifically military targets, such as a factory producing weapons or economically critical goods. An airfield well behind the lines might be considered a tactical or operational target, something between ground attack and a strategic attack, whereas an airplane or aero-engine factory would be a strategic target. Despite the technological immaturity of airplanes and airships, both sides launched strategic bombing campaigns early in the war. The most sustained strategic bombing campaign was the German attempt to force Great Britain out of the war by air attack, first by airships, then by airplanes.

◀ **The first 'Battle of Britain'**
A British home lies in ruins after a Zeppelin raid. In early 1915 Germany launched the world's first strategic bombing campaign, using Zeppelins in a futile attempt to drive Britain out of the war. When the Zeppelins failed, airplanes carried on the campaign until May 1918.

Zeppelins over England
1915–AUGUST 1918

In an attempt to drive Britain out of the war, Zeppelins undertook the world's first strategic bombing campaign.

A PORTENT OF THINGS to come arrived on 21 December 1914, when a German Friedrichshafen FF29 seaplane, No. 203 of *SFA 1* (*see Flieger Abteilung 1*) attempted to bomb Dover, but the bombs fell into the sea. However, on the 24th, FF29 No. 204 of the same unit dropped a single 10kg (22lb) bomb on Dover that broke some windows. The next day FF29 No. 203 made its second bombing attempt, this time against the London dock area, but was driven off by a prototype Vickers Gunbus of No. 7 Squadron, RFC. These modest efforts, which continued into 1917, hardly qualify as strategic and succeeded merely in alerting the defences.

Early in 1915 things became more serious as the event some Britons had dreaded for years finally took place; the first Zeppelin bombing attack occurred on the night of 19/20 January when *L.3* bombed Great Yarmouth and *L.4*, having got completely lost, bombed King's Lynn. Four people were killed. Two defence sorties by Vickers F.B.5 Gunbuses failed to intercept the raiders.

This first Zeppelin attack set the pattern as airship raids on Britain grew in intensity. The Zeppelins could not find their way at night and dropped their bombs on any targets that presented themselves; likewise the British interceptors could not find the Zeppelins at night. On the rare occasions when British pilots did see a Zeppelin, they could not catch it before it disappeared in the clouds and darkness.

Three more Zeppelin attacks were made in April with little damage and few casualties. On 16 April a lone Albatros B.II from *FFA.41* made the first army airplane attack on England; no casualties resulted. Attacks continued and on the night of 31 May /1 June, Army Zeppelin *LZ38* finally found London and dropped a string of bombs; seven people were killed and 35 injured. British defenders flew 15 sorties attempting to intercept *LZ38*; only one pilot

▲ **L 33 in September 1916**
On 24 September 1916, L 33 was forced down during her first raid on England. Her design was copied by the British Admiralty and was reproduced as post-war British airships R 33 and R 34. Together with sister ships L 31 and L 32, her loss marked the turning point of the airship raids.

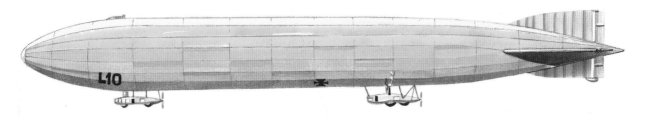

▲ L.10

German Naval Airship Division / Nordholz, Western Front / Summer 1915

L.10, an early P-class Zeppelin, raided Britain a number of times before being destroyed by a lightning strike on 3 September 1915. There were no survivors among her 19-man crew, the first German naval airship crew to be lost in the war.

Specifications

Crew: 18	Dimensions: diamater 18.7m (61ft 4in);
Powerplant: 4 x 156.6kW (210hp)	length 163.5m (536ft 5in); height 24.2m
Maybach C-X engines	(79ft 4in)
Maximum speed: 93km/h (57mph)	Weight: 15,876kg (35,000lb) max take-off
Range: 4345km (2700 miles)	Armament: 3–4 MGs, plus 2649kg (5840lb)
Service ceiling: 3200m (10,500ft)	bomb load

even saw the Zeppelin and another crashed fatally while landing at night. *LZ38* flew at altitude and the motley collection of interceptors could hardly have caught it if they had seen it.

The next attack took place on the night of 6/7 June, when one Navy Zeppelin, *L.9*, and three Army Zeppelins, *LZ37, LZ38* and *LZ39,* bombed Hull and London, killing 24 and injuring 40. The British public was indignant at the ineffective defences and serious rioting broke out. However, if the defences were unable to prevent the attack, they finally succeeded in hurting the attackers. Just after *LZ38* returned to her shed in Belgium she was bombed and destroyed by Henri Farmans of No. 1 RNAS Squadron. Even better from the Allied viewpoint, Flt Sub-Lt Warneford, flying Morane Parasol No. 3253, spotted *LZ37* during her return flight over Ostende; after an hour-long chase he was able to position his airplane above the Zeppelin, then dive down and drop six 9kg (20lb) bombs on it. *LZ37* exploded in flames, and Warneford was awarded the Victoria Cross for the first air-to-air destruction of a Zeppelin, only the second VC awarded to an airman. Miraculously, one of the ten airship crewmen (the helmsman), survived his 2000m (7000ft) fall, crashing through the roof of a convent, and landing in a bed.

The fact that it took Warneford an hour to close on the Zeppelin after first sighting it was clear indication of the inadequate performance of contemporary aircraft. Only modest improvement was made in interceptor performance until 1917, but better ground organization, tactics, weaponry, and experience gradually improved the defenders' chances.

The turning point

Zeppelins raided sporadically during the summer of 1915, the short summer nights giving insufficient cover of darkness for more extensive operations. London was not bombed again until the night of 9/10 August; on its return *L.12* was damaged by anti-aircraft gun fire over Dover and came down in the sea off Zeebrügge. Despite this loss, additional raids quickly followed. Anti-aircraft fire also destroyed the next Zeppelin to fall, *L.15* ditching off Margate on the night of 31 March/1 April 1916, after being damaged, all but one of her crew being rescued.

The biggest airship raid of the war occurred on the night of 2/3 September 1916, when German Army and Navy airships combined for the first, and only, time to raid London. Twelve Navy and four Army airships sortied, but bad weather dispersed the raiders and little damage was done. Moreover, Army airship Schütte-Lanz *SL11* was shot down by Lt Robinson flying a BE.2c, becoming the first German airship brought down on British soil. The next attack on Britain was the night of 23/24 September by 12 Navy Zeppelins. Two of them were destroyed, *L.33* by a BE.2c nightfighter and *L.32* by anti-aircraft damage and prolonged attack by another BE.2c. Two nights later seven Navy Zeppelins attacked Britain with limited results. On the night of 1/2 October 11 Navy Zeppelins sortied and *L.31* was lost with all hands to a BE.2c.

The loss of three of the latest-model Zeppelins in three raids marked a turning point in the strategic airship bombing campaign. It was clear that airship attacks could not continue without unacceptable losses. The German services re-examined the campaign and reached different decisions. The German Army, concerned about the high cost to build and operate airships and their demonstrated vulnerability in combat, stopped building the expensive airships and finally disbanded their airship service after the *LZ.107* executed the last Army raid on 16 February 1917. The Army was able to turn to G-type and larger airplanes for its needs.

The German Navy, on the other hand, decided to persevere. A major reason for this was the iron determination of *Fregattenkapitän* Peter Strasser, Chief of the German Naval Airship Division, to continue the strategic bombing campaign against Britain. This decision was made easier by the German Navy's great need for the long-range, long-endurance naval reconnaissance that only airships could provide. The Army could abandon airships as nonessential; the Navy could not.

The question then became how best to improve Zeppelin performance in order to avoid interception over Britain. An obvious approach was to add more power to increase speed. More power required more engine weight, limiting ceiling to that already achieved, which had proved inadequate against the new defences. Moreover, the rapid pace of airplane development meant that airplane speed could increase faster than airship speed. On the other hand, lightening the airships significantly increased ceiling at the expense of no speed increase. Both approaches were seriously considered, and the decision was to made increase ceiling. Existing airships were modified and these changes, together with additional measures, were incorporated into new-production Zeppelins.

Operating altitudes immediately increased from 3050–4000m (10,000–13,000ft) to 4875–6100m (16,000–20,000ft). In addition, beginning early in 1917 the undersides were painted black to make them less visible to detection by searchlights.

With this one stroke, the entire British defence system was rendered obsolete. Anti-aircraft guns caused no further losses to the high-altitude airships, and the existing interceptors, with ceilings of 3350–4000m (11,000–13,000ft), could not reach them. Only late in the war did newer nightfighters have ceilings of 5500–6100m (18,000–20,000ft), which enabled them to attack the 'height-climber' Zeppelins. Despite this, Naval airships were only able to bomb London once after 1916.

The end of the Zeppelin raids

Despite their new, high-altitude capabilities, airship losses due to bad weather, operational accidents, attacks on their sheds and combat losses over the continent and North Sea continued apace. Raids over Britain dropped significantly in 1917 and even more in 1918. Determined to strike Britain in the face of a flagging war effort, Strasser flew aboard *L.70*, one of the last two Zeppelins to be completed during the war, on a raid over Britain on the night of 5/6 August 1918 with four other Naval airships. Flying at 17,400 feet, *L.70* was intercepted and shot down by a DH.4; all hands were lost. The other Zeppelins, one bombing from an altitude of 6300m (20,700ft), evaded interception but caused no damage. With the death of Strasser, Leader of Airships, aboard the most modern Zeppelin, airship raids on Britain ceased.

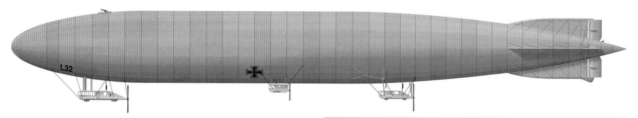

▲ L.32

German Naval Airship Division / Nordholz, Western Front / Summer 1916

L.32, an R-class Zeppelin, was destroyed over Britain on 24 September 1916 by Second Lt Frederick Sowrey flying BE.2c #4112. Sister ship *L.33* was downed by AAA fire on the same raid. The loss of two new Zeppelins to British defences on the same raid was a turning point in the strategic bombing campaign heralding its ultimate failure.

Specifications

Crew: 22

Powerplant: 6 x 179kW (240hp) Maybach HSLu engines

Maximum speed: 101km/h (63mph)

Range: 7403km (4600 miles)

Service ceiling: 3993m (13,100ft)

Dimensions: diameter 24m (78ft 5in); length 198m (649ft 7in); height 27.7m (90ft)

Volume: 55,206m³ (1,949,600 cu ft)

Armament: 10 x MGs, plus 4196kg (9250lb) bombs

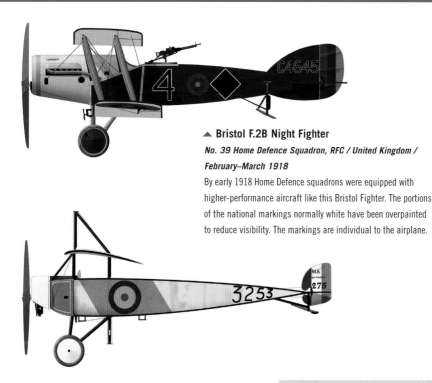

Bristol F.2B Night Fighter

No. 39 Home Defence Squadron, RFC / United Kingdom / February–March 1918

By early 1918 Home Defence squadrons were equipped with higher-performance aircraft like this Bristol Fighter. The portions of the national markings normally white have been overpainted to reduce visibility. The markings are individual to the airplane.

Specifications

Crew: 2
Powerplant: 1 x 205kW (275hp) Rolls-Royce
  Falcon III V-12
Maximum speed: 182km/h (113mph)
Endurance: 3hrs
Service ceiling: 6096m (20,000ft)
Dimensions: span 11.96m (39ft 3in); length
  7.90m (25ft 11in) height 2.95m (9ft 8in)
Weight: 650kg (2,779lb)
Armament: 1 x 7.7mm (.303in) fixed Vickers
  MG and 1 or 2 x .7.7mm (.303in) flexible
  Lewis MG

Morane-Saulnier Type L

No.1 Squadron, RNAS / Furnes Aerodrome, France / June 1915

On 7 June 1915 in this airplane Flt Sub-Lt Reginald A.J. Warneford became the first pilot to destroy a German airship, Army Zeppelin *LZ.37*, in flight; he was awarded the Victoria Cross for his accomplishment. Unfortunately, Warneford was killed in a flying accident ten days later.

Specifications (Type L)

Crew: 1 or 2
Powerplant: 1 x 60kW (80hp) Le Rhône 9C
  rotary piston engine
Maximum speed: 116km/h (72mph)
Endurance: 2hrs 30mins
Service ceiling: 3000m (9,843ft)

Dimensions: span 11.20m (36ft 9in);
  length 6.86m (22ft 7in); height 3.66m
  (12ft)
Weight: 650kg (1441lb) max take-off
Armament: 1 x 8mm (0.315in) Hotchkiss MG
  and 1 x .7.7mm (.303in) Lewis MG, or up to
  6x 20lb bombs

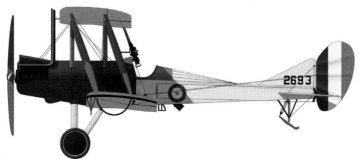

RAF BE.2C Night Fighter

No. 39 Home Defence Squadron, RFC / Suttons Farm Aerodrome, United Kingdom / September 1916

On the night of 2 September 1916 Leefe Robinson flew this airplane to shoot down Schutte Lanz airship *SL11*, the first airship to be brought down over British soil. This was a significant morale boost for a population stunned by losses during the Battle of the Somme that was still raging, and Robinson was awarded the Victoria Cross for his achievement.

Specifications

Crew: 1
Powerplant: 1 x 52kW (70hp) Renault V-8 and
  1 x 67kW (90hp) RAF 1a V-8
Maximum speed: 121km/h (75mph)
Endurance: 3hrs 15mins
Service ceiling: 3048m (10,000ft)

Dimensions: span 12.42m (40ft 9in); length
  8.31m (27ft 3in); height 3.66m (12ft)
Weight: 972kg (2142lb) max take-off
Armament: 1 x 7.7mm (.303in) Lewis MG

GERMAN NAVAL AIRSHIP OPERATIONS						
Mission	1914	1915	1916	1917	1918	Total
North Sea Scouting Sorties	48	297	253	242	131	971
Baltic Scouting Sorties	10	53	59	98	0	220
Raid Flights North Sea	0	47	187	54	18	306
Flights over England	0	27	111	28	11	177
Raid Flights over Baltic	0	4	15	27	0	46
Losses	0	10	16	16	11	53

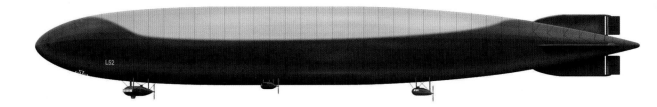

▲ L.52

German Naval Airship Division / Nordholz, Western Front / October 1917

L.52, a U-class Zeppelin, survived the war. On 23 June 1919 airship crews destroyed it, along with six other surviving Zeppelins, to prevent its capture and use by revolutionary forces within Germany.

Specifications

Crew: 20

Powerplant: 5 x 179kW (240hp) Maybach HSLu
    engines

Maximum speed: 106km/h (66mph)

Range: 12230km (7600 miles)

Service ceiling: 6,000m (20,000ft)

Dimensions: diameter 24m (78ft 5in);
    length 196.5m (644ft 8in); height 28.1m
    (92ft 4in)

Volume: 55,792m³ (1,970,300 cu ft)

Armament: 5 x MGs, plus 2018kg (4450lb)
    bombs

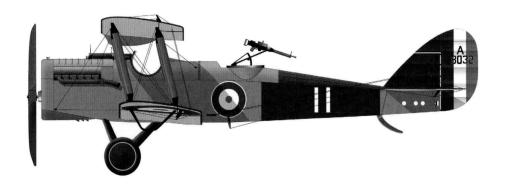

▲ Airco DH.4

No. 4 Group, RAF / Great Yarmouth NAS, United Kingdom / August 1918

Britain pressed many high-performance airplanes into the anti-Zeppelin role and this DH.4 was particularly successful. On 5 August 1918, Eagle-powered A8032 flown by Major E.Cadbury and Capt R. Leckie, downed *L.70* that was carrying Peter Strasser, commander of the German naval airships. They were experienced: Cadbury had downed *L.21* on 27/28 Nov. 1916 while flying BE.2c #8625 and Leckie had flown Curtiss H-12 #8666 when it downed *L.22* on 14 May 1917.

Specifications

Crew: 2

Powerplant: 1x 280kW (375hp) Rolls-Royce
    Eagle VIII inline piston engine

Maximum speed: 230km/h (143mph)

Endurance: 3hrs 45mins

Service ceiling: 6705m (22,000ft)

Dimensions: span 12.92m (42ft 4in);
    length 9.35m (30ft 8in); height 3.35m (11ft)

Weight: 1575kg (3742lb) max take-off

Armament: 4 x 7.7mm (0.303in) Vickers MGs
    (two forward-firing, two in rear cockpit), plus
    provision for 209kg (460lb) of bombs

Gothas over England
SUMMER 1917

Although the German Army gave up its costly airships, it planned to carry on its strategic bombing of Britain with airplanes. Daylight raids by twin-engine Gothas came first.

RAIDS on Britain by German floatplanes began late in 1914. Never true strategic bombing, these raids were little more than a nuisance. They continued, primarily against coastal targets, into the spring of 1917, although a single LVG C.IV succeeded in bombing London in broad daylight on 28 November 1916, the first airplane to do so. What prompted this bold attack is unknown; it was likely an individual effort. However, it was likely one reason why British Intelligence predicted large scale airplane raids late in 1916. On the night of 6/7 May 1917, a single-engine Albatros C.VII of *Flieger Abteilung* 19 bombed London, the first airplane to do so at night. This attack was very much a personal effort of an enthusiastic crew, and earned them a reprimand from higher authority, doubtless for alerting the defences prior to the planned Gotha bombing offensive.

First Gotha raid on England

The German Army was already planning airplane attacks on London when the LVG C.IV performed its raid. The Army, never as enthusiastic about airships as the Navy, was already looking for a more effective method, both operationally and financially, to mount a strategic bombing offensive when the British defences inflicted heavy airship losses in the autumn of 1916. One reason the Army abandoned airship attacks at that time was twin-engine bombers appeared to offer more potential for success at less cost than the airship campaign had demonstrated.

The airplane offensive finally got under way on 25 May 1917 when 21 twin-engine Gotha G.IV bombers crossed the British coast headed for London. Heavy cloud barred the way, so the bombers instead dropped their loads on Folkestone. The long lull between predictions of airplane raids and their appearance contributed to complete strategic surprise. Tactical surprise was also achieved; during their 90 minutes over Britain the Gothas were not intercepted, although one bomber was brought down on the return flight by RNAS fighters from Dunkirk. Casualties were 95 people killed and 195 injured.

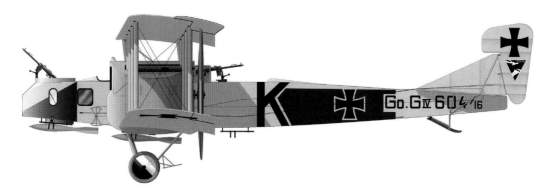

▲ **Gotha G.IV**

Kagohl 3 / Nieuwmunster Aerodrome, Flanders / 1917

This Gotha G.IV is camouflaged for day bombing missions over Britain in summer 1917. It carries the letter 'K', probably an initial, as an individual marking. The green trim on the nose and aft fuselage may identify its *Kasta* within *Kagohl 3*. The Gotha logo is on the rudder. It was based at Nieuwmunster on the Flanders coast.

Specifications

Crew: 3	Dimensions: span 23.70m (77ft 9in); length
Powerplant: 2 x 194kW (260hp)	12.22m (40ft 1in) height 3.90m (12ft 9.5in)
Mercedes D.IVa inline engines	Weight: 3648kg (8042lb) max take-off
Maximum speed: 140km/h (87mph)	Armament: 2 x 7.92mm (0.313in) parabellum
Range: 491km (305 miles)	MGs, up to 500kg of bombs
Service ceiling: 6500m (21,325ft)	

On 5 June a second raid of 22 Gothas attacked Sheerness and Shoeburyness, one being lost. As before, London had been the desired target but weather again prevented that.

First Gotha raid on London

On 13 June 1917 the Gothas finally reached London, 18 bombers of the 20 dispatched attacking. Over London the German formation broke up so the Gothas could bomb targets individually; they then reformed into several groups for the return flight. Casualties were the most severe for any raid of the entire war; 160 dead and 414 injured by bombs; including self-inflicted casualties from AA fire the totals rose to 162 and 432 respectively.

Despite having lost the element of surprise because of the two previous daylight attacks, not a single British fighter was able to intercept the Gothas before they bombed London, and only a few were able to intercept the bombers on their return. All of the

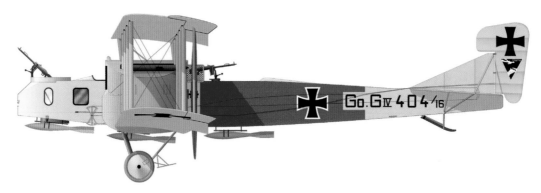

▲ Gotha G.IV

Kagohl 3 / Nieuwmunster Aerodrome, Flanders / May 1917

This was the Gotha of *Hptm* Ernst Brandenburg, Commanding Officer of *Kagohl 3*. The fuselage was painted red to make it easier to lead the other Gothas in formation during daylight raids over Britain. The serial number was in the series 401/14–412/16; the last two digits are not known and an entire number is depicted here to represent its appearance because it was so prominent. Brandenburg was awarded the Pour le Mérite for his achievements.

Specifications

Crew: 3

Powerplant: 2 x 194kW (260hp) Mercedes D.IVa inline engines

Maximum speed: 140km/h (87mph)

Range: 491km (305 miles)

Service ceiling: 6500m (21,325ft)

Dimensions: span 23.70m (77ft 9in); length 12.22m (40ft 1in) height 3.90m (12ft 9.5in)

Weight: 3648kg (8042lb) max take-off

Armament: 2 x 7.92mm (0.313in) parabellum MGs, up to 500kg of bombs

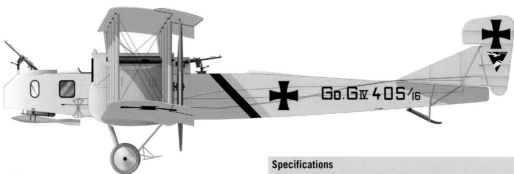

▲ Gotha G.IV

Kagohl 3 / Nieuwmunster Aerodrome, Flanders / 1917

This Gotha G.IV is camouflaged for day bombing missions over Britain. The black and yellow stripe is the personal insignia of *Oblt.* von Trotha, deputy commander of *Kagohl 3*. The Gotha logo is on the rudder. It was based at Nieuwmunster on the Flanders coast.

Specifications

Crew: 3

Powerplant: 2 x 194kW (260hp) Mercedes D.IVa inline engines

Maximum speed: 140km/h (87mph)

Range: 491km (305 miles)

Service ceiling: 6500m (21,325ft)

Dimensions: span 23.70m (77ft 9in); length 12.22m (40ft 1in) height 3.90m (12ft 9.5in)

Weight: 3648kg (8042lb) max take-off

Armament: 2 x 7.92mm (0.313in) parabellum MGs, up to 500kg of bombs

German bombers returned safely and the observer of a Bristol Fighter was killed by the Gothas' return fire.

If the physical damage from the raid was modest, the psychological impact was huge. The sight of German bombers over the capital of the British Empire leisurely bombing anything they wanted, coupled with the civilian casualties, shocked the British populace and created upheaval in the defence establishment. No. 56 Squadron, the premier British fighter squadron on the Western Front, was recalled to England along with two other first-line fighter squadrons, No. 46 and No. 66. Three more fighter squadrons had to be formed for home defence instead of reinforcing the RFC on the critical Western Front. However, more importantly in the long run, the British War Cabinet agreed to double the size of both the RFC and RNAS as a direct result of the raid.

Gotha daylight bombing raids continued until 22 August, for a total of nine attempts, with one raid aborted. The second and final raid on London took place on 7 July, when 21 Gothas leisurely bombed the city. One raider was shot down but two defenders were lost. Again the bombers made a strong impression on the populace despite relatively light damage. Such was the concern at the top level of the British government that the second raid eventually lead to the combination of the RFC and RNAS into the RAF, effective 1 April 1918, to eliminate inter-service wrangling and wasteful duplication of effort.

The British government immediately reorganized the air defence system and strongly reinforced it with more interceptors and anti-aircraft guns. Gotha losses mounted, leading to the end of daylight bombing and a switch to night bombing to avoid severe losses.

Giants over England
SEPTEMBER 1917–MAY 1918

As Britain strengthened her air defences, German day-bombing losses increased. The Gothas switched to night bombing and were soon joined by Giant bombers.

JUST AS THE BRITISH defences got the measure of the Gothas in daylight, the German switch to night bombing caught them unaware. The extensive training in daylight defence had then to be followed by extensive retraining in night defence. While this was forced on the Germans by the success of the British defences, ironically it was more inconvenient for the British than for the Germans.

Initially the Germans had hoped that the new Gotha G.V would offer sufficient performance improvement over the G.IV that day raids could continue. However, with the same engine being used and only minor differences between the two types, the performance improvement was minor. Accordingly, the switch to night bombing was done quickly; the first Gotha night raid fell on 3/4 September, less than two weeks after the last day raid.

The British interceptors were immediately forced back to the frustrating tactics employed against Zeppelins, with the added challenge that the Gothas were tougher, faster and much smaller targets to hit, making interception even more difficult. Even worse for the fighter pilots deployed to intercept Gotha day raids, most had limited night-flying experience, and the fighters lacked night-flying equipment. Flying difficulties and operational accidents immediately rose as the pilots struggled to gain night-flying experience. The challenges of night flying had also to be mastered by the Gotha crews, but in compensation they were now far less likely to be intercepted by British fighters.

First Giant raid
The pace of Gotha raids immediately picked up, with seven night raids in September alone, five of those against London. Worse was to come, however. On the night of 28/29 September the Gothas were joined by two formidable new Giant bombers. The Giant

bombers had a wingspan of 42m (138ft), nearly twice that of the 24m (78ft) span Gotha. Powered by four to six engines depending on type, they typically carried almost four times the bomb load to London carried by the Gothas.

The Giant bombers had first served on the Eastern Front, where longer-range planes were an advantage where long distances were involved, and had extensive operational experience prior to their debut over England. Their dimensions surprised British pilots, who had great difficulty appreciating their huge size at night. The result was the fighters usually opened fire at much greater range than intended and with far less effect. In turn, the British ground defence organization, calibrated for the twin-engine Gothas, was far less effective against the Giants. For example, a Giant 32km (20 miles) distant sounded like a Gotha overhead, frustrating attempts to locate and track them accurately. Furthermore, when intercepted the well-armed Giant bombers roughly

▲ **Gotha G.IV**

Kagohl 3 / Nieuwmunster Aerodrome, Flanders / November 1917

This Gotha G.IV is in dark camouflage for night bombing raids over Britain in autumn 1917. The name *MoRoTaS* was derived from the crewmembers' names. *MoRoTaS* crashed into a Belgian farmhouse on 11 November 1917.

Specifications

Crew: 3

Powerplant: 2 x 194kW (260hp)
  Mercedes D.IVa inline engines

Maximum speed: 140km/h (87mph)

Range: 491km (305 miles)

Service ceiling: 6500m (21,325ft)

Dimensions: span 23.70m (77ft 9in); length
  12.22m (40ft 1in) height 3.90m (12ft 9.5in)

Weight: 3648kg (8042lb) max take-off

Armament: 2 x 7.92mm (0.313in) Parabellum
  MGs, up to 500kg of bombs

▲ **Staaken R.IV**

Rfa 501 / Ghent Aerodrome, Flanders / Winter 1917–18

Giant Staaken R.IV type R.12/15 was the only Giant airplane to serve on both Eastern and Western Fronts. She is seen here in the night camouflage she wore for night raids over Britain in winter 1917–1918. R.12/15 was the most successful R-plane and, despite striking a barrage balloon cable the night of 10 February 1918, survived the war.

Specifications

Crew: 7

Powerplant: 2 x 119kW (160hp) Mercedes D.III
  plus 4 x 164kW (220hp) Benz Bz.IV engines

Maximum speed: 125km/h (77.5mph)

Endurance: 6–7hrs

Service ceiling: 3700m (12,139ft)

Dimensions: span 42.40m (138ft 6in); length
  23.20m (76ft 1in) height 6.80m (22ft 3in)

Weight: 13,035kg (28,742lb) max take-off

Armament: 7 x 7.92mm (0.312in) Parabellum
  MGs and 1500kg (3307lb) bombs

GIANT AND GOTHA RAIDS ON ENGLAND				
Raids	Sorties	Attacked	Downed	Accidents
8 Daylight (Gothas only)	383 Gothas	297 Gothas	24 Gothas shot down or missing	36 Gothas lost or damaged in crashes
19 Night (Gothas & Giants)	30 Giants	28 Giants	None	2 Giants lost in crashes
			6 British aircraft shot down or forced down	10 British aircraft lost or damaged in crashes

▲ Zeppelin Staaken R.VI

Rfa 501 / Ghent Aerodrome, Flanders / early 1918

Staaken R.VI R.27/16 flew night bombing raids on Britain. The R.VI type was the largest airplane placed in mass production during the war. All Staaken types used similar airframes; they differed in their engine configurations as designers searched for better reliability and performance. No R-planes were lost over Britain.

Specifications

Crew: 7

Powerplant: 4 x 194kW (260hp) Mercedes D.IVa engines

Maximum speed: 130km/h (80mph)

Endurance: 7–8hrs

Service ceiling: 3800m (12,467ft)

Dimensions: span 42.40m (138ft 6in); length 22.10m (72ft 6in) height 6.30m (20ft 8in)

Weight: 11,460kg (25,269lb) max take-off

Armament: 6 x 7.92mm (0.312in) Parabellum MGs and 1650kg (3638lb) bombs

▲ Gotha G.V

Bogohl 3 / Western Front / March 1918

The main visual difference between the Gotha G.IV and the early G.V shown here is the engine nacelles; on the G.V they are supported between the wings on struts. The black markings on this G.V indicate the unknown Bosta within *Bogohl 3* to which it was assigned; the letters are individual markings for *Ltn* von Korff and *Ltn* von Zedlitz, captured with their gunner, *Gefr* Speyer, on 21 March 1918 after being downed over French lines. This G.V is in standard night camouflage.

Specifications

Crew: 3

Powerplant: 2 x 194kW (260hp) Mercedes D.IVa 6-cylinder inline piston engines

Maximum speed: 140km/h (87mph)

Range: 500km (310.7 miles)

Service ceiling: 6500m (21,325ft)

Dimensions: span 23.70m (77ft 9in); length

11.86m (38ft 11in); height 4.30m (14ft 1in)

Weight: 3975kg (8763lb) loaded

Armament: 2 x 7.92mm (0.312in) Parabellum MGs on flexible mount in nose, 2 x 7.92mm (0.313in) Parabellum MGs on flexible mount in dorsal position; plus max bomb load of 500kg (1102lb)

Specifications

Crew: 1

Powerplant: 1 x 149kW (200hp) Hispano-
Suiza engine

Maximum speed: Unknown

Endurance: 3hrs

Service ceiling: 5486m (18,000ft)

Dimensions: span 11.28m (37ft); length
8.33m (27ft 3in) height 3.38m (11ft 1in)

Weight: Unknown

Armament: 1–2 x 7.7mm (0.303in) Lewis
MGs and 2 x 45.36kg (100lb) bombs

▲ **Royal Aircraft Factory BE.12B Night Fighter**

Unknown Home Defence Squadron, RFC / United Kingdom / 1918

The BE.12b served in British Home Defence squadrons as a night fighter. This
example has had the white of the insignias modified to reduce visibility at night.
It may have served at Detling.

▲ **Sopwith Camel 'Comic' Night Fighter**

AFC Training Unit / United Kingdom / 1918

The Sopwith Camel made a useful night fighter, and a number were converted to
'Comic' configuration with over-wing Lewis guns; moving the guns prevented the
pilot being blinded from the muzzle flash when firing at night. This one served
with the AFC Training Camp in Leighterton in September 1918.

Specifications

Crew: 1

Powerplant: 1 x 97kW (130hp) Clerget
9-cylinder air-cooled rotary piston engine

Maximum speed: 188km/h (117mph)

Endurance: 2hr 30mins

Service ceiling: 5790m (19,000ft)

Dimensions: span 8.53m (28ft);
length 5.72m (19ft); height 2.60m (9ft)

Weight: 659kg (1450lb) max take-off

Armament: 2 x 7.7mm (0.303in) fixed
forward-firing Lewis MGs

Specifications

Crew: 1

Powerplant: 1 x 97kW (130hp) Clerget
9-cylinder air-cooled rotary piston engine

Maximum speed: 188km/h (117mph)

Endurance: 2hr 30mins

Service ceiling: 5790m (19,000ft)

Dimensions: span 8.53m (28ft);
length 5.72m (19ft); height 2.60m (9ft)

Weight: 659kg (1450lb) max take-off

Armament: 2 x 7.7mm (0.303in) fixed
forward-firing Lewis MGs

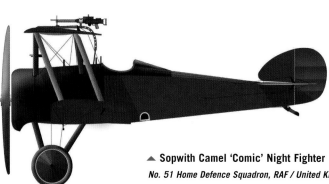

▲ **Sopwith Camel 'Comic' Night Fighter**

No. 51 Home Defence Squadron, RAF / United Kingdom / Autumn 1918

This Sopwith Camel 'Comic' night fighter served with No. 51 Home Defence
Squadron, RAF, in autumn 1918. All markings have been overpainted to reduce its
visibility at night.

BRITISH AIR DEFENCES, 1918					
Area and Date	Guns	Searchlights	Balloon Aprons	Fighter Squadrons	Aircraft Authorized
London, January	249	323	4	8	192
London, November	304	415	10	11	264
Northern Air Defence Area, November	176	291	0	5	120
Total at Armistice	480	706	10	16	384

Note: Fighter squadrons authorized 24 aircraft each, not always at full strength

handled the night fighters, and during the war no Giants were lost over England. One Giant even struck the barrage balloon defences of London, spun round, got clear of the cables, and went on to bomb the city. The only casualty was the flight engineer, who grabbed a hot exhaust manifold to keep from being thrown out when the Giant spun round.

Final night raid

A total of 19 night-bombing raids were flown against Britain, the last against London (again) on the night of 19/20 May 1918. After that German night bombing was confined to tactical raids over the continent in an attempt to prevent the defeat of the German Army on the Western Front.

The German strategic bombing offensive against Britain continued from January 1915 to May 1918 and progressed from night airship raids to daylight Gotha raids to night raids by Gothas and Giants. Results were mixed. The primary desire, to drive Britain out of the war by bombing and demoralizing the populace of London, was not achieved, and in fact goaded the British first to greatly enlarge the RFC and RNAS, then to combine them into the RAF. Nor was extensive damage done to military targets. On the other hand, civilian morale was affected, there was sometimes a negative impact on war production and the British War Cabinet was distracted. Most importantly, extensive resources of men, airplanes and heavy guns were diverted from the crucial Western Front to defend Britain against air attack. While at first this was balanced by the extensive resources needed to prosecute the airship offensive, the much less expensive airplane bombing campaign clearly diverted more resources from the Front than it cost the Germans.

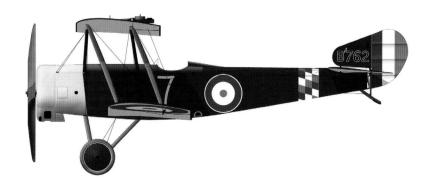

▲ **Sopwith 1½ Strutter Single-seat 'Comic' Night Fighter**

No. 78 Home Defence Squadron, RFC / Martlesham Heath Aerodrome, United Kingdom / November 1917

The adaptable Sopwith 1½ Strutter was also modified to 'Comic' configuration for use as a night fighter. This example was attached to No. 78 Home Defence Squadron at Martlesham Heath Aerodrome in November 1917. The red, white and blue bands around the rear fuselage were an individual marking.

Specifications

Crew: 1	Dimensions: span 10.21m (33ft 6in);
Powerplant: 1 x 97kW (130hp) Clerget rotary	length 7.97m (25ft 3in); height 3.12m
engine	(10ft 3in)
Maximum speed: 164km/h (102mph)	Weight: 1062kg (2342lb) max take-off
Range: n/a	Armament: 1 x 7.7mm (0.303in) fixed forward-
Service ceiling: 3960m (13,000ft)	firing Lewis MG, plus up to four 25kg (56lb)
	bombs or equivalent weight of smaller bombs

French and British Strategic Bombing
1914–1918

The French bombed strategic targets intermittently throughout the war, but never expected to drive Germany out of the war by it. Britain wanted to retaliate for the airship and Gotha raids.

FRENCH LONG-RANGE bombing started early; G.B.1 (*Groupe de Bombardement* 1) was formed 23 November 1914 with three squadrons totalling 18 single-engine, pusher Voisin bombers. G.B.1 flew its first day bombing mission to Germany on 4 December, repeating the raid on 19 December. Similarly, G.B.2 was established on 16 January 1915 and G.B.3 and G.B.4 were both created in March 1915. As battles raged along the Front, these units initially busied themselves more with bombing raids on rail hubs, gun batteries and airfields than on industrial targets. On 26 May 1915 G.B.1 bombed

poison gas factories at Ludwigshafen, in a flight of more than five hours. A bombing raid on Karlsruhe followed on 15 June. Joined by G.B.2 and soon G.B.3, more day raids followed, and German opposition grew. First two-seat Aviatiks, faster than the pusher Voisins, attacked the bombers with their observers' flexible gun. From September 1915 the Aviatiks were joined by Fokker monoplane fighters with a machine gun synchronized to fire through the propeller arc. Simultaneously, German anti-aircraft guns expanded in number and accuracy. French losses in daylight raids grew, and by the end of the year

▼ **No. 104 Squadron RAF Independent Force**
This graphic shows the basic markings of 104 Squadron, Independent Force. The 18 assigned airplanes were grouped in three flights of six; each flight had its own unique wheel covers (probably red for A Flight, white for B Flight and blue for C Flight, but this is not confirmed) and assigned letters to identify individual airplanes within the flight. Missions were often flown by a single flight.

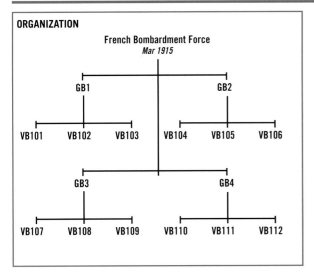

ORGANIZATION

French Bombardment Force
Mar 1915

GB1   GB2

VB101   VB102   VB103   VB104   VB105   VB106

GB3   GB4

VB107   VB108   VB109   VB110   VB111   VB112

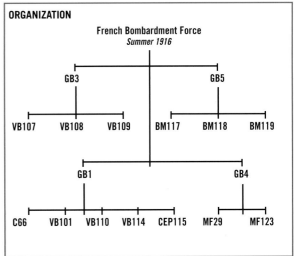

ORGANIZATION

French Bombardment Force
Summer 1916

GB3   GB5

VB107   VB108   VB109   BM117   BM118   BM119

GB1   GB4

C66   VB101   VB110   VB114   CEP115   MF29   MF123

became too high. Despite being escorted by fighters, it was recognized that the Voisin was simply too slow and vulnerable for day bombing. Moreover, the fighters did not have the range to escort the bombers to many of the desired targets.

On 11 March 1916 G.B.3 officially became a night-bombing unit. On 12 March several of G.B.1's units were detached to train in Nieuports for fighter duty. The escadrilles of G.B.2 were assigned to artillery spotting, although a new Caproni escadrille

was assigned for night bombing. These moves greatly diluted the power of the bomb groups. However, long-range day bombing lingered on in isolated attacks until the Oberndorf raid of 12 October 1916. During 1916 before Oberndorf the most notable daylight attack was made on Habsheim airfield on 18 March. That day 23 airplanes from G.B.4, 13 of them Voisins, were intercepted by 10 German Aviatiks and Fokkers; the resulting combat was a large one for the time. The French had the numerical

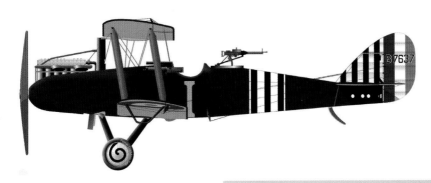

▲ Airco DH.9

No. 211 Squadron, RAF / Petite Synthe Aerodrome, France / Summer 1918

Derived from the excellent DH.4 by moving the pilot's cockpit aft and substituting the low-powered and unreliable Puma engine, the DH.9 suffered greatly from the attentions of German fighters during its daylight bombing raids. The flamboyant markings are likely those of a formation leader, making it easier for the formation members to see his airplane and form up on it.

Specifications

Crew: 2

Powerplant: 1 x 172kW (230hp) Siddeley Puma inline engine

Maximum speed: 185km/h (115mph)

Endurance: 4hrs 30mins

Service ceiling: 5105m (15,500ft)

Dimensions: span 12.90m (42ft 4in);

length 9.30m (30ft 6in); height 3.40m (11ft 2in)

Weight: 1664kg (3669lb) max take-off

Armament: 1 x 7.7mm (0.303in) fixed Vickers MG and 1–2 x 7.7mm (0.303in) flexible Lewis MGs, two 104kg (230lb) bombs or equivalent weight

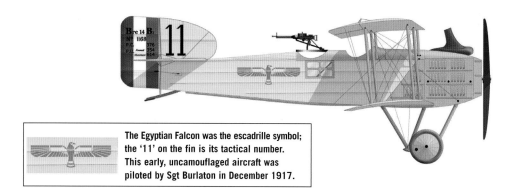

The Egyptian Falcon was the escadrille symbol; the '11' on the fin is its tactical number. This early, uncamouflaged aircraft was piloted by Sgt Burlaton in December 1917.

▲ Breguet Br14

Escadrille Br 66 / France / December 1917

The Breguet 14 was one of the war's great airplanes. Arriving at the Front in late 1917, it had a strong metal airframe and good flying characteristics. It was the best day bomber of the war. The French mounted large, heavily escorted day bombing raids with them and the Germans could not stop them.

Specifications

Crew: 2	Dimensions: span 14.36m (47ft 2in);
Powerplant: 1 x 224kW (300hp) Renault 12 Fe	length 8.87m (29ft 1in); height 3.03m
liquid-cooled V-12 engine	(9ft 11in)
Maximum speed: 177km/h (110mph)	Weight: 1765kg (3883lb) max take-off
Range: 2hr 45 mins	Armament: 1 x fixed and 2 x flexible 7.7mm
Service ceiling: 5750m (18,850ft)	(.303in) Lewis MGs, up to 320kg (705lb) bombs

advantage; the Germans had the technical advantage. Both sides pressed their attack and two burning bombers managed to ram and destroy German interceptors. Four planes were lost on each side, but nine French aircrew died, others were wounded, and every French airplane was damaged.

French day bombers

Then came the Oberndorf raid. The target was the big Mauser arms factory that produced 240,000 rifles per month. That day a large, motley collection of French and British bombers and fighters set out in daylight and collected a swarm of German fighters. Allied losses were heavy and long-range daylight bombing temporarily came to an end pending arrival of better airplanes. The pusher bombers were just too vulnerable to survive in daylight, even when escorted.

In fact, the new day bomber had participated in some numbers in the Oberndorf raid, where it was used in its two-seat fighter configuration. This was the Sopwith Strutter, used as both a single-seat bomber and two-seat fighter. Powered by a 97kW (130hp) engine, it had good handling characteristics, good performance for 1916 and modest payload. The French used the Sopwith, a British design, throughout 1917 for day bombing, with the two-seat fighter version escorting the single-seat bombers. Later, the excellent SPAD fighters provided

additional fighter escort. But the need for SPAD escort limited day bombing to shorter, tactical ranges because, to be fully effective, the fighter escort had to be continuous. By November 1917 the Sopwith Strutter was outmoded, and the pilots considered it too slow and hard to defend.

Another French day bomber introduced in the Spring of 1917 was the Paul-Schmitt. Stemming from a 1914 design, its development and service introduction took far too long. It was not fast or manoeuvrable enough in combat and its long wingspan precluded close formation flying, a necessity for mutual defence. Obsolete when it reached service, it was quickly replaced by other types.

With the failure of the Paul-Schmitt and the Sopwiths limited to short-range missions because they needed fighter escort, the significant French bombardment development for 1917 was the improvement in night bombing, largely brought about by improved airplanes and operational techniques. The old Voisins were replaced by newer machines, especially the Voisin 8 which, together with its development, the more powerful Voisin 10, formed the backbone of French night bombing to the end of the war. The Voisin 8 and 10 were still slow pushers but carried a much larger bomb load than their predecessors. France also used three-engine Capronis of Italian design; they carried heavy bomb loads and were also effective in long-range night bombing, but they were never very numerous in French service.

In November 1917 the new Breguet 14 B2 made its debut. Fast, tough and well-armed, the Breguet 14 became the best day bomber of the war and enabled the French to again attack long-range targets by day. As deliveries increased, in 1918 the French were able to mount large day bombing raids of 60–100 Breguet 14's escorted by single-seat SPAD fighters and, starting in July, three-seat Caudron R.11 escort fighters. Determined interception by German fighters often inflicted serious losses, especially after the Fokker D.VII entered service, but this was not able to stop these large formations. Most 1918 French day bombing was tactical or operational, not strategic, as the final offensives of the war were launched first by the Germans, then by the Allies.

Very late in the war, the French introduced the twin-engine Farman F.50 for night bombing, finally giving them an airplane comparable to the Gotha, Friedrichshafen, and AEG twin-engine bombers long used for night bombing by the Germans.

French bombing was a mixture of bombing tactical targets near the front lines and at longer distance plus some strategic bombing. This varied depending on operational conditions, particularly the technology of the airplanes compared to German interceptors, and after the early part of the war strategic bombing was done only on occasion. The French were realistic and never considered their strategic bombing operations would force Germany out of the war.

British long-distance bombing operations started 22 September 1914 with the first RFC raid into Germany at Düsseldorf, and RNAS aircraft made a number of attacks on Zeppelin sheds, which destroyed several airships, starting in October 1914. At the time, long-distance bombing was anything not directly in support of the British ground forces. The attacks on Zeppelins in their sheds would today be considered operational, not strategic, bombing. The first British bombing campaign that might be considered strategic was that of No. 3 Wing RNAS from July 1916 until the carnage of Bloody April forced its withdrawal from these operations. No. 3 Wing operated with French bombers against German industrial targets, including the costly attack on Oberndorf.

Revived interest

The shocking daylight Gotha attacks on London revived British interest in strategic bombing. Despite limited support among senior RFC officers, in October 1917 the British War Cabinet decided to retaliate with raids on German towns, and tasked No. 41 Wing RFC with the job. In February 1918 the Wing was renamed No. VIII Brigade, RFC, and on 6 June 1918 this brigade became the Independent Force, RAF. The IF was based south of Nancy, France, putting it within range of German factories near the border. From October 1917 to May 1918, No. 41 Wing consisted of only three squadrons; No. 55 with DH.4 day bombers, No. 16 Squadron RNAS (later

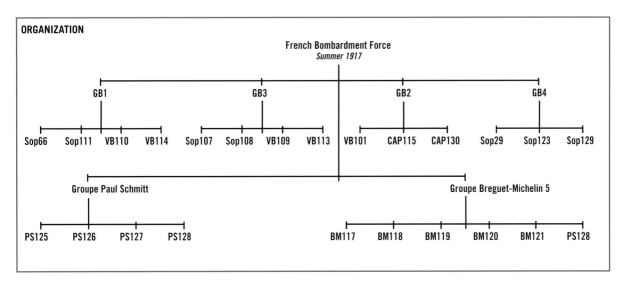

ORGANIZATION

French Bombardment Force
Summer 1917

GB1 — Sop66 Sop111 VB110 VB114
GB3 — Sop107 Sop108 VB109 VB113
GB2 — VB101 CAP115 CAP130
GB4 — Sop29 Sop123 Sop129

Groupe Paul Schmitt — PS125 PS126 PS127 PS128
Groupe Breguet-Michelin 5 — BM117 BM118 BM119 BM120 BM121 PS128

No. 216 Squadron, RAF) with Handley Page O/100 twin-engine night bombers, andNo. 100 with the FE.2b for night bombing. New squadrons were added starting in June, and by war's end there were nine squadrons in the Independent Force. Four squadrons were day bombers (Nos. 55 with DH.4s, 99 and 104 with DH.9s, and 110 with DH.9As), each with 18 aircraft. The five night bomber squadrons (Nos. 97, 100, 115, 215 and 216) were each equipped with 12 Handley Page O/400 bombers, which were improved developments of the earlier O/100.

There was a great deal of discussion about the actual aims of the Independent Force and specific targets to be bombed, but a coherent policy was never implemented. Most serving officers, tasked to win the war, thought that the airplanes and crews of the Independent Force would be more effectively utilized in direct support of the army in the field. Government officials, however, felt compelled to impress the voting public by bombing German civilians in retaliation for German attacks on London and other British cities.

▲ **Pfalz D.VIII**

Kest 1a / Germany / October 1918

The Pfalz D.VIII had exceptional climb due to its innovative Siemens-Halske Sh.III counter-rotary engine and was a frequent opponent of Independent Force day bombers. This one was flown by *Vzfw* Heinrich Forstmann, who scored one confirmed victory, a DH.4, on 7 September 1918 before being killed in a crash with this airplane on 10 October 1918. The fuselage band was his personal marking.

Specifications

Crew: 1

Powerplant: 1 x 119kW (160hp) Siemens-
Halske Sh.III rotary engine

Maximum speed: 180km/h (111.8mph)

Endurance: About 2 hours

Service ceiling: 7000m (22,966ft)

Dimensions: span 7.52m (24ft 8in); length
5.65m (18ft 6.4in) height 2.85m (9ft 4in)

Weight: 767kg (1691lb) max take-off

Armament: 2 x 7.92mm (0.313in) Spandau
MGs

▲ **SSW D.III**

Kest 4b / Germany / September 1918

Having the same engine as the Pfalz D.VIII, the SSW D.III combined its exceptional climb with better manoeuvrability and was a similarly excellent interceptor. This one was flown by *Vzfw* Reimann in September 1918. The black and white tail markings were Reimann's personal markings.

Specifications

Crew: 1

Powerplant: 1 x 119kW (160hp) Siemens-
Halske Sh.III or IIIa rotary piston engine

Maximum speed: 180km/h (112mph)

Endurance: 2hrs

Service ceiling: 8000m (26,245ft)

Dimensions: span 8.43m (27ft 7.75in);
length 6.7m (18ft 8.5in); height 2.8m
(9ft 2.25in)

Weight: 725kg (1598lb) max take-off

Armament: 2 x 7.92mm (0.313in) fixed
forward-firing LMG 08/15 MGs

Major Lord Tiverton, later Second Earl of Halsbury, and probably Britain's most sophisticated bombing strategist of the war, did much of the detailed planning for the strategic bombing campaign and envisioned concentrated daylight bombing of German industrial targets by 100 squadrons employing 1000 or more DH.9 bombers, an effort requiring a total force of 1630 DH.9 bombers and 370 SE.5A escort fighters. Tiverton's primary aim was the destruction of German industry, although he acknowledged the potential positive effect on the population's morale. This came to nothing because the required force was far beyond the actual Independent Force strength of 132 bombers at its peak.

Major General Sir Hugh Trenchard, now commander of the Independent Force, did not share the view that such a small force could be in any way decisive in strategic bombing, and ordered the Independent Force to bomb many tactical targets. Attacks on aerodromes and railways, which were not even on the official Independent Force target list, rose from 70 per cent of the sorties in June to 80 per cent in August, with half of all August sorties bombing aerodromes. While these were legitimate and useful targets, they were not the targets the Independent Force had been created to attack. However, they were convenient targets, being closer to the Front than industrial targets; moreover, railways were much easier to identify at night, especially for novice crews.

The Independent Force suffered heavy casualties, especially the daylight bombers, which suffered greatly from German fighters. From June to mid-October, 104 day bombers and 34 night bombers were lost, plus 320 airplanes that crashed behind

TONS OF BOMBS DROPPED PER MONTH

Date	Zeppelin	Gotha/Giant	Independent	Date	Zeppelin	Gotha/Giant	Independent
Jan 1915	1.815	–	–	Jan 1917	–	–	–
Feb 1915	–	–	–	Feb 1917	–	–	–
Mar 1915	–	–	–	Mar 1917	7.840	–	–
Apr 1915	5.303	–	–	Apr 1917	–	–	–
May 1915	7.864	–	–	May 1917	9.449	5.720	–
Jun 1915	9.015	–	–	Jun 1917	3.586	10.340	–
Jul 1915	–	–	–	Jul 1917	–	15.510	–
Aug 1915	14.438	–	–	Aug 1917	11.496	4.428	–
Sep 1915	17.214	–	–	Sep 1917	16.264	25.108	–
Oct 1915	11.325	–	–	Oct 1917	26.764	10.967	11.851
Nov 1915	–	–	–	Nov 1917	–	–	0.681
Dec 1915	–	–	–	Dec 1917	–	16.385	4.346
Jan 1916	20.946	–	–	Jan 1918	–	7.370	12.407
Feb 1916	–	–	–	Feb 1918	–	5.775	12.259
Mar 1916	14.241	–	–	Mar 1918	16.610	5.522	18.924
Apr 1916	37.335	–	–	Apr 1918	16.670	–	13.496
May 1916	9.217	–	–	May 1918	–	15.999	57.553
Jun 1916	–	–	–	Jun 1918	–	–	76.749
Jul 1916	17.536	–	–	Jul 1918	–	–	91.321
Aug 1916	41.741	–	–	Aug 1918	16.435	–	111.221
Sep 1916	75.782	–	–	Sep 1918	–	–	200.000
Oct 1916	12.989	–	–	Oct 1918	–	–	109.590
Nov 1916	11.509	–	–	Nov 1918	–	–	22.761
Dec 1916	–	–	–	Dec 1918	–	–	–

MONTHLY SORTIES IN WHICH BOMBS WERE DROPPED

Date	Zeppelin	Gotha/Giant	Independent	Date	Zeppelin	Gotha/Giant	Independent
Jan 1915	2	–	–	Jan 1917	–	–	–
Feb 1915	–	–	–	Feb 1917	1	–	–
Mar 1915	–	–	–	Mar 1917	4	–	–
Apr 1915	5	–	–	Apr 1917	–	–	–
May 1915	4	–	–	May 1917	5	21	–
Jun 1915	4	–	–	Jun 1917	2	40	–
Jul 1915	–	–	–	Jul 1917	–	61	–
Aug 1915	7	–	–	Aug 1917	6	21	–
Sep 1915	9	–	–	Sep 1917	10	63	–
Oct 1915	6	–	–	Oct 1917	11	35	63
Nov 1915	–	–	–	Nov 1917	–	–	6
Dec 1915	–	–	–	Dec 1917	–	34	39
Jan 1916	9	–	–	Jan 1918	–	11	71
Feb 1916	–	–	–	Feb 1918	–	6	76
Mar 1916	9	–	–	Mar 1918	6	5	129
Apr 1916	20	–	–	Apr 1918	5	–	69
May 1916	9	–	–	May 1918	–	33	340
Jun 1916	–	–	–	Jun 1918	–	–	472
Jul 1916	14	–	–	Jul 1918	–	–	486
Aug 1916	20	–	–	Aug 1918	5	–	420
Sep 1916	33	–	–	Sep 1918	–	–	562
Oct 1916	7	–	–	Oct 1918	–	–	363
Nov 1916	9	–	–	Nov 1918	–	–	125
Dec 1916	–	–	–	Dec 1918	–	–	–

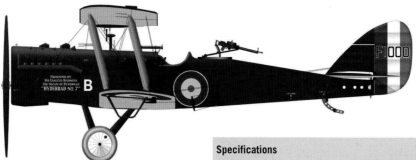

▲ Airco DH.9A

No. 110 Squadron, RAF (Independent Force) / Western Front / September 1918
By substituting the powerful 280kW (375hp) Rolls Royce Eagle or American Liberty
engine for the wretched Puma and enlarging the wing, the resulting DH.9A had
excellent speed and ceiling. It was second only to the Breguet 14B2 as a day bomber.

Specifications
Crew: 2
Powerplant: 1 x 313kW (420hp) Packard Liberty
  12 vee-12 piston engine
Maximum speed: 198km/h (123mph)
Endurance: 5hrs 15mins
Service ceiling: 5105m (16,750ft)
Dimensions: span 14.01m (45ft 11in);

length 9.22m (30ft 3in); height 3.45m
(11ft 4in)
Weight: 1575kg (3742lb) max take-off
Armament: 1 x 7.7mm (0.303in) Vickers MG
  and 1–2 x 7.7mm (0.303in) Lewis MGs in rear
  cockpit; external pylons with provision for
  299kg (660lb) of bombs

Allied lines. This was from a nominal peak establishment of 72 day bombers and 60 night bombers. No. 55 Squadron, the most experienced day-bombing unit and flying the excellent DH.4, lost 167 per cent of its aircrew strength in 1918. Squadrons flying the inferior DH.9, with its lower speed and ceiling and less reliable engine, suffered even more heavily from fighter attacks.

Unsurprisingly, daylight attacks, while more costly in casualties, were also more effective. For the 90 per cent of the raids for which it is possible to determine for certain, 93 per cent of the daylight raids hit their target, while only 66 per cent of night raids hit theirs. In fact, these numbers are generous, but they are indicative of the relative effectiveness of day compared to night raids.

British strategic bombing lacked coherence, and most of the targets actually bombed were tactical.

INDEPENDENT FORCE SORTIES AND LOSSES				
Aircraft Type	Sorties	Planes Bombing	Planes Missing	Planes Damaged
DH.4	1125	948	31	19
DH.9	1328	1053	55	13
DH.9A	100	79	17	0
FE.2	763	579	11	10
HP O/100 HP O/400	810	562	23	20

Strategic bombing was viewed both by the government and citizens primarily as retaliation for German strategic bombing; military officers generally preferred bombing tactical targets as a way to win the crucial ground war. Independent Force operations were tactically useful albeit at high cost, but were ineffective strategically.

Strategic bombing in retrospect
1914–1918

Truly effective strategic bombing was far beyond the reach of the technology and weaponry available during World War I.

THE AIRCRAFT OF WORLD WAR I simply were not powerful enough, numerous enough, nor accurate enough to deliver decisive results from strategic bombing; that would have to wait for later wars with much improved technology. However, this does not mean that strategic bombing was totally ineffective. The prolonged German strategic assault on Britain tied down a disproportionate amount of British resources needed on the crucial Western Front. This was an indirect German victory, but in the long run was not decisive.

French daylight strategic bombing efforts were brought to an early and ineffective end by German fighters, although limited strategic night bombing continued throughout the war. Most French bombing operations, both day and night, were tactical. In 1918 large French daylight tactical bombing formations could not be stopped by German fighters and directly aided the French army in its winning effort. French strategic bombing was

never expected to be decisive; it was just viewed as an important part of the war effort.

Early British daylight strategic bombing efforts were also brought to an end by German fighters, which inflicted heavy casualties on the Independent Force day bombers in 1918 as well. However, the Independent Force never had the strength or the technology to strike a significant, let alone decisive, blow. The British bombed strategic and tactical targets by night throughout the war, but never had the number of aircraft needed to be a real threat to German industry. The large Handley Page V/1500 four-engine bomber, arriving just too late to see combat before the Armistice, would finally have given the RAF the range to strike Berlin by night. However, hundreds would have been needed to achieve significant military results.

Though it was attempted by both sides in World War I, truly effective strategic bombing required far better technology than was available at the time.

Chapter 4

Maritime Aviation

Flight over water puts a premium on reliability, long range and endurance, key advantages of airships, which became prominent in maritime reconnaissance and anti-submarine warfare. As airplanes became more powerful and reliable, they gained an increasing role in those missions and started attacking ships with bombs and torpedoes, then started to provide shipboard interception capability and power projection over land via carrier air strikes.

◄ **Early Aircraft Carrier**
A Sopwith Pup is hoisted up to the flight deck of an early British aircraft carrier. The modest performance of seaplanes, burdened with greater weight and drag, created a need to bring higher-performance landplanes to sea, and the aircraft carrier was developed in response.

Naval aviation versus land aviation
1914–1918

The special demands of flight over water initially gave airships the advantage but seaplanes and, finally, landplanes became increasingly important.

THE BIRTH OF THE AIRPLANE had an impact on naval operations in World War I similar to that on land warfare. Naval aviation means flight over water, and that puts a premium on reliability and robustness. Many early army aviators were forced down by a minor fault they were able to correct, then take off again to resume their mission. Faults over water are not as minor. If a landplane has to ditch, the flight is over and the crew, if they survive ditching, are now in a life-threatening situation. If the plane is a seaplane or flying boat, the odds are improved. Providing the sea is not too rough, the seaplane or flying boat may be able to float indefinitely, or even take off again if repair is possible.

Flying off a ship raises additional challenges. Does the airplane have enough power to take off in a short distance? Can a catapult be used? Or does the airplane have to take off from the water? And how does the airplane get back on board the ship? Can it land on a flat deck, or must it alight alongside the ship and be raised on a crane? All of these operations are challenging and require skill, practice and practical, robust technology.

Navigation is one of the most critical and difficult challenges in naval aviation, and this was especially true during World War I before reliable electronic

▲ **Flying boat spots for naval guns**
An Italian flying boat spots gunfire for the Italian monitor *Faa' Di Bruno*'s two 381mm (15in) guns.

means of navigation had become available. There are few landmarks at sea, and celestial navigation is generally not practical except for the largest aircraft that were stable and could carry skilled navigators.

Over the open ocean, long range and endurance are also important, both to accomplish long-distance scouting missions and to have reserve fuel to find the ship after completion of the mission.

Aerial attack on other ships was another goal, one more difficult than merely finding them. Would bombs or torpedoes be most effective against ships? And how could an under-powered airplane carry a torpedo or enough bombs to be effective? And what about launching an aerial attack on land targets from ships?

Potential too great to ignore

The admirals instantly saw the potential of exploiting naval aviation for long-range scouting and the direction of naval gunfire. But given the challenging realities they were faced with, they realized that it was going to take a great deal of time and effort before naval aviation could become established as a practical and reliable combat arm. Beyond the aircraft themselves, even the means for successfully launching and retrieving them were going to needed. But the potential was too great to ignore.

Considering that the best qualities of airships, long range, long endurance, and relative reliability, closely matched the critical requirements of naval aviation, it is not surprising that airships played a major role in World War I naval aviation. In Germany, Zeppelins of the Naval Airship Division found more employment in North Sea scouting that any other mission, including their highly publicized raids over Britain. When the German Army grew disenchanted with the airship, the German Navy took them over. In fact, long-range, long-endurance scouting missions by Zeppelins over the North Sea were essential to the German High Seas Fleet, which could not risk letting itself be trapped away from its bases by the larger British Battle Fleet.

Anti-submarine warfare
1914–1918

Anti-submarine warfare was a necessity for all combatants, and especially for the Allies. Airships were essential for this mission because of their long range and endurance.

IF SCOUTING FOR the High Seas Fleet was the Zeppelins' most important role, for the Allied airships it was anti-submarine warfare. Like the airplane, the submarine was a weapon that saw its first major combat in World War I. Unable to compete effectively with the Royal Navy's long-term supremacy at sea, the smaller German Navy sought to redress that balance with submarines. After the Royal Navy adopted the distant blockade strategy against Germany, which ultimately lead to Allied victory, the Germans embarked on several submarine campaigns against merchant shipping in an attempt to starve Britain of resources. As an island nation, this was especially threatening to Britain; if she were starved of food and resources by submarines sinking her merchant fleet, she would lose the war.

Allied anti-submarine operations quickly grew in size, technical complexity and intensity to prevent a successful submarine campaign against merchant shipping supplying Britain, and airships played a major role. Britain alone built 213 naval airships during the war, 103 of which were in commission at the Armistice.

Harassing the submarine
The table overleaf shows only eight German submarines lost to air attack during the entire war, including one bombed in dry dock. This raises the question of how effective naval aviation was against submarines. If only submarine losses are considered, the answer would be, 'not very'. However, direct submarine losses to air attack are only a small part of the story. More important was the harassment of submarines by aircraft that prevented the submarines from sinking ships.

These early submarines are more accurately called submersibles; they spent most of their time on the surface scouting and charging their batteries, and only submerged to stalk ships. The sight of an aircraft forced them to dive to avoid detection and attack.

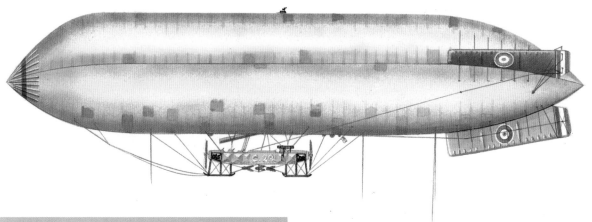

Specifications

Crew: 4	Dimensions: length 59.74m (196ft)
Powerplant: 1 x 112kW (150hp) Sunbeam and	Volume: 170,000 cu ft
1 x 164kW (220hp) Renault	Armament: 2 x 7.7mm (.303in) Lewis MGs, 4 x
Maximum speed: 76km/h (47mph)	51kg (112lb) or 2 x 104kg (230lb) bombs or
Endurance: 20 hours	depth charges

▲ **Coastal Class Airship**
Capel/Folkestone RNAS Station / United Kingdom / Spring 1917
Coastal class airships were designed for anti-submarine duties and 27 were built. *C.23* is shown here in standard markings. On 1 May 1917 *C.23* collapsed owing to the upper Lewis gun striking the envelope and it was deleted on 11 May 1917.

Underwater the submarines had to run on batteries, which reduced their speed, range and endurance, and limited their ability to stalk and attack ships. And if the submarine were detected by an aircraft, it could expect an immediate attack plus surface warships being summoned by the aircraft. Accordingly, naval aircraft extensively patrolled routes the submarines transited, forcing them to dive frequently and reducing their time on station during their patrol. This lowered the submarines' effectiveness as ship killers even if they were never directly subjected to an effective air attack. Therefore the true measure of effectiveness for anti-submarine operations is not the number of submarines sunk, but the number of ships that safely reach port.

As the war ground on, Allied airmen flew an astronomical number of dreary but hazardous hours on anti-submarine patrols. Complete statistics are not available, but a few will illustrate the magnitude of the operations. During the three months of 1 July–30 September 1918, three groups of anti-submarine aircraft in Britain, each composed of landplanes, seaplanes and airships, flew a total of 24,309 hours against German submarines. In the period June 1917–October 1918, British airships flew 9,069 patrols for a total of 59,703 hours aloft. Despite

SUBMARINES LOST TO AIRCRAFT		
Nationality	**Number**	**Notes**
British	3	1 bombed in harbour, 1 strafed and total loss, 1 bombed and sunk by French airship by mistake
French	1	Sunk by Austrian Lohner flying boat
German	8	1 bombed by seaplane under way, 1 bombed in dry dock, 3 sunk by surface vessels after being located by LTA craft, 2 sunk by joint attack of surface vessels and airship, 1 interned after being bombed by seaplanes

arriving late to war, even the US Navy flew at least 5,170 anti-submarine sorties covering 506,784 miles.

Although the preponderance of the anti-submarine effort was by the Allies, the first aerial attack on a submarine was by Zeppelin *L.5* when it unsuccessfully bombed British submarine *E 11* on Christmas Day, 1914. Ironically, the first confirmed sinking of a submerged submarine in the open sea was of the French submarine *Foucault* by Austro-Hungarian Lohner flying boat L135 in the Adriatic on 22 September 1916. Without the use of

▲ SSZ Class Airship

Longside Air Station / United Kingdom / 1918

Seventy-six Submarine Scout Zero, or SSZ, class airships were built for anti-submarine duties; two (*SSZ 23* and *SSZ 24*) were delivered to the US Navy. *SSZ 65* is in standard markings. *SSZ 65* was deleted in October 1919 having flown a total of 254 hours; 252 in 1918, 2 in 1919.

Specifications	
Crew: 3	Dimensions: length 44m (143ft 4in); beam
Powerplant: 1 x 56kW (75hp)	12.04m (39ft 6in) height 14.32m (47ft)
Rolls-Royce Hawk engine	Volume: 2000m³ (70,000ft³) loaded
Maximum speed: 83.4km/h (52mph)	Armament: 1 x 7.7mm (.303in) Lewis MG, plus
Range: n/a	29.4kg (65lb) bombs
Service ceiling: n/a	

sophisticated locating technology the Austrian aircrew saw the submerged *Foucault* through the clear waters and dropped depth charges on it. The damaged (and surprised) *Foucault* sank, but her crew was able to force her to the surface by pumping out the seawater. Then the second officer fired a machine gun at the Lohner, which dropped another bomb. The submarine's crew abandoned ship as she sank and the Lohner, together with sister L132, landed and rescued all 29 of the *Foucault*'s crew. After an Austrian torpedo boat arrived and took the prisoners, the Lohners took off and flew back to base.

▲ North Sea Class Airship
East Fortune Air Station / United Kingdom / 1918
Sixteen North Sea class airships were delivered for anti-submarine duties. *N.S.7*, shown in standard markings, was on the starboard bow of the High Seas Fleet when it sailed into captivity. *N.S.7* was the last non-rigid airship in service with the RAF; it completed 450+ flight hours, the last on 25 October 1921.

Specifications
Crew: 10	Dimensions: length 79.86m (262ft); beam
Powerplant: 2 x 179kW (240hp) Fiat engines	16.5m (54ft 2in) height 21.1m (69ft 3in)
Maximum speed: 92km/h (57mph)	Capacity: 10,000m³ (360,000 cu ft)
Endurance: 24 hours	Useful lift: 3900kg (8500lb)
Service ceiling: 2900m (9500ft)	Armament: 3–4 x 7.7mm (.303in) Lewis MGs,
	plus 363kg (800lb) bombs

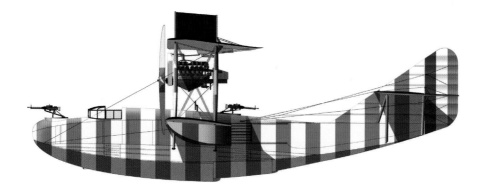

▲ Felixstowe F.2A
NAS Great Yarmouth / United Kingdom / late 1918
The Felixstowe F.2A was active on anti-submarine patrols over the North Sea. Many were painted flamboyantly to increase their visibility in case they needed rescue after ditching. This one was flown by FSL Robert Leckie, who had flown Curtiss H-12 #8666 on 14 May 1917 when it downed *L.22*. On 5 August 1918 Leckie destroyed *L.70* while flying in a DH.4 with Cadbury.

Specifications
Crew: 2	Dimensions: span 29.15m (95ft 8in); length
Powerplant: 2 x 257kW (345hp) Rolls-Royce	14.10m (46ft 3in) height 5.33m (17ft 6in)
Eagle VIII Vee piston engines	Weight: 4980kg (10,978lb) max take-off
Maximum speed: 153km/h (95.5mph)	Armament: 3-6 x 7.7mm (.303in) Lewis MGs
Endurance: 6 hours	(1–2 forward-firing; 1–2 rearward-firing; 1–2
Service ceiling: 2925m (9,600ft)	lateral-firing), 209kg (460lb) bombload

Seaplanes and flying boats
1914–1918

Because most of the Earth's surface is water, seaplanes were very important. The difficulty was making them both sturdy enough to survive the water environment yet light enough to fly.

LIKE THEIR LANDPLANE brothers, seaplanes (meaning both flying boats and floatplanes), developed quickly during the war. But seaplanes were even more limited by inadequate engine power than landplanes. By the nature of their operating environment, seaplanes had to be more robust, and thus heavier, and this is especially true for flying boat hulls. Additionally, floats were an extra weight not carried by landplanes. The greater weight of seaplanes in addition to the water drag made take-offs more difficult and limited their load-carrying ability.

On the other hand, the greater safety and operational flexibility of seaplanes over water spurred their development, and many designs were built. The Austrians preferred flying boats, the Germans generally chose floatplanes, and the British and French built both in quantity. As aviation technology advanced, Germany built multi-engine floatplanes and flying boats to supplement their expensive Zeppelins for maritime scouting.

One of the more interesting uses of a floatplane was by the German merchant raider SMS *Wolf*. Sailing from Kiel on 30 November 1916 to raid Allied merchant shipping, *Wolf* carried a Friedrichshaffen FF 33E floatplane, Marine Number 841, called

SURFACE WARSHIPS AND AUXILIARIES LOST TO AIRCRAFT		
Nationality	**Number**	**Notes**
Austrian	1	Minesweeper bombed and sunk in harbour
British	7	1 net trawler bombed by Austrian seaplanes, 6 motor torpedo boats sunk/interned after seaplane attack
German	3	3 bombed and sunk in harbour
Russian	2	1 destroyer sunk by mine laid by seaplane, 1 torpedo boat bombed by seaplanes, subsequently destroyed by storm
Turkish	1	Destroyer sunk by bombing

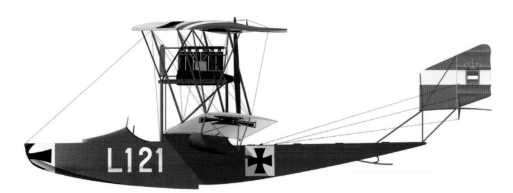

▲ **Lohner L**

Unknown Squadron / Adriatic Sea / late 1916

On 22 September 1916 a Lohner like this sank the French submarine *Foucault* in the Adriatic. This was the first time a submarine under way in the open ocean was sunk by an aircraft. The interestng application of the national insignia on the nose was common on Austro-Hungarian flying boats, as was application of the red-white-red national colors on the wings and tail.

Specifications

Crew: 2

Powerplant: 1 x 104kW (140hp) Austro-Daimler inline engine

Maximum speed: 105km/h (65.2mph)

Endurance: 4 hours

Service ceiling: 3500–4000m

(11,483–13,123ft)

Dimensions: span 16.20m (53ft 1.6in); length 10.26m (33ft 8in) height 3.85m (12ft 7.5in)

Weight: 1700kg (3748lb) max take-off

Armament: 1 x 8mm Schwarzlose MG, plus 200kg (441lb) bomb load

Wölfchen (wolf cub), for scouting. *Wolf* was the first merchant raider so equipped. *Wölfchen* had a wireless transceiver to summon *Wolf* when prey was spotted, and could also carry a few small bombs it typically used to persuade the victim to stop trying to escape *Wolf* and surrender. During its 15-month cruise the *Wölfchen* flew a total of 56 flights serving as the long-range eyes of *Wolf* and helping *Wolf* capture or sink 28 Allied merchant ships. Maintaining and operating *Wölfchen* demanded a lot of skill and effort; flights could only be made in calm weather, when *Wölfchen* could be lowered into

▲ Sopwith Baby

RNAS Yarmouth / United Kingdom / 1918

This Sopwith Baby is armed with two Lewis machine guns, one synchronized to fire forwards and the other fixed to fire upwards, as armament for intercepting airships. The design on the nose is an individual marking.

Specifications

Crew: 1	Dimensions: span 7.82m (25ft 8in); length
Powerplant: 1 x 82kW (110hp) Clerget rotary	6.96m (22ft 10in) height 3.05m (10ft)
engines	Weight: 717kg (1580lb) max take-off
Maximum speed: 148km/h (92mph)	Armament: 1 or 2 x 7.62mm (.303in) Lewis MG
Range: 2 hours 15mins	
Service ceiling: n/a	

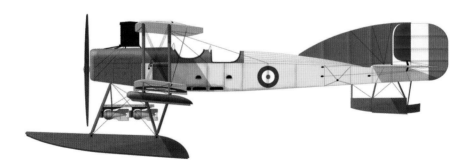

▲ Short 184

HMS Ben-my-Chree / Dardanelles / August 1915

This Short 184 flew from the seaplane tender HMS *Ben-my-Chree* in the Dardanelles. On 15 August 1916 Cdr C.R. Samson used it to lead the bombing raid on El Afulch; the fin was painted red for this raid to make it easy to identify the leader in flight.

Specifications

Crew: 2	Dimensions: span 19.36m (63ft 6in); length
Powerplant: 1 x 194kW (260hp) Sunbeam	12.38m (40ft 7in); height 4.11m (13ft 6in)
Maori Vee piston engine	Weight: 2433kg (5363lb) max take-off
Maximum speed: 142km/h (88mph)	Armament: 1 x 7.62mm (.303in) Lewis MG in
Endurance: 2 hours 45 mins	rear cockpit; plus 1 x 35.6cm (14in) torpedo
Service ceiling: 2745m (9000ft)	or up to 236kg (520lb) of bombs

the water to take off. *Wölfchen* soon became essential to *Wolf*'s survival and success on seas the Royal Navy dominated. *Wolf* and *Wölfchen* returned to Germany on 24 February 1918 to a hero's welcome after having sailed the Atlantic, Indian and Pacific Oceans.

In Africa, the light cruiser *Königsberg*, after sinking a merchant vessel and the British cruiser *Pegasus*, had engine trouble and took refuge in the Rufiji River delta for repairs. This raider was viewed as a serious threat to Allied shipping in the Indian Ocean; fear of her caused the French to hold seven vessels at Diego Suarez for two months and Winston Churchill to direct that even individual troop transports be escorted by warships. On 30 October 1914 British cruisers sighted *Königsberg*, but she simply moved upriver and out of sight. The British cruisers drew more water than *Königsberg*, so could not follow her.

It quickly became apparent that only aerial reconnaissance would break the impasse, and a Curtiss flying boat was brought to the scene of action. On 22 November the pilot spotted *Königsberg*; now *Königsberg* could be kept under surveillance.

Two shallow-draft monitors, *Severn* and *Mersey*, were sent by the Royal Navy. In April three Short Folder floatplanes arrived. On 6 July the monitors' attack on the *Königsberg* finally began, but failed.

MERCHANT VESSELS LOST TO AIRCRAFT		
Nationality	Number	Notes
British	5	3 torpedoed by aircraft, 2 captured by German raider *Wolf* and seaplane *Wölfchen*, later sunk
Turkish	5	1 bombed in harbour, 3 torpedoed (2 unverified), 1 sunk by balloon-guided naval gunfire
Misc	4	1 each American and Japanese captured by German raider *Wolf* and seaplane *Wölfchen*, 1 Dutch captured by seaplane, and 1 Norwegian captured by Zeppelin

The attack was renewed on 11 July; this time *Severn* hit *Königsberg* with her eighth salvo and those after, but the Farman spotting the fire was hit and downed by the *Königsberg*. A Caudron took over the spotting and *Königsberg* was destroyed, although confirmation had to await arrival of a new Caudron. The major threat posed by the *Königsberg* was lifted, freeing up numerous warships for other duties.

Elsewhere in Africa, on 10 June 1916 a Short seaplane in Belgian service actually damaged the German armed steamer *Graf Goetzen* in Lake Tanganyika by bombing, which was a rare and impressive feat at the time.

Landplanes and aircraft carriers
1914–1918

Flying boats generally did not have the speed or climb rate to intercept airships shadowing the fleet. The need for landplanes at sea lead to the development of aircraft carriers.

THE ADDITIONAL WEIGHT and drag associated with seaplanes motivated some navies to experiment with flying landplanes off ships. The first successful flight of a landplane from a naval vessel was in the United States on 14 November 1910 by Eugene Ely, and the same pilot made the first landing on a naval vessel on 18 January 1911. However, at this early date, with airplane performance and reliability still very modest, seaplanes and airships were much preferred and the United States put the idea of flying landplanes from ships on hold until after World War I.

However, the US Navy developed the first successful catapult system for launching seaplanes from shipboard in 1912.

As the leading seapower of the time, it is hardly surprising that Britain developed naval aviation beyond any other contemporary nation during World War I. The initial motivation was the desire to shoot down Zeppelins. The German airships were shadowing Royal Navy ships and reporting their positions, and the Royal Navy was determined to stop them. The limited performance of the seaplanes

▲ **Sopwith Camel 2F1**

HMAS Sydney / *North Sea / Summer 1918*

The 2F1 was a navalized Camel for shipboard use as an interceptor and attack airplane. The whitewashed tire treads provided the pilot with a visual aid when flying off the small platform on HMAS *Sydney*.

Specifications

Crew: 1
Powerplant: 1 x 112kW (150hp) Bentley
  BR.1 Rotary
Maximum speed: 185km/h (115mph)
Endurance: 2 hours 30 mins
Service ceiling: 5790m (19,000ft)
Dimensions: span 8.2m (26ft 11in); length
  5.72m (18ft 9in); height 2.59m (8ft 6in)
Weight: 659kg (1453lb) max take-off
Armament: 1 x 7.62mm (.303in) fixed
  forward-firing Vickers MG, 1 x 7.62mm
  (0.303in) Lewis MG, plus 2 x 22.7kg (50lb)
  bombs carried on fuselage sides)

▲ **Sopwith Camel 2F1**

HMS Furious / *North Sea / July 1918*

This Camel was flown on the raid against the Zeppelin sheds at Tondern from HMS *Furious* by Lt Smart; the blue and white nose was an individual marking. The Camel had a short take-off run, which was important for a shipboard aircraft.

Specifications

Crew: 1
Powerplant: 1 x 112kW (150hp) Bentley
  BR.1 Rotary
Maximum speed: 185km/h (115mph)
Endurance: 2 hours 30 mins
Service ceiling: 5790m (19,000ft)
Dimensions: span 8.2m (26ft 11in); length
  5.72m (18ft 9in); height 2.59m (8ft 6in)
Weight: 659kg (1453lb) max take-off
Armament: 2 x 7.62mm (0.303in) fixed
  forward-firing Vickers MG, plus 2 x 22.7kg
  (50lb) bombs carried on fuselage sides)

of the time ruled them out as a practical alternative for intercepting the Zeppelins, and the concept of launching landplanes from ships to intercept and destroy Zeppelins increasingly took shape.

The HMS *Vindex* was an early solution, but landplanes flying off *Vindex* were on a one-way trip because it was not possible to recover landplanes back on the ship. A few Bristol Scouts flew from *Vindex* but were not successful in downing Zeppelins because better performance and weapons were needed. The Royal Navy needed a true aircraft carrier, one that could recover landplanes as well as launch them. HMS *Furious*, ready for operations by the middle of 1917, was the first ship with this capability. In addition, by the time the *Furious* was operational, the Sopwith Pup was obsolete on the Western Front and therefore the RNAS considered it expendable.

Initially the Pups launched from *Furious* were at first either landed on shore or ditched at sea. However, the navy soon realized that the Pups were capable of landing on *Furious* if the ship steamed into the wind, thereby reducing the Pups' landing speed relative to the ship to about three knots. On 2 August 1917 Squadron Commander Dunning made the first landing on a ship under way on *Furious*. While Dunning was unfortunately killed on his third landing attempt, he had proved the concept.

The first aircraft carrier strike in history was flown on 19 July 1918 when six Sopwith Camels launched from *Furious* attacked the Zeppelin sheds at Tondern. Two Zeppelins, *L.54* and *L.60*, were destroyed in their sheds. Unfortunately, all the airplanes either ditched or were captured ashore, but five of the six pilots survived.

North Sea air battles
1914–1918

Throughout the war the North Sea was strongly contested by Britain and Germany, and this naval struggle stimulated a major evolution of maritime aviation development.

JUST AS THE WESTERN FRONT was the pivotal ground arena of the war, the adjacent North Sea was the pivotal naval arena. The British Battle Fleet and German High Seas Fleet were based on opposite sides of the North Sea and there were several battles between their heavy surface units. In addition, the North Sea had to be transited by German submarines en route to and from their patrol areas. Finally, the Royal Navy initiated many raids by light surface units on the German coast.

All of these activities required aviation support. In addition to scouting for their fleet units, both sides got involved in actions around the terminus of the trench lines, which was essentially a seaward extension of the land battle. Moreover, the British

steadily expanded their anti-submarine operations, and the Germans sought to counter them.

Strategically, the greatest impact of naval aviation over the North Sea was the long-range reconnaissance capability of the Zeppelins. With an endurance and range unmatched by any other aircraft, they gave the German Navy a great reconnaissance advantage. The operations of the Royal Navy, the most powerful navy in the world at the time, were inhibited over the North Sea by the presence of Zeppelins. Despite its superior power, the Royal Navy worried it could sail into a devastating trap caused by the reconnaissance from Zeppelins and German submarines. The British knew that defeat of the Royal Navy likely meant loss of the war, so the Zeppelin threat kept them cautious.

For this reason the Royal Navy took extreme steps to destroy them. One of the early rounds in this fight was a British raid against the Zeppelin sheds at Cuxhaven on Christmas Day 1914. The Royal Navy launched floatplanes from the tenders *Engadine*, *Riviera*, and *Empress* to bomb the sheds. Though the raid failed it was the first naval battle in which aircraft were the sole striking weapons on both sides. The opposing warships did not fire a single shot and submarines, present on both sides, proved ineffective.

Battle of Jutland

Naval aviation played a very minor role at the Battle of Jutland, the largest fleet action in history, in May 1916. The seaplane carrier HMS *Engadine* had only four airplanes aboard, but was still able to launch a Short 184 (which had sighted German warships and radioed their position to *Engadine*), when needed. Soon afterwards the Short's fuel line broke. It was forced down, but *Engadine* later retrieved it. This was the first time a heavier-than-air craft had participated in a major fleet action. HMS *Campania*, the other available seaplane carrier, missed her sailing order due to bad visibility. *Campania* sailed later, but being unescorted, was ordered back to port with her ten seaplanes. On the other side, high winds kept the

▲ **Curtiss H-12 at Felixstowe**
Pitched battles were fought over the North Sea between these large, well armed flying boats and Hansa-Brandenburg floatplane fighters.

Zeppelins on the ground until the battle had already started, so played no major role. Only *L.11* actually sighted British warships the morning after the main battle; she reported them reasonably accurately (and was fired on by the main batteries of British battleships for her trouble). Both the German and British naval commanders were under the mistaken impression that the Zeppelins were far more effective at Jutland than was actually the case. Despite the fact that only *L.11* had sighted Royal Navy ships, many

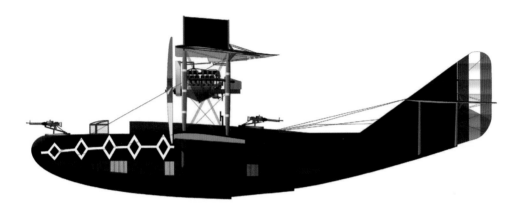

▲ Curtiss H-16

No. 257 Squadron, RAF / Dundee NAS, United Kingdom / late 1918

The American-built Curtiss H-16 was closely related to the Felixstowe flying boats and was used the same way. This H-16 was based at Dundee NAS; the white diamond markings on the nose were an individual marking for air-to-air identification.

Specifications

Crew: 4	Dimensions: span 31.7m (104ft); length
Powerplant: 2 x 268kW (360hp) Rolls-Royce	14.07m (46ft 2in) height 5.38m (17ft 8in)
Eagle V12 engines	Weight: 3252kg (10,670lb) max take-off
Maximum speed: 140km/h (87mph)	Armament: 4–7 x 7.62mm (.303in) Lewis MGs
Endurance: 11 hours	and 208.7kg (460lb) bombs
Service ceiling: 3810m (12,500ft)	

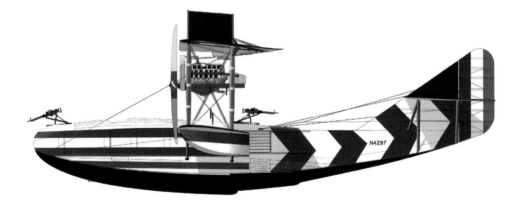

▲ Felixstowe F.2A

Felixstowe NAS / United Kingdom / November 1918

The heavily armed Felixstowe flying boats constantly flew anti-submarine patrols over the North Sea, sometimes in groups of five or more, and some were painted with unique and flamboyant patterns to identify them in air combat and to make them more visible in case rescue was needed. This one was based at Felixstowe NAS in November 1918.

Specifications

Crew: 4	length 14.10m (46ft 3in); height 5.33m
Powerplant: 2 x 257kW (345hp) Rolls-Royce	(17ft 6in)
Eagle VIII Vee piston engines	Weight: 4980kg (10,978lb) max take-off
Maximum speed: 153km/h (95.5mph)	Armament: 3–6 x 7.7mm (.303in) Lewis MGs
Endurance: 6 hours	(1–2 forward-firing; 1–2 rearward-firing; 1–2
Service ceiling: 2925m (9600ft)	lateral-firing), 209kg (460lb) bomb load
Dimensions: span 29.15m (95ft 7.5in);	

GROWTH OF NAVAL AVIATION				
Country	Airplanes	Airships	Balloons	Personnel
Austria-Hungary				
28 Jul 1914	22	–	–	–
4 Nov 1918	249	–	–	–
France				
4 Aug 1914	8	–	–	208
11 Nov 1918	1,264	37	198	11,059
Germany				
1 Aug 1914	24	1	–	200
11 Nov 1918	1,478	19	–	16,122
Great Britain				
4 Aug 1914	93	6	2	727
1 Apr 1918	2,949	111	200	55,066
Italy				
23 May 1915	15	3	2	385
4 Nov 1918	638	36	16	4,382
Russia				
1 Aug 1914	24	–	–	–
30 Jun 1917	200	–	–	–
United States				
6 Apr 1917	54	1	2	267
11 Nov 1918	2,107	20	117	39,871

ships had sighted her over a period of several hours, giving the impression that many Zeppelins were in contact. This lead British authorities to ascribe the successful German escape at Jutland to Zeppelin reconnaissance. In reality, it was essentially worthless. Yet this belief made the British still more cautious.

Worst airship blunder of the war

On the night of 18 August 1916 the High Seas Fleet again sailed to bombard Sunderland. Warned of the sortie by German radio chatter, the Grand Fleet and other British naval forces sailed to intercept. Zeppelins were out in force to scout for the High Seas Fleet, and *L.13* sighted British units and made two accurate reports. With the British and German fleets sailing within 65km (40 miles) of each other and converging at right angles, but out of sight of each other, Scheer, commanding the High Seas Fleet, then received an erroneous sighting message from *L.13* indicating inferior forces were astern of him. Based on this report, he reversed course to intercept them, unknowingly avoiding a clash with a much superior force, which could have been decisive – to the Royal Navy's advantage. *L.13's* erroneous sighting report has been called the worst airship blunder of the war. It was directly

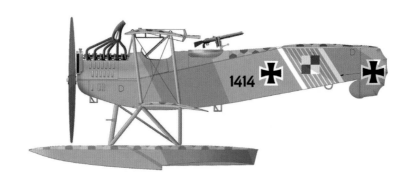

▲ **Hansa-Brandenburg W.12**

Seeflugstation Zeebrugge / Flanders / December 1917

This Brandenburg W.12 was flown by *Ltn* Becht from *Zeebrügge* in December 1917. The two-seat W.12 seaplane fighter was as fast and manoeuvrable as the single-seaters it replaced with the additional effectiveness of a gunner. The W.12 and its derivatives fought pitched battles with the large British Curtiss and Felixstowe flying boats on patrol over the North Sea.

Specifications

Crew: 2

Powerplant: 1 x 119kW (160hp) Mercedes D.III
6-cylinder inline piston engine

Maximum speed: 160km/h (99mph)

Endurance: 3 hours 30mins

Service ceiling: 5000m (16,405ft)

Dimensions: span 11.2m (36ft 9in); length
9.6m (31ft 6in); height 3.3m (10ft 10in)

Weight: 1454kg (3206lb) max take-off

Armament: 1–2 fixed forward-firing 7.92mm
(.313in) LMG 08/15 MGs; 1 x 7.92mm
(.313in) Parabellum MG in rear cockpit

responsible for preventing possibly the greatest naval battle never fought, with massive, but unknowable, consequences for the war.

Other North Sea air battles were less momentous but possibly more dramatic, mostly motivated by the continuous skirmishing around the search for submarines. Britain developed the large Felixstowe series of flying boats from American Curtiss designs to hunt German submarines. These long-range, twin-engine machines, tough and well armed, patrolled regular routes in the North Sea hoping to find and bomb submarines transiting on the surface to and from their patrol areas. These missions posed a significant hazard to German submarine operations and had to be countered by German seaplanes. By 1918 the airplanes on both sides were well developed, and aerial combats between them were frequent and often intense. German floatplane fighters brought down the British airship *C27* in flames and dispatched all six of a group of torpedo boats on armed reconnaissance. They even shot up surfaced British submarine *C.25* so badly she could not submerge and had to return to port.

At the same time, small British surface combatants, supported by floatplanes and flying boats, constantly worried the German minefields and mine tenders off the coast, and German floatplanes and Zeppelins maintained as continuous scouting coverage as was practical.

Although a British flying boat brought down *L.43*, generally the flying boats and floatplanes did not have the speed, climb rate, and ceiling to intercept Zeppelins. With few aircraft carriers available, the Royal Navy was forced to try another means to protect itself from Zeppelin observation, intercepting them with Sopwith 2F1 Camels flown from lighters towed behind destroyers. Of course, landing back on the lighter was not possible, and the airplane had to be either ditched or flown to land. Testing of the new method started in May 1918, with the first successful flight on 31 July 1918. The first operational attempt was made on 11 August, when Lt Culley flew his Camel from a lighter and intercepted and destroyed Zeppelin *L.53*. This was the second Zeppelin shot down by airplanes in six days and ended the effectiveness of the German Naval Airship Division.

Ironically, because of the *L.13* incident and others, World War I naval aviation is mainly notable for the fact that it did not deliver what was expected of it. Its impact was significant, but mostly in its failure to meet expectations, which were likely unrealistic given the immature state of aviation technology.

▲ Hansa-Brandenburg W.29

Seeflugstation Zeebrügge / Flanders / July 1918

For greater speed the monoplane W.29 two-seat fighter was developed from the W.12. The W.29 was very effective against British flying boats and light surface craft. This one was flown by *Oblt zur See* Friedrich Christiansen, who scored 13 victories, including British airship *C27* and British submarine *C25*, and was awarded the Pour le Mérite.

Specifications

Crew: 2	Dimensions: span 13.5m (44ft 3.5in);
Powerplant: 1 x 112kW (150hp) Benz Bz.III	length 9.36m (30ft 8.5in);
inline piston engine	height 3m (9ft 10in)
Maximum speed: 175km/h (109mph)	Weight: 1494kg (3294lb) max take-off
Endurance: About 4 hours	Armament: 1 x 7.92mm (0.312in) LMG 08/15
Service ceiling: n/a	forward-firing MG; 1 x 7.92mm (.312in) LMG
	14 Parabellum trainable rearward-firing MG

Chapter 5

The Eastern Front

Cavalry could still function on the Eastern Front, which covered too vast an area for trench warfare to predominate. Aircraft, too, soon showed their value and became the primary means of reconnaissance. German long-range reconnaissance and bombing was largely carried out by airships, later supplemented by Giant airplanes. With no practical airships, the Russians relied on their innovative Sikorsky Ilya Muromets four-engine reconnaissance bombers for long-range missions. Lacking the critical importance of the decisive Western Front, and with a more permissive combat environment, on the Eastern Front, both sides used their second-string airplanes.

◀ **Imperial Russian Air Service, Spring 1917**
Members of the 7th Corps Detachment, Imperial Russian Air Service, stand in front of the Nieuport 17 of Ensign Vasili Yanchenko. Credited with 16 victories, Yanchenko was the second-ranked Russian ace of the war. His Dux-built Nieuport 17 carries a fixed, synchronized Vickers machine gun on the fuselage and a Madsen gun above the wing. The open spaces of the Eastern Front stretch away in the background.

A different combat environment
1915–1917

German technology and production capacity ensured air superiority over an under-developed Russia struggling with social collapse.

THE COMBAT ENVIRONMENT on the Eastern Front was substantially different from that on the Western Front. The large distances and lower population density permitted a war of movement in the East, although transport capability via roads and railways was poor compared to the West. In addition, neither Russia nor Austria-Hungary were highly industrialized empires, so neither could field large numbers of airplanes. Germany had the industrial capacity, but concentrated its airplanes on the decisive Western Front. The long distances placed a priority on long-range reconnaissance missions, and the low density of combat airplanes and the lower priority of the Front for Germany resulted in a much less intense air combat environment than the West.

Older airplane types lasted longer in service on the Eastern Front, and second-rate French and German airplanes, like the SPAD SA series, Roland D.II, and Aviatik C.II, were often assigned there, where they could be of use; first-rate airplanes were frequently reserved for the more demanding Western Front. On the other hand, weather extremes on the Eastern Front meant airplanes had to be robust and reliable.

Russia had the world's largest air force at the start of the war, but only a small aviation industry. This meant it had a limited production capacity and could not keep pace with attrition. Inadequate supply of airplane engines was a chronic problem for Russia. The country produced only 1511 aero-engines during the entire war, and was largely dependent on France for airplane designs built under licence, for completed airplanes, and especially for aero-engines. Engines from downed airplanes, both Russian and enemy, were eagerly salvaged for re-use.

Sikorsky Ilya Muromets

The shortage of aero-engines was particularly troublesome for the production of the Sikorsky Ilya Muromets, the four-engine reconnaissance bomber that was the only native Russian design of particular merit. The long distances in Russia motivated Igor Sikorsky to design large airplanes of long range, and the resulting *Grand* was the world's first successful four-engine airplane. First flown with two engines on 2 March 1913, the *Grand*'s performance was marginal and two more engines were added as pushers, with the first flight in a four-engine configuration on 13 May 1913. In June the two pusher engines were moved to the front of the wings outboard of the original engines. In this, its final configuration, the *Grand* was renamed *Russkiy Vityaz* (Russian Knight).

THE IMPERIAL RUSSIAN AIR SERVICE, 2 AUGUST 1914		
Unit	**Location**	**Subordinate Units**
1 Air Co	Petrograd	1st, 5th, 16th, 18th, 22nd Air Detachments and the Guards Air Detachment
2 Air Co	Warsaw	14th, 15th, 19th and 23rd Air Detachments
3 Air Co	Kiev	9th, 11th, 12th Corps Air Detachments and the 3rd Field Air Detachment
4 Air Co	Lutzk	2nd, 3rd, 4th, 6th, 10th, 20th, 21st Corps Air Detachments
5 Air Co	Bronnitza	13th and 17th Corps Air Detachments and Grenadiers Air Detachment
6 Air Co	Odessa	7th, 8th, 24th and 25th Air Detachments, 3rd Siberian Air Corps Detachment and 8 Fortress Air Detachments

LEADING RUSSIAN ACES	
Ace	**Score**
Maj Aleksandr Kosakov †	20
Ens Vasili Yanchenko	16
Capt Paul d'Argueff	15
Lt Ivan Smirnov	11

Note: † indicates killed in the war.

The next four-engine design crashed on its first flight, on 11 December 1913, fortunately without serious injury to the crew. By January 1914 the airplane was modified and repaired and testing resumed. On 12 February, Sikorsky flew 16 passengers to an altitude of 300m (1000ft), an impressive accomplishment for the time. In March the new design was named Ilya Muromets after a legendary Russian knight. The next Ilya Muromets was completed in April and was considerably improved. Span was 30m (101ft) and length was 19m (62ft); the inboard engines were 104kW (140hp) Argus and the outboard engines 93kW (125hp)

Argus. Using two different engine types on the Ilya Muromets was typical; the shortage of suitable engines frequently prevented all four being the same. On 5 June 1914 Sikorsky established a new world record, carrying five passengers for 650km (400 miles). Setting out on 29 June the airplane made a round-trip flight from St Petersburg to Kiev, a distance of 1290km (800 miles) each way. There were some challenges during the flight, the round trip of which took three days, but it was an impressive achievement before the start of the war, and influenced the Imperial Russian Air Service to create the *Eskadra Vozdushnykh Korablei* (Squadron of

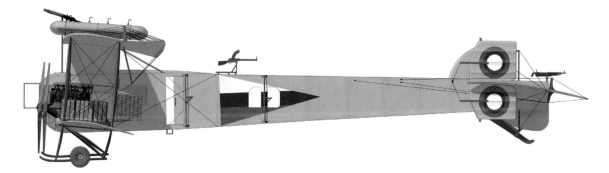

▲ **Sikorsky Ilya Muromets**

Squadron of Flying Ships, IRAS / Russia / Winter 1916–17

Sikorsky's Ilya Muromets, the world's first successful four-engine airplane, was developed specifically to handle the vast distances in Russia and was used for long-range reconnaissance and bombing. Most Ilya Muromets were assigned to the Squadron of Flying Ships. The paintwork and markings were very plain. This is a later model, which featured the world's first tail gun position.

Specifications (for E2)

Crew: 4–8

Powerplant: 4 x 164kW (220hp) Renault piston engines

Maximum speed: 137km/h (85mph)

Range: 560km (348 miles)

Service ceiling: 3200m (10,500ft)

Dimensions: span 34.50m (113ft 2in); length 18.80m (61ft 8in); height 4m (13ft 1in)

Weight: 7460kg (16,450lb) loaded

Armament: Up to six MGs including Lewis, Maxim, Madsen and Browning

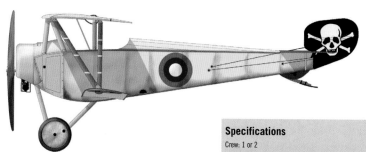

▲ **Nieuport 10**

19th Corps Detachment, IRAS / Russia / Autumn 1916

The Nieuport 10 was widely used by the IRAS. The skull and crossbones on the rudder was the unit insignia of the 19th Corps Detachment.

Specifications

Crew: 1 or 2

Powerplant: 1 x 59.65kW (80hp) Le Rhône rotary engine

Maximum speed: 146km/h (91.3mph)

Endurance: 3 hours

Service ceiling: About 4000m (13,123ft)

Dimensions: span 7.92m (25ft 11.8in); length 7.05m (23ft 2in) height 2.67m (8ft 9in)

Weight: 660kg (1452lb) max take-off

Armament: 1–2 x 7.7mm (.303in) Lewis MGs

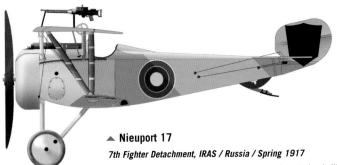

Specifications
Crew: 1
Powerplant: 1 x 82kW (110hp) Le Rhône 9J
 rotary piston engine
Maximum speed: 170km/h (106mph)
Range: 250km (155 miles)
Service ceiling: 1980m (6500ft)
Dimensions: span 8.2m (26ft 11in); length
 5.96m (19ft 7in); height 2.44m (8ft)
Weight: 560kg (1235lb) max take-off
Armament: 1 x 7.7mm (.303in) fixed Vickers
 MG , 1 x 7.7mm (.303in) Lewis overwing MG

▲ **Nieuport 17**

7th Fighter Detachment, IRAS / Russia / Spring 1917

Most Russian airplanes were French types either imported or built under licence.
This Nieuport 17 was flown by Ensign Vasili Yanchenko, with 16 victories the
second-ranking Russian ace of the war. The black shield on the rudder is
Yanchenko's personal marking. The style of the cockade is characteristic of
Dux-built Nieuports.

Specifications
Crew: 2
Powerplant: 1 x 59.65kW (80hp)
 Le Rhône 9c rotary engine
Maximum speed: 140km/h (87mph)
Endurance: 3 hours
Service ceiling: n/a
Dimensions: 9.55m (31ft 4in); length 7.35m
 (24ft 1in) height 2.65m (8ft)
Weight: 674kg (1486lb) max take-off
Armament: 1 x 7.7mm (.303in) Lewis MG

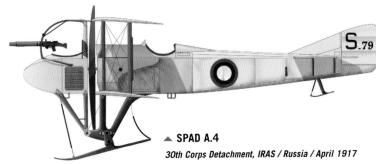

▲ **SPAD A.4**

30th Corps Detachment, IRAS / Russia / April 1917

Flying this airplane Private Nedzevetsky and gunner *Korporal* Rodin shot down a
Brandenburg C.I of *Flik 1* on 22 April 1917. The Austrian crew of pilot *Ltn* Fiala
and observer *Oblt* Baumgartner were captured.

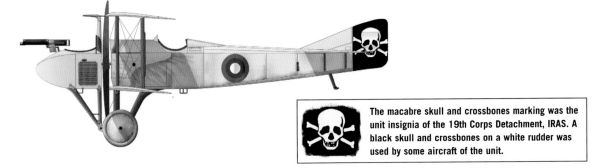

The macabre skull and crossbones marking was the
unit insignia of the 19th Corps Detachment, IRAS. A
black skull and crossbones on a white rudder was
used by some aircraft of the unit.

▲ **SPAD A.4**

19th Corps Detachment, IRAS / Russia / September 1916

This strikingly marked SA.4 was flown by the 19th Corps Detachment. While flown
by 2/Lt Bashinsky and gunner 2/Lt Huber, this airplane scored the first confirmed
victory by a SPAD A.4 on the Eastern Front on 6 September 1916. The downed two-
seater was from *Feldflieger Abteilung 46*.

Specifications
Crew: 2
Powerplant: 1 x 59.65kW (80hp) Le Rhône 9c
 rotary engine
Maximum speed: 140km/h (87mph)
Endurance: 3 hours
Service ceiling: n/a
Dimensions: span 9.55m (31ft 4in); length
 7.35m (24ft 1in) height 2.65m (8ft)
Weight: 674kg (1486lb) max take-off
Armament: 1 x 7.7mm (.303in) Vickers MG

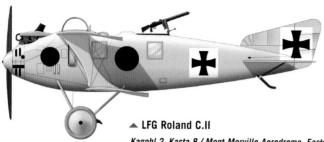

▲ **LFG Roland C.II**

Kagohl 2, Kasta 8 / Mont-Morville Aerodrome, Eastern Front / May–June 1916
Before becoming a fighter pilot, Manfred von Richthofen flew this Roland C.II in
Kasta 8 of *Kagohl 2* from Mont-Morville Aerodrome on the Eastern Front. When
introduced to combat the streamlined Roland C.II was as fast as opposing fighters.

Specifications

Crew: 2

Powerplant: 1 x 119kW (160hp) Mercedes
D.III inline engine

Maximum speed: 165km/h (103mph)

Endurance: 4 hours

Service ceiling: 4000m (13,120ft)

Dimensions: span 10.33m (33ft 10in);
length 7.70m (25ft 3in); height 2.90m
(9ft 6in)

Weight: 1309kg (2886lb) max take-off

Armament: 1 x 7.92mm (.313in) Parabellum
MG for observer

Specifications

Crew: 1

Powerplant: 1 x 119kW (160hp) Mercedes
D.III inline engine

Maximum speed: 180km/h (112mph)

Endurance: About 2 hours

Service ceiling: About 6000m (19,685ft)

Dimensions: span 8.90m (29ft 2in); length
6.93m (22ft 9in) height 3.11m (10ft 2in)

Weight: 815kg (1797lb) max take-off

Armament: 2 x 7.92mm (.313in) Spandau MGs

▲ **LFG Roland D.II**

Unknown Unit / Eastern Front / 1917

This Pfalz-built Roland D.II served on the Eastern Front. Developed from the larger,
two-seat C.II, the D.II was strong, fast and heavily armed with two synchronized
guns, but was not as manoeuvrable as opposing Nieuport fighters. The white zig-
zag on the fuselage was a personal marking.

Flying Ships, or EVK) in December 1914 composed
of the seven Ilya Muromets then available.

The Ilya Muromets was outstanding for long-
range reconnaissance and bombing over the
extended distances of the Eastern Front. They were
slow, but were usually armed with three or four
machine guns and proved tough opponents in air
combat. Most missions were by individual airplanes
flying at about 2440m (8,000ft) at a speed between
100–112km/h (62–70mph). Targets were usually
railway stations, trains, artillery and supply depots,
divisional headquarters and airfields. There were
never enough airplanes for large formations, and the
smaller airplanes often could not fly the necessary
distance for escort duties. Only three were downed
by enemy aircraft, including one on 6 July 1915
when four two-seaters from *Feldflieger Abteilung 21*
attacked and downed the *Keivsky II*, whose over-
confident crew had carried only one machine
gun and a rifle for defence. On 23 September 1916

the prototype KDW floatplane fighter, Marine
Nr. 748, intercepted and forced down Ilya
Muromets *Ship VI*.

On 25 September 1916, in a large air combat by
Eastern Front standards, *Ship XVI* was downed by a
number of airplanes from *Feldflieger Abteilung 45*.
The mission was flown by two Ilya Muromets
escorted by a number of Morane Parasols and
Voisins, to bomb the headquarters of the German
89th Division in Boruny as well as the adjacent rail
station and airfield. Some of the smaller airplanes left
their guns behind to carry more bombs, while others
flew as escorts. Over the target the Russian
formation was dispersed by heavy anti-aircraft fire
and *Ship XVI* was attacked by four German two-
seaters. *Ship XVI* drove off three of the attacking
airplanes, but the fourth, Aviatik C.I(Han) 2106/16
crewed by *Ltn* Lode and *Ltn* Wolf, closed in and
exchanged determined machine-gun fire with *Ship
XVI*. Its right outboard engine was put out of action,

and *Ship XVI* started descending and then spun and crashed, the bombs exploding when it hit; all four of the Russian crew were killed. The Aviatik C.I also took a lot of damage including 70 bullet holes and ripped open oil and reserve fuel tanks, but the crew was unhurt.

Four of the smaller Russian airplanes were also shot down. As a result, the Russians decided that only the Ilya Muromets would carry bombs on these missions from then on, with all the smaller aircraft acting as escorts. Voisins and Morane Parasols were no longer considered suitable escorts; the faster SPAD 7s and Nieuports were needed. The largest such mission was one flown in 1917 with seven Ilya Muromets and 26 escorting fighters.

In addition to the three Ilya Muromets downed by aircraft, German anti-aircraft fire shot down *IM-III* on 28 November 1915. However, at least 17 enemy aircraft were shot down in combat with Ilya Muromets and many others damaged, showing how dangerous an opponent it was.

Many more Ilya Muromets were lost in accidents than in combat. The airplane evolved through a number of different versions, and in 1916 the G-2 variant introduced a tail gun position, the first in the world. A total of 76 Ilya Muromets were ordered, with 38 accepted by February 1917.

Sikorsky and others designed a number of other airplanes, some of which were produced in limited numbers, but the Ilya Muromets was the only Russian design that stood out.

Initially lacking a counterpart to the Ilya Muromets, Germany relied on its airships for long-range bombing and reconnaissance. In the war on the Eastern Front the number of airships varied between two to eight, and they were very active. A dozen German airships were lost on the Eastern Front to a combination of accidents, bad weather and Russian ground fire.

German Long-Range Operations

One notable mission was by Army airship LZ.120. Starting on 26 July 1917 it made a record-breaking 101-hour patrol over Oesel Island and the western Baltic covering 6105km (3795 miles). Later, LZ.120 participated in Operation Albion, a successful air-land-sea combined arms assault on Oesel, Moon, Runo and Dago Islands in the Gulf of Riga.

Another significant airship operation launched from Bulgaria was the mission of *L.59*. Taking off on 21 November 1917, *L.59* left for German East Africa with 12 tonnes (13.5 tons) of supplies to assist German troops. On the 23rd *L.59* received a recall signal when it was 200km (125 miles) west of Khartoum, and returned to its base of Jamboli in Bulgaria on the 25th. At the time this was the longest non-stop flight ever made by any type of aircraft.

As in the West, shorter-range missions were flown by airplanes. *KG2* (*Kampfgeschwader* 2 or Battle Group 2) had six *Kastas* (*Kampfstaffeln*) and was transferred to the Eastern Front in July 1916. Five of its *Kastas* had Albatros C.III and Rumpler C.I two-seaters, but the

▲ **LFG Roland D.IIA**

Jasta 25 / Macedonia / 1917

This Roland D.IIa of *Jasta 25* was flown by *Vzfw* Gerhard Fieseler in Macedonia. Fieseler scored 19 confirmed victories; after the war he started his own aviation company (the Fieseler 'Storch' was his most famous product) and was five times World Aerobatic Champion. The letter 'F' is Fieseler's personal marking. The iron cross insignia on Roland-built airplanes was thicker than usual.

Specifications

Crew: 1	Dimensions: span 8.90m (29ft 2in); length
Powerplant: 1 x 134kW (180hp) Argus As.III	About 7m (23ft) height 2.95m (9ft 8in)
inline	Weight: 795kg (1753lb) max take-off
Maximum speed: 180km/h (112mph)	Armament: 2 x 7.92mm (.313in) Spandau MGs
Endurance: About 2 hours	
Service ceiling: About 6000m (19,685ft)	

▲ Albatros C.III

Flieger Abteilung 41 / 1916

The robust, reliable Albatros C.III was widely used on both the Eastern and Western Fronts for reconnaissance and occasional light bombing. Like many two-seaters during the early and middle period of the war, this aircraft is in plain factory finish with no personal or unit markings.

Specifications

Crew: 2
Powerplant: 1 x 112kW (150hp) Benz Bz.III
 or 119kW (160hp) Mercedes D.III inline
 piston engine
Maximum speed: 140km/h (87mph)
Endurance: About 4 hours
Service ceiling: 3350m (11,000ft)
Dimensions: span 11.69m (38ft 4in);
 length 8m (26ft 3in); height (Benz engine)
 3.07m (10ft), (Mercedes engine)
 3.10m (10ft 2in)
Weight: 1353kg (2983lb) max take-off
Armament: 1 x 7.92mm (.313in) Parabellum MG,
 later aircraft 1 x 7.92mm (.313in) LMG 08/15
 fixed forward-firing MG; plus internal bomb bay

Specifications

Crew: 2
Powerplant: 1 x 134kW (180hp)
 Argus As.III 6-cylinder water-cooled
 in-line piston engine
Maximum speed: 150km/h (93mph)
Endurance: 4 hours
Service ceiling: 5000m (16,200ft)
Dimensions: span 12.15m (39ft 10in);
 length 7.85m (25ft 9in);
 height 3.05m (10ft)
Weight: 1300kg (2860lb) max take-off
Armament: 1 x 7.92mm (.313in) LMG 08/15
 MG and 1 x 7.92mm (.313in) Parabellum
 MG, 100kg (220lb) of light bombs

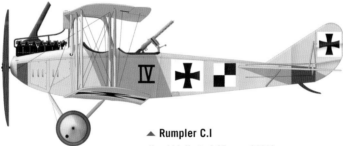

▲ Rumpler C.I

Kagohl I, Kasta 4 / France / 1916

The Rumpler C.I was an excellent airplane that had a long service life on both the Eastern and Western Fronts. On this aircraft the Roman 'IV' is the *Kasta*; the black and white insignia may be a personal marking.

Specifications

Crew: 2
Powerplant: 1 x 138kW (185hp)
 Daimler inline engine
Maximum speed: 165km/h (102.5mph)
Endurance: 2 hours
Service ceiling: 4600m (15,092ft)
Dimensions: span 11.19m (36ft 9in); length
 7.22m (23ft 8in) height 3m
 (9ft 10in)
Weight: 1125kg (2481lb) max take-off
Armament: 1 x 8mm (.315in) fixed
 Schwarzlose and 1 x 8mm (.315in) flexible
 Schwarzlose MG

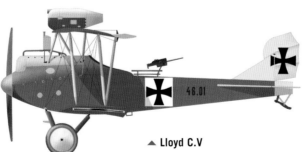

▲ Lloyd C.V

Flik 13 / Russia / October 1917

The Lloyd C.V was a fast, manoeuvrable two-seater and was a handful to fly. The C.V served on the Eastern and Italian fronts with the Austro-Hungarian *Luftfahrtruppe*. This example was attached to *Flik 13* on the Eastern Front.

sixth had twin-engine AEG G.III and Rumpler G.II bombers. In October 1916 *KG2* was transferred back to the Western Front. At the end of June 1916 *KG1* was transferred to the Eastern Front with four *Kastas* flying Albatros C.VII two-seaters and AEG G.III, Rumpler G.II, Friedrichshafen G.II and Gotha G.II twin-engine bombers. In late September it was transferred to northern Bulgaria for bombing operations against Romania. In January or February 1917 *KG1* was transferred to southern Bulgaria for service on the Macedonian Front and apparently served there until May 1917, when it was transferred back to the Western Front.

Since the early part of the war Germany had been developing large, long-range airplanes called *Riesenflugzeugen* (Giant airplanes), with three to six engines that could be repaired in flight by the flight mechanics, a necessary feature given the unreliability

of contemporary engines. The most successful series was that by Zeppelin Staaken, which was later used to bomb Britain.

Rfa 500 (Rfa – *Riesenflugzeugeabteilung*, or Giant Airplane Unit) was established 1 February 1916 and assigned Zeppelin-Staaken VGO.II, powered by three 179kW (240hp) Maybach engines. Its first mission was delayed until 13 August by engine problems. On 8 September VGO.II was joined by VGO.III, which made about seven bombing missions around Riga, mostly against rail installations, before suffering a crash-landing that destroyed it, killing five crew members. On 30 April 1917 DFW R.I arrived at the unit. Technical problems forced its return to the factory for repairs, and it was restored to the unit in May. Its only successful bombing mission was on 13 June, when it bombed rail lines at Schlock. On a mission in September engine failure forced an

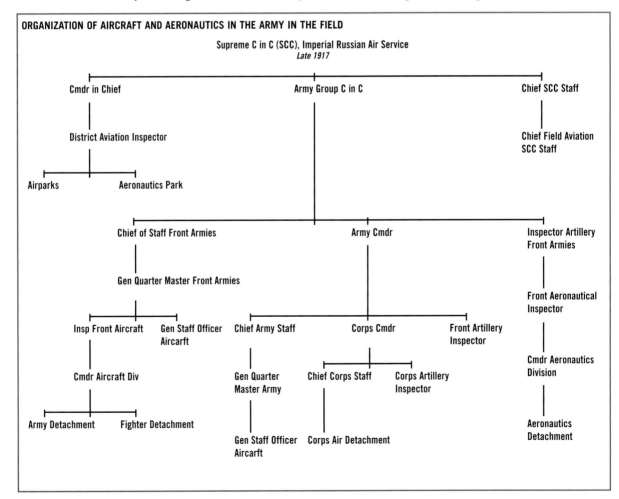

ORGANIZATION OF AIRCRAFT AND AERONAUTICS IN THE ARMY IN THE FIELD

emergency landing; the airplane caught fire and the bomb load exploded, killing one crew member.

R.IV R.12/15, the most successful R-plane of all, arrived at *Rfa 500* in the middle of June 1917. R.IV had six engines coupled in pairs to drive three propellers; if an engine failed it would be disengaged from its propeller. R.IV had 895kW (1200hp) and the formidable armament of seven machine guns. On its first mission on 28/29 June it dropped 1500kg (3300lb) of bombs on the Wolmar train station.

Another raid that carried the same bomb load was made on 8/9 July against coastal gun batteries at Zerel on the southwest tip of Oesel Island. On 18 July the R.12 was transferred to the Western Front for the strategic assault against Britain. There, it somehow survived a collision with the balloon apron guarding London. R.12 was the only R-plane to serve on both Eastern and Western Fronts and survived the entire war after dropping approximately 25,000kg (55,000lb) of bombs during its missions.

▲ Albatros C.X

Unknown Unit / 1917

The Albatros C.X had disappointing performance and was used primarily on the less demanding Eastern Front. Like many two-seaters it is in plain factory finish without any personal or unit markings.

Specifications

Crew: 2

Powerplant: 1 x 194kW (260hp) Mercedes D.IVa inline piston engine

Maximum speed: 175km/h (109mph)

Endurance: 3 hours 25 mins

Service ceiling: 5000m (16,405ft)

Dimensions: span 14.36m (47ft 1in); length 9.15m (30ft); height 3.40m (11ft 2in)

Weight: 1668kg (3677lb) max take-off

Armament: 1 x 7.92mm (.313in) forward-firing MG; 1 x 7.92mm (.313in) rearward firing MG, provision for light bombs

Specifications

Crew: 2

Powerplant: 1 x 194kW (260hp) Mercedes D.IVa inline piston engine

Endurance: 3 hours 15 mins

Service ceiling: 5000m (16,405ft)

Dimensions: span 14.37m (47ft 2in);

length 8.85m (29ft); height 3.25m (10ft 8in)

Weight: 1639kg (3613lb) max take-off

Armament: 1 x 7.92mm (.313in) forward-firing MG and 1 x 7.92mm (.313in) rearward-firing MG; plus provision for light bombs

▲ Albatros C.XII

Flieger Abteilung 46 / France / June 1917

Developed from the C.X, the elegant C.XII inherited its predecessor's disappointing performance and, like the C.X, was used primarily on the less demanding Eastern Front. This example was flown by *Ltn* Gieger and *Ltn* Rein of *Flieger Abteilung 46* in June 1917. The lightning-bolt fuselage band is a unit marking.

Rfa 501, officially formed on 3 August 1916, was assigned Siemens-Schuckert R-planes. Arriving on 7 August, SSW R.VI flew a number of bombing missions starting on 3 September. SSW R.VI was joined by R.IV, R.V and R.VII, and their targets were rail facilities. In August 1917 both *Rfa 500* and *Rfa 501* were transferred to Doberitz, near Berlin, to be reformed for service on the Western Front.

Russian Hydro-Cruisers in the Black Sea

Beside the Ilya Muromets there was one other bright spot in Russian aviation. These were the hydro-cruisers (*gidrokresiesera*) in the Black Sea. The Black Sea Fleet's principal seaplane carriers were the *Imperator Nikolai I* and *Imperator Aleksandr I*, converted from British-built cargo liners, and the *Almaz*, built originally as a vice-regal yacht for the Far East. The two *Imperators* were classed as hydro-cruisers and formed a separate division in the fleet. After Romania entered the war the three Russian ships were augmented by five Romanian ships, four of which were merchant ships converted to auxiliary cruisers. However, all occasionally operated seaplanes. The fifth, *Romania*, was rated as a 'hydroplane transport' but functioned as a carrier.

The carriers were active from early 1915 until Russia dropped out of the war, and their seaplanes, initially mostly Curtiss floatplanes and flying boats, bombed harbour installations and ships in port. In coastal waters, the aircraft flew extensive reconnaissance missions, escorted troop convoys, screened mine-laying operations and spotted for battleship and cruiser bombardments.

The hydro-cruisers were capable of launching as many as seven seaplanes aloft in 15 minutes. They could carry as many as eight seaplanes each and on at least two occasions managed to put 18 seaplanes in the air in conjunction with other carriers. This was the largest number of airplanes flown from shipboard anywhere during the war, and it was a remarkable achievement at the time.

Shipboard aviation was tightly integrated into the Black Sea Fleet structure, even more so than in the Royal Navy of that day, and the carriers were involved in almost all fleet operations. In some operations the carriers were the sole or principal strike units, with battleships screening them. In fact, it was the Black Sea Fleet that pioneered the battleship-carrier task force. These remarkable achievements, never well known, were quickly forgotten.

Typical Operations

While long-range reconnaissance and bombing by Zeppelins and giant airplanes were important as well as dramatic operations on the Eastern Front, short-range reconnaissance missions flown by individual two-seaters were more typical, and involved occasional light bombing and scattered air combats. Observation balloons were important, as was shooting them down. Like those of the Russians and

▲ **Lebed XII**

Unknown IRAS Unit / Russia / 1916

The Lebed XII was a mediocre performer but was used in numbers by an IRAS desperate for airplanes. Other than the Russian pennant on the fuselage, this airplane is in plain factory finish.

Specifications

Crew: 2	Dimensions: span 13.15m (43ft 1in); length
Powerplant: 1 x 112kW (150hp) Salmson radial	7.86m (25ft 9in) height n/a
engine	Weight: 1212kg (2672lb) max take-off
Maximum speed: 135km/h (84mph)	Armament: 1 x flexible MG, plus 90.7kg (200lb)
Endurance: 3 hours	of bombs
Service ceiling: 3500m (11,483ft)	

Germans, Austro-Hungarian air operations were primarily reconnaissance flights by two-seaters. Both sides frequently attacked railway targets because, in the huge, undeveloped regions of the Eastern Front, trains were essential for moving troops and supplies.

Within the IRAS were a couple of interesting historical firsts. The first woman combat pilot in the world was Russian Princess Eugenie M Shakhovskaya, who had earned her pilot's licence on 16 August 1911 at Johannisthal, near Berlin. As soon as Russia declared war on Germany, Princess Shakhovskaya wrote to the Tsar requesting assignment to active duty as a pilot. The Tsar granted her request and in November 1914 she was ordered to First Field Air Detachment as an artillery and reconnaissance pilot with the rank of *Praporshik* (Ensign). Subsequent Russian woman combat pilots include Lyubov A. Golanchikova, Helen P. Samsonova, Princess Sophie A. Dogorukaya and Nadeshda Degtereva, who in the spring of 1915 became the first woman pilot wounded in combat.

Marcel Pliat, half-French and half-black, served as a gunner in Ilya Muromets airplanes. When a new Ilya Muromets with tail gun arrived, Pliat requested assignment as the tail gunner. While on a combat mission in late 1916/early 1917, three German fighters attacked and Pliat returned fire, surprising the fighters who had not expected a tail gun. Pliat damaged one fighter and shot down another,

becoming the first black aviator to shoot down an airplane in combat. In November 1917 Eugene Bullard, a black American flying for France, was credited with one confirmed victory, making him the first black pilot, but the second black aviator, to shoot down an aircraft in combat.

In his book *Memories and Impressions of War and Revolution in Russia 1914–1917*, Russian General Basil Gruko, former commander of the Russian 5th Army, sums up the Russian aviation experience, 'Of course the Germans had far fewer machines on our front, taking its extent in consideration, than they had on their Western Front, which showed their need of having aviation power equal to our Allies' flying forces. Nevertheless, the Germans were always able to have superiority over us in aviation.' Similarly, Russian General A.A. Brusilov, in his book *A Soldier's Note Book*, states, 'during the whole of the war, we were badly handicapped by the shortage of machines… As for dirigibles, we had none, for one cannot take seriously the few specimens that we had bought, at a high price, from foreign countries; they were out of date, inefficient and of no practical value. Altogether it must be recognized that, compared with that of the enemy, our technical equipment was quite inferior.' Although the Austro-Hungarian air service had at best marginal superiority over the Russians, it was German technical superiority that made all the difference in the East.

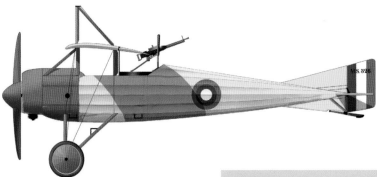

▲ **Morane-Saulnier P**

Unknown IRAS Unit / Russia / 1917

A small number of Morane-Saulnier P reconnaissance two-seaters were purchased by Russia. They were used as escorts for Ilya Muromets reconniassance bombers in addition to their usual reconnaissance duties.

Specifications

Crew: 2	Dimensions: span 11.16m (36ft 7in); length
Powerplant: 1 x 82kW (110hp)	7.18m (23ft 7in) height 3.47m (11ft 5in)
Salmson engine	Weight: 730kg (1609lb) max take-off
Maximum speed: 162km/h (101mph)	Armament: 1 or 2 machine guns of various
Endurance: 4 hours	manufacture in Russian service
Service ceiling: 4800m (15,748ft)	

Chapter 6

The Italian Front

Italy's entry into the war started a long struggle over rugged territory, making aerial reconnaissance as important as it was on the Western Front. Italy was more industrialized than the Austro-Hungarian Empire and France was able to provide Italy with more aero-industry support than Germany could provide to her ally. As a result, Italy generally enjoyed air superiority.

◀ **Italian SVA 5 flies a reconnaissance mission**
Italian SVA 5 of *87a Squadriglia* on a reconnaissance mission in 1918 shows its mottled camouflage. Flown by *Tenente* Gino Allegri, the number '4' on both stabilizers is the tactical number; three white streamers fly from the tailplane. The SVA series was fast and excelled at long-range reconnaissance.

A third Front opens
MAY 1915–NOVEMBER 1918

Italy's entry into the war on the Allies' side caused insurmountable problems for an under-developed Austro-Hungarian Empire already embroiled in Russia.

BEFORE WORLD WAR I ITALY was loosely allied with Germany and the Austro-Hungarian Empire, but decided to stay neutral when war broke out. Considering the opportunities, on 23 May 1915 Italy declared war on the Austro-Hungarian Empire in hope of winning territorial gains, such as the city of Trieste. The Italian war death toll of 651,000 soldiers and 589,000 civilians, nearly 3.5 per cent of Italy's population of 35.6 million, was a higher price than expected.

Italian industry was more developed than that of the Austro-Hungarian Empire, her primary adversary. Despite the usual combination of technical problems and managerial mistakes, Italy produced more than twice as many airplanes and three times as many aero-engines as Austria, not least because Austria was plagued with similar technical and managerial problems. This larger aviation production gave Italy a long-term air superiority advantage over Austria. Moreover, as an ally of France, Italy was able to import French airplanes and aero-engines as well as produce them under licence in Italy.

Although Austria was able to import a few German airplanes for her air service and built a number of German designs under licence, Germany never had an adequate number of aero-engines and sold very few to Austria. This inadequate production of aero-engines was to handicap Austria's *Luftfahrtruppen* throughout the war.

When Italy entered the war the Italian air service primarily flew French two-seat reconnaissance airplanes like the Voisin 3 and Caudron G.3 and G.4. As air combat developed, Italy purchased Nieuport, then Hanriot and SPAD fighters from France and also produced them under licence in Italy. Only one original Italian fighter design, the Balilla, saw limited service, and scored just one confirmed victory. Produced for commercial, not military, reasons, the Balilla was a fast airplane but was not manoeuvrable enough for combat with other fighters and its technical problems had not been resolved before the Armistice. The French Hanriot HD.1, not used by France itself, which preferred the SPAD, was the fighter of choice in Italian service.

The Italian SVA series, produced in both single-seat and two-seat configurations and as a floatplane, was an excellent design. Fast, strong and long-ranged, the SVA series made excellent reconnaissance

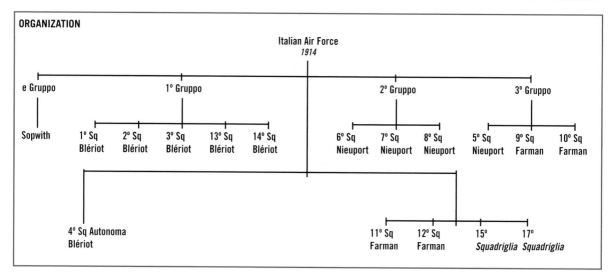

ORGANIZATION

airplanes. Together with the SVA series, the Caproni tri-motor bombers were the most significant Italian designs to see service. When first entering service the Caproni Ca.3 series biplanes were the best bombers available to the Western Allies and were sold to France and even built under licence in France. The Austrians were never able to introduce a bomber comparable to the Caproni and eventually had to purchase Gotha G.IVs from Germany.

The Caproni Ca.4 series were immense triplane, tri-motor airplanes used mainly for night bombing. Only a few entered service due to production and development challenges, but the type served briefly with the RNAS in Italy and was even considered for American production. The Caproni Ca.5 series was developed from the earlier Ca.3 biplanes but had more power. Unfortunately, the Ca.5 was full of defects, especially with the engines, and despite huge production preparations, few were delivered to Italian units. Some were delivered to the American Northern Bombing Group in France for night bombing, but many were lost on the delivery flight. The situation was so bad that the old Ca.3 had to be re-introduced into production, and hundreds of Ca.5s were quickly scrapped after the war.

Like other Allied nations, Italy retained the obsolete pusher configuration for reconnaissance airplanes for far too long, but the SP.2 and SP.3 pushers were reliable airplanes that served into 1918.

The reliable SAML S.2 was derived from an Aviatik design but powered by the 149kW (200hp) Fiat A.12 engine. Although later two-seat designs had more performance, the SAML S.2 was the 'old reliable' two-seater that could always be counted on. The SIA 7b was a much different proposition. Powered by a 212kW (285hp) Fiat A.12 engine, the SIA 7b was a handsome two-seater usefully faster than the SAML. However, it had a fatal flaw. Structurally it was so weak the wings sometimes fell off in normal flight. This lead to its early withdrawal from service, a substantial blow to the Italian air service, followed by a parliamentary inquiry. The SIA 7b was followed by the redesigned Fiat R.2, which, despite using many components from the SIA 7b, was a much better airplane. A few R.2s arrived just in time for the final battles and served into the 1920s.

Predominant Pomilio

The Pomilio company was another supplier of reconnaissance two-seaters; like the SIA 7b the Pomilio PD, powered by the 186kW (250hp) Fiat A.12, was much faster than the old pusher designs, but the PD was far more robust than the SIA. The refined PE, powered by the 224kW (300hp) Fiat A.12 bis, followed the PD in production and was even faster. The Pomilio was the predominant Italian reconnaissance two-seater at the Armistice, when it equipped 17 squadrons completely and another five

▲ Voisin III

25a Squadriglia / Italy / 1915

The Voisin III was one of the numerous French designs used by Italy. Like many Italian airplanes the undersides of the lower wings are painted in the national colors of red to port and green to starboard; the inboard sections of the wings were left in the overall light brown.

Specifications

Crew: 2	Dimensions: span 14.74m (48ft 4.3in);
Powerplant: 1 x 89.5kW (120hp)	length 9.50m (31ft 2n); height 2.95m
Salmson M9 engine	(9ft 8in)
Maximum speed: 98km/h (60.5mph)	Weight: 1350kg (2976lb) max take-off
Range: 200km (124miles)	Armament: 1 x 8mm (0.315in) Hotchkiss MG
Service ceiling: 4000m (13,123ft)	

The Caudron G.4 had four rudders; the airplane's serial number was shown on the outside of each inner rudder.

▼ Caudron G.4
48a Squadriglia / Italy / April 1917

Two engines gave the French-designed Caudron G.4 useful climb and ceiling for flying over mountainous terrain despite its obsolete pusher-style design. This example carries two machine guns for use by the observer in the front cockpit. There are no unit or personal markings.

Specifications
Crew: 2
Powerplant: 1 x 60kW (80hp) Le Rhone 9C
  rotary engine
Maximum speed: 130km/h (81mph)
Endurance: 5 hours
Service ceiling: 4300m (14,110ft)
Dimensions: span 16.89m (55ft 4.75in);
  length 7.19m (23ft 7in); height 2.55m
  (8ft 4.5in)
Weight: 1232kg (2716lb) max take-off
Armament: 1–2 x 7.7mm (0.303in) MGs

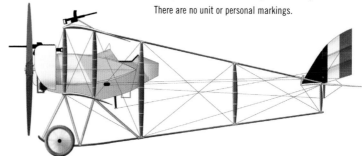

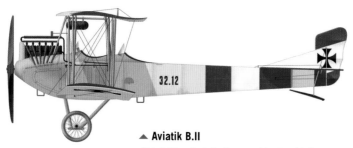

▲ Aviatik B.II
Flek 4 / Szombathely, Hungary / October 1915

This B.II, flown by *Hptm* Karl Banfield, is in transitional markings; early crosses are applied but the red-white-red national colors are still used. The airplane serial number, 32.12, is applied in later style from that used on delivery. There are no unit or personal markings.

Specifications
Crew: 2
Powerplant: 1 x 89kW (120hp) Mercedes
  D.III 6-cylinder inline piston engine
Maximum speed: 110km/h (68.3mph)
Endurance: n/a
Service ceiling: 2900m (9514ft)
Dimensions: span 14.0m (45ft 11in);
  length 8.63m (28ft 3.7in); height 3.15m
  (10ft 4in)
Weight: 1250kg (2756lb) max take-off
Armament: None

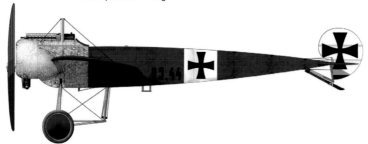

▲ Fokker A.III (Austrian designation for Fokker E.I & E.III)
Flik 19 / Aisovizza, Italian Front / August 1916

The German-built Fokker A.III was the first Austro-Hungarian fighter to see service. Flown by *Feldwebel* Stefan Szucse, this one was lost in a mid-air collision with Fokker A.III 03.52 of *Flik 28* flown by *Feldwebel* Franz Gregel during an air combat on 15 August 1916, killing both pilots. The serial number is on the fuselage; there are no unit or personal markings.

Specifications
Crew: 1
Powerplant: 1 x 75kW (100hp) Oberusel U.I 9-
  cylinder rotary engine
Maximum speed: 140km/h (87mph)
Range: 200km (124 miles)
Service ceiling: 3500m (11,500ft)

Dimensions: span 14.04m (46ft .8in); length
  7.20m (23ft 7in); height 2.40m (7ft 10.5in)
Weight: 635kg (1400lb) max take-off
Armament: 1 x 7.92mm (0.313in) fixed
  forward-firing LMG 08/15 MG

▼ Brandenburg CC

Kriegsmarine Air Station Pola / Italian Front / Spring 1917

The Brandenburg CC was a strong, fast, effective flying-boat fighter. This is a late model with more powerful 149Kw (200hp) Hiero engine and twin Schwarzlose M7/12 machine guns. It was replaced in service by the W.18. The rudder and upper wing are in the red-white-red national colors; the serial number is on the nose.

Specifications

Crew: 1
Powerplant: 1 x 149kW (200hp) Hiero engine
Maximum speed: 180km/h (112mph)
Endurance: 3 hours
Service ceiling: 4300m (14,107ft)

Dimensions: span 9.3m (30ft 6in); length 7.65m (25ft 11.8in); height 3.2m (10ft 6in)
Weight: 1030kg (2271lb) max take-off
Armament: 2 x 8mm (0.315in) Schwarzlose MGs

▼ Brandenburg W.18

Kriegsmarine Air Station Trieste / Italian Front / Spring 1918

Fhr d. Res Josef Niedermeyer was shot down and killed in this seaplane on 4 May 1918 by five-victory ace *Tenente* Frederico Martinengo, who was flying a Macchi M.5 of *260a Squadriglia*. The rudder and upper wing are in the red-white-red national colors; the serial number is on the nose.

Specifications

Crew: 1
Powerplant: 1 x 171.5kW (230hp) Hiero engine
Maximum speed: 180km/h 112mph)
Range: 400km (248.5 miles)
Service ceiling: 4000m (13,123ft)

Dimensions: span 10.7m (35ft 1in); length 8.64m (28ft 4in); height 3.45m (11ft 4in)
Weight: 1092kg (2407lb) loaded
Armament: 2 x 8mm (0.315in) Schwarzlose MGs

Specifications

Crew: 2
Powerplant: 186.4kW (250hp) Benz engine
Maximum speed: 160km/h (99.4mph)
Endurance: 3 hours 30 mins
Service ceiling: 5000m (16,404ft)
Dimensions: span 12.3m (40ft 4in);
    length 8.35m (27ft 4.7in); height 3.33m
    (10ft 11in)
Weight: 1381kg (3045lb) loaded
Armament: 1 x 8mm (0.315in) fixed
    Schwarzlose MG and 1 x 8mm (0.315in)
    flexible Schwarzlose MG

▲ Brandenburg C.I(U)

Flik 105/G / Italian Front / Summer 1918

The sturdy, reliable C.I was the most successful Austro-Hungarian warplane. Comprising about one-quarter of all combat airplanes produced, it was built by several manufacturers with frequent performance boosts as more powerful engines were installed. The complex camouflage was painted using stencils. The serial number is on the fuselage; there are no unit or personal markings.

in part. The Pomilio PD and PE were faster than the reliable SAML and far more reliable than the SIA 7b. A single-engine, two-seat day bomber that saw service in small numbers was the SIA 9b. Powered by the 522kW (700hp) Fiat A.14, the most powerful aero-engine used in the war, the SIA 9b was faster than opposing Austro-Hungarian fighters but inherited much of the fragility of its SIA 7b predecessor, limiting its use.

Seaplanes and flying boat fighters

Seaplanes were important to both combatants, which faced each other across the Adriatic. The Austrians used a bewildering variety of reconnaissance flying boats, with the Lohner being so successful that Italy put it into production after capturing one. Both sides used flying boats for reconnaissance and bombing, with frequent clashes. Interestingly, both sides used flying boat fighters, a concept that seems odd because of the weight and drag of the hull and floats. The most common flying boat fighter in Austrian service was the Brandenburg CC. Late in the war Italy introduced the Macchi M.5 flying boat fighter. Sharing its basic configuration with the Brandenburg CC, the M.5 was faster than the Nieuport landplane fighters used earlier and was very effective.

As in the Atlantic, anti-submarine warfare grew in importance. Merchant ships lost to German submarines caused serious problems, especially coal shortages, for Italian industry. By late 1917 many anti-submarine squadrons equipped with flying boats were formed to reduce shipping losses. Together with increased naval protection, this plan was successful, but many experienced pilots had to be re-assigned from duty in the Adriatic to fly them.

The Austro-Hungarian Empire

Developments in Austro-Hungarian aviation were not as positive as those of Italy. Largely agricultural and riven by ethnic strife, the Austro-Hungarian Empire was less developed industrially and had fewer raw materials, all of which greatly hampered its airplane and aero-engine production. Austria started the war with a motley collection of *Taube* monoplanes and biplane two-seaters used for reconnaissance. The *Taube,* considered reliable prewar for its stability, soon proved itself a poor combat aircraft and biplanes replaced it. After using a number of mediocre biplanes from Knoller and others, the major Austrian success was the Brandenburg C.I reconnaissance two-seater. So robust, reliable and tractable was the Brandenburg C.I that it was continually developed to accommodate engines of greater power and was purchased in multiple production batches from a number of manufacturers. Used successfully until the end of the war, it comprised about one-quarter of all warplanes built for the *Luftfahrtruppe.*

When fighter airplanes were needed, Austria did not have a satisfactory design in hand and so bought some Fokker *Eindeckers* from Germany. The first fighter produced in Austria was the Brandenburg D.I, a German design built under licence but not used by the Germans, which should have been a warning. While strong and fast, the D.I (also known as the KD, for *Kampf Doppeldecker,* or battle biplane) had poor, even vicious, handling characteristics. More pilots were killed in flying accidents in this airplane than than were downed in combat. The KD had another problem. Thanks to the shortage of synchronizers, its gun was mounted above the upper wing, However, it was in a streamlined container, which prevented pilots from clearing jams in flight.

Phönix uncovered the KD's problems while producing it under licence so, starting with the KD as a basis, the company developed its own Phönix D.I fighter. The wings and struts were redesigned and a more powerful engine was fitted. Prototypes were built and test flown until handling characteristics

AUSTRO-HUNGARIAN FLIEGERTRUPPE, AUGUST 1914		
Northeast Front	Southeast Front	Not Yet Assigned
Flik 1 (Stanislau)	Flik 2 (Brezovopoljet)	Flik 3 (Aspern)
Fliks 5 & 7 (Nisko)	Flik 4 (Rogatica)	Flik 6 (Mostar)
Flik 8 (Radymno)		Flik 9 (Krakau)
Flik 10 (Cieszanow)		Flik 12 (Fischamend)
Fliks 11 & 14 (Lemberg)		Fliks 13 & 15 (Wiener Neustadt)

AUSTRO-HUNGARIAN FLIEGERTRUPPE, AUTUMN 1915		
Russian Front	Balkan Front	Italian Front
Flik 1, 3, 5, 10, 11, 13, 14	Flik 6, 9, 15	Flik 2, 4, 7, 8, 12, 16, 17

▲ Brandenburg D.I

Flik 41/J / Sesana, Italian Front / August 1917

The D.I was strong and fast but its dangerous handling characteristics seriously limited its combat effectiveness. This one was flown by *Oblt* Frank Linke-Crawford, fourth-ranked Austrian ace with 27 victories. The red-and-white design was a personal marking. The over-wing gun was not accessible during flight.

Specifications

Crew: 1

Powerplant: 1 x 138kW (185hp) Daimler engine

Maximum speed: 185km/h (115mph)

Endurance: n/a

Service ceiling: n/a

Dimensions: span 8.5m (27ft 10.6in); length 6.3m (20ft 8in); height 2.79m (9ft 1.8in)

Weight: 1047kg (2308lb) max take-off

Armament: 1 x 8mm (0.315in) Schwarzlose MG

Specifications

Crew: 2

Powerplant: 1 x 149kW (200hp) Fiat A.12 engine

Maximum speed: 151km/h (93.8mph)

Endurance: 3 hours 30 mins

Service ceiling: About 4000m (13,123ft)

Dimensions: span 12.25m (40ft 2in); length 8.5m (27ft 10.6in); height 2.95m (9ft 8in)

Weight: 1395kg (3075lb) max take-off

Armament: 1 x 6.5mm (0.256in) fixed Fiat-Revelli MG and 1 x 6.5mm (0.256) flexible Fiat-Revelli MG

▲ SAML 2

115a Squadriglia / Italian Front / 1918

The number '115' indicates the *squadriglia*, the devil is a personal marking. Derived from an Aviatik design, the SAML 2 was a sturdy, reliable reconnaissance airplane used until the end of the war despite the appearance of faster two-seaters intended to replace it. The SIA 7B was too fragile and the handling characteristics of the Pomilio PD and PE were not as safe.

▲ SAML 2

118a Squadriglia / Italian Front / June 1918

The number 118 indicates the *squadriglia*, the fuselage band in national colors is a personal marking. The SAML found popularity because of its good handling qualities and was widely used as a trainer as well as in combat.

Specifications

Crew: 2

Powerplant: 1 x 149kW (200hp) Fiat A.12 engine

Maximum speed: 151km/h (93.8mph)

Endurance: 3 hours 30 mins

Service ceiling: About 4000m (13,123ft)

Dimensions: span 12.25m (40ft 2in); length 8.5m (27ft 10.6in); height 2.95m (9ft 8in)

Weight: 1395kg (3075lb) max take-off

Armament: 1 x 6.5mm (0.256in) fixed Fiat-Revelli MG and 1 x 6.5mm (0.256) flexible Fiat-Revelli MG

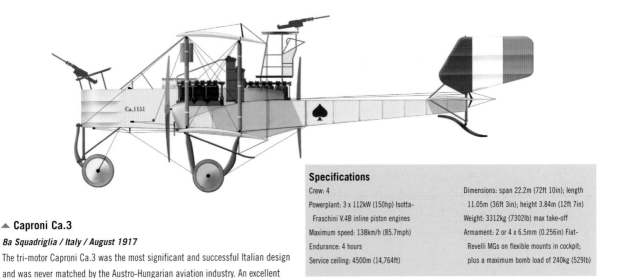

▲ Caproni Ca.3

8a Squadriglia / Italy / August 1917

The tri-motor Caproni Ca.3 was the most significant and successful Italian design and was never matched by the Austro-Hungarian aviation industry. An excellent airplane, it was also used by France. D'Annunzio often flew in this particular airplane with pilots Pagliano and Gori. The ace of spades was the unit insignia.

Specifications

Crew: 4

Powerplant: 3 x 112kW (150hp) Isotta-
Fraschini V.4B inline piston engines

Maximum speed: 138km/h (85.7mph)

Endurance: 4 hours

Service ceiling: 4500m (14,764ft)

Dimensions: span 22.2m (72ft 10in); length
11.05m (36ft 3in); height 3.84m (12ft 7in)

Weight: 3312kg (7302lb) max take-off

Armament: 2 or 4 x 6.5mm (0.256in) Fiat-
Revelli MGs on flexible mounts in cockpit;
plus a maximum bomb load of 240kg (529lb)

▼ Caproni Ca.4

181a or 182a Squadriglia / Italian Front / 1918

The Ca.3 biplane was followed by the huge Ca.4 triplane, tri-motor bomber for heavy night bombing. Much too slow and cumbersome for daylight use, only a few were built. Half a dozen were briefly used by the RNAS.

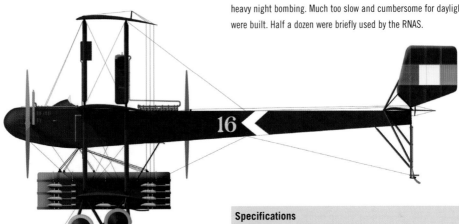

Specifications

Crew: 4–5

Powerplant: 3 x 201kW (270hp)
Fiat A.12bis engines

Maximum speed: 134km/h (83mph)

Endurance: 4 hours 40 minutes

Service ceiling: 3000m (9842ft)

Dimensions: span 29.9m (98ft 1in); length
8.50m (27ft 10.6in); height 6.30m (20ft 8in)

Weight: 6150kg (13,558) loaded

Armament: 4 x 6.5mm (0.256in) Fiat-Revelli
MGs (2 in nose, 2 in dorsal positions); 945kg
(2083lb) bomb load

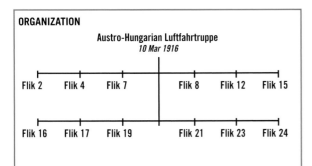

ORGANIZATION

Austro-Hungarian Luftfahrtruppe
10 Mar 1916

Flik 2	Flik 4	Flik 7	Flik 8	Flik 12	Flik 15
Flik 16	Flik 17	Flik 19	Flik 21	Flik 23	Flik 24

were acceptable, and the resulting Phönix D.I was a reliable, manoeuvrable fighter with two synchronized guns. Development continued with the D.II, which weighed less and had better manoeuvrability. The D.IIa, with a more powerful engine and better performance, followed in production. The D.III and D.IV both arrived too late to be used in combat.

Specifications

Crew: 2

Powerplant: 1 x 138kW (185hp)
Daimler engine

Maximum speed: 178km/h (110.6mph)

Endurance: n/a

Service ceiling: n/a

Dimensions: span 8.4m (27ft 6.7in);
length 7.68m (25ft 2in); height 2.92m
(9ft 7in)

Weight: 976kg (2152lb) max take-off

Armament: 2 x 8mm (0.315in) Schwarzlose MGs

▲ **Aviatik (Berg) C.I**

Flik 46P / Prosecco, Isonzo Front / Winter 1917–1918

The Aviatik (Berg) C.I was a fast, lightly built airplane that was small and yet very manoeuvrable for a two-seater. This example in a common camouflage scheme flew from Divalla in Setpember 1917. The letter 'F' is a personal marking. The serial number is on the fuselage.

▲ **Aviatik (Berg) C.I**

Flik 22D / Isonzo Front / early 1918

This Lohner-built Series 214 C.I had a more powerful 149kW (200hp) Daimler engine and wore a more elaborate camouflage pattern than the C.I above. It flew from Corbolone in spring 1918. Some C.Is were modified as fast, single-seat photo-reconnaissance fighters. The serial number is on the fuselage.

Specifications

Crew: 2

Powerplant: 1 x 149kW (200hp) Daimler engine

Maximum speed: 178km/h (110.6mph)

Endurance: n/a

Service ceiling: n/a

Dimensions: span 8.4m (27ft 6.7in); length
7.68m (25ft 2in); height 2.96m (9ft 8.5in)

Weight: 1045kg (2304lb) max take-off

Armament: 2 x 8mm (0.315in) Schwarzlose MGs

Specifications

Crew: 1

Powerplant: 1 x 149kW (200hp)
Daimler engine

Maximum speed: 195km/h (121mph)

Endurance: n/a

Service ceiling: About 6500m (21,325ft)

Dimensions: span 8m (26ft 3in); length
6.86m (22ft 6in); height 2.92m (9ft 7in)

Weight: n/a

Armament: 2 x 8mm (0.315in) Schwarzlose MGs

▲ **Aviatik (Berg) D.I**

Flik 42J / Motta di Livensa, Italian Front / November 1917

The Aviatik (Berg) D.I fighter of five-victory *Off Stv* Friedrich Hefty. On 22 August 1918 Hefty became the first Austro-Hungarian pilot to use a parachute to save his life, bailing out of his burning Albatros D.III(Oef) 253.71.

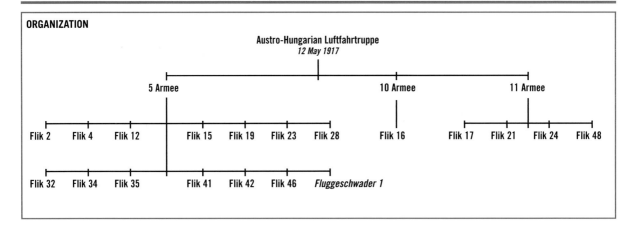

ORGANIZATION

Austro-Hungarian Luftfahrtruppe
12 May 1917

5 Armee | 10 Armee | 11 Armee

Flik 2 — Flik 4 — Flik 12 — Flik 15 — Flik 19 — Flik 23 — Flik 28 — Flik 16 — Flik 17 — Flik 21 — Flik 24 — Flik 48

Flik 32 — Flik 34 — Flik 35 — Flik 41 — Flik 42 — Flik 46 — *Fluggeschwader 1*

Closely resembling its fighter siblings, the Phönix C.I reconnaissance airplane was an excellent design fully comparable with any other airplane of its type. It was fast, manoeuvrable and robust, and its gunner had a good field of fire enhanced by the unusual tail design. It was a tough opponent in combat and was credited with bringing down Major Francesco Barraca (with 34 victories the leading Italian ace), on 19 June 1918. The UFAG C.I was similar to the Phönix C.I and produced in parallel with it. The UFAG had better climb and ceiling, the Phönix C.I was faster and more manoeuvrable. Eventually UFAG was tasked to build the Phönix C.I under licence.

Fragile fighters

The Austrian Aviatik company, with *Oberingenieur* Julius von Berg as designer, built the Aviatik (Berg) C.I two-seat reconnaissance airplane and the D.I single-seat fighter. Both offered good performance and the D.I in particular had good manoeuvrability and handling characteristics. Unfortunately, both were fragile designs plagued by structural failures, especially the fighter version, which was subjected to greater manoeuvring stress in combat.

The D.I was initially hampered by lack of synchronizers and early production D.Is had one gun firing over the propeller arc. Later production airframes had two synchronized guns. Fitting more powerful engines made the D.I even faster and gave it better climb, but its fragile structure was always a potential problem. With 27 victories, fourth-ranking Austrian ace Frank Linke-Crawford was killed in a combat with two Hanriots on 31 July 1918. During the combat Linke-Crawford's Berg D.I was seen to go into a spin, usually the result of wing failure, from

which he recovered. He was then seen to fly straight and level, possibly to keep his wing from falling off, but was again attacked by the Hanriots. His Berg D.I then disintegrated in flight. Linke-Crawford's body had no bullet wounds, substantiating the theory that the Berg's structural failure lead to his downfall. He was *Caporale Pilota* Aldo Astolfi's single victory of the war.

The best Austrian fighter to see combat was probably the Albatros D.III built under licence. The major shortcomings of the KD lead Austrian authorities to move with uncommon speed to seek a suitable replacement at the time the Albatros fighters were proving themselves on the Western Front. The Austrian Oeffag company obtained a licence from Albatros, and production of the Albatros D.II was well under way when the contract was signed for the airplanes on 4 December 1916. Only 16 D.II fighters were built, production then switching to the D.III.

When Oeffag took up Albatros D.III production they used a more powerful engine than the German original (138kW [185hp] compared to 119kW [160hp]) and, more importantly, they strengthened the wing and fuselage. The resulting fighter was fast, tough, manoeuvrable and able to use more powerful engines as they became available. Wing failures, as suffered by Albatros D.III, and especially D.V fighters, were eliminated. The Albatros D.III(Oef) was produced in quantity in several series, the final 253 series featuring a 168kW (225hp) engine reaching the Front in June 1918. *Flik 63/J* considered the new fighter as 'equal to all combat requirements, it is very much liked, only the squadron does not receive sufficient numbers'. *Flik 61/J* considered it 'first class and superior to any fighter'.

▲ Aviatik (Berg) D.I
Flik 74/J / Italian Front / August 1918

The Aviatik (Berg) D.I fighter was closely related to the C.I reconnaissance airplane. It was manoeuvrable and fairly fast, but was a lightly built airplane that sometimes experienced structural failures in combat. 'MIZZI' was a personal marking of *Korporal* Josef Kunz.

Specifications
Crew: 1
Powerplant: 1 x 149kW (200hp)
 Daimler engine
Maximum speed: 195km/h (121mph)
Endurance: n/a
Service ceiling: About 6500m (21,325ft)
Dimensions: span 8m (26ft 3in); length
 6.86m (22ft 6in); height 2.92m (9ft 7in)
Weight: n/a
Armament: 2 x 8mm (0.315in) Schwarzlose MGs

Specifications
Crew: 1
Powerplant: 1 x 89kW (120hp) Le Rhône 9Jb
 9-cylinder rotary piston engine
Maximum speed: 186km/h (115.6mph)
Range: 2hr 30 mins
Service ceiling: 6000m (19,700ft)
Dimensions: span 8.69m (28ft 6in); length
 5.84m (19ft 2in); height 2.94m (9ft 7.7in)
Weight: 605kg (1334lb) max take-off
Armament: 1 x 7.7mm (.303in) Vickers
 machine gun with 110 rounds

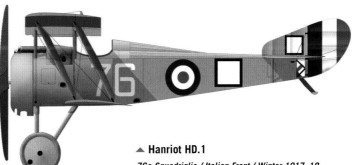

▲ Hanriot HD.1
76a Squadriglia / Italian Front / Winter 1917–18

This Hanriot HD.1 was flown by *Tenente* Silvio Scaroni; with 26 victories Scaroni was the second-ranked Italian ace. The Hanriot was a stronger airplane than the similarly-powered Nieuport and was liked better by Italian pilots.

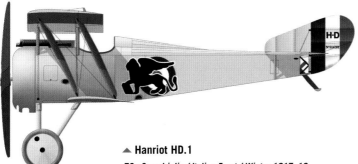

▲ Hanriot HD.1
72a Squadriglia / Italian Front / Winter 1917–18

The Hanriot HD.1 was a French design not used by France, which preferred the sturdy SPAD fighters. The manoeuvrable HD.1 was both imported from France and built under licence in Italy. The winged lion over the cockade was a unit style.

Specifications
Crew: 1
Powerplant: 1 x 82kW (110hp) Le Rhône 9Jb
 9-cylinder rotary piston engine
Maximum speed: 183km/h (114mph)
Range: 2hr 30 mins
Service ceiling: 6000m (19,700ft)
Dimensions: span 8.5m (27ft 10.6in);
 length 5.84m (19ft 2in); height 2.5m
 (8ft 2in)
Weight: 600kg (1323lb) max take-off
Armament: 1 x 7.7mm (.303in) Vickers MG
 with 110 rounds

Specifications

Crew: 1

Powerplant: 1 x 82kW (110hp) Le Rhône 9Jb
9-cylinder rotary piston engine

Maximum speed: 183km/h (114mph)

Range: 2hr 30 mins

Service ceiling: 6000m (19,700ft)

Dimensions: span 8.5m (27ft 10.6in);
length 5.84m (19ft 2in); height 2.5m
(8ft 2in)

Weight: 600kg (1323lb) max take-off

Armament: 1 x 7.7mm (.303in) Vickers MG

▲ Hanriot HD.1

85a Squadriglia / Valona, Albania / 1918

This highly decorated HD.1 was flown by Franco Sarrocchi from Valona, Albania, in
1918. The Hanriot was the most popular fighter used by Italy during the war
despite mounting only a single machine gun.

▲ Nieuport 10

Unknown Squadriglia / Italian Front / Winter 1915–16

Like other Allied air services Italy flew single-seat versions of the Nieuport 10 as
fighters before the smaller, more manoeuvrable Nieuport 11 became available.
This example was built under licence by Macchi in Italy.

Specifications

Crew: 1

Powerplant: 1 x 59.65kW (80hp)
Le Rhône engine

Maximum speed: 146km/h (91.3mph)

Endurance: 3 hours

Service ceiling: About 4000m (13,123ft)

Dimensions: span 7.92m (25ft 11.8in);
length 7.05m (23ft 1.5in); height 2.67m
(8ft 9in)

Weight: 660kg (1452lb) max take-off

Armament: 1 x 7.62mm (0.303in) Lewis MG

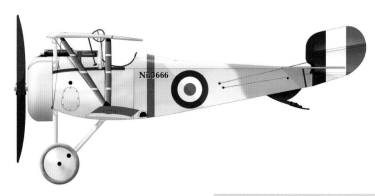

▲ Nieuport 17

Unknown Squadriglia / Italian Front / 1917

The Nieuport 17 was as popular a fighter in Italy as it was in other Allied air
services. Many Italian airplanes had the underside of their wings painted in the
national colors of red on the port side and green on the starboard side, with the
middle being a lighter shade, in this case silver.

Specifications

Crew: 1

Powerplant: 1 x 89kW (120hp) Le Rhône 9Jb
rotary piston engine

Maximum speed: 170km/h (106mph)

Endurance: 2 hours

Service ceiling: 5500m (18,045ft)

Dimensions: span 8.2m (26ft 11in); length
5.7m (18ft 8in); height 2.40m (7ft 10in)

Weight: 590kg (1300lb) max take-off

Armament: 1 x 7.7mm (0.303in) fixed forward-
firing Vickers MG

Specifications

Crew: 1

Powerplant: 1 x 97kW (130hp) Le Rhône
rotary piston engine

Maximum speed: 172km/h (107mph)

Endurance: 2hours 15 mins

Service ceiling: 5550m (18,210ft)

Dimensions: span 8.21m (26ft 11in); length
5.87m (19ft 2in); height 2.40m (7ft 11in)

Weight: 535kg (1179lb) loaded

Armament: 1 x 7.7mm (0.303in) Vickers MG

◢ Nieuport 27

73a Squadriglia / Macedonia / Spring 1918

The last Nieuport design used by Italy during the war was the Nieuport 27; most
Italian pilots preferred the stronger Hanriot. This example was used in Macedonia
in Spring 1918.

◢ Phönix C.I 121.17

Flik 28/D / Godega, Italian Front / June 1918

The fast, tough, manoeuvrable Phönix C.I was the best Austro-Hungarian two-
seater. While flying this example on 19 June 1918, pilot *Feldwebel* Max Kauer and
observer *Oblt* Arnold Barwig shot down an attacking SPAD fighter, ending the life
of the leading Italian ace, *Maggiore* Francesco Barraca. Well-flown two-seaters
were dangerous opponents for even the best aces.

Specifications

Crew: 2

Powerplant: 1 x 171.5kW (230hp)
Hiero engine

Maximum speed: 175km/h (108.7mph)

Endurance: n/a

Service ceiling: 6850m (22,474ft)

Dimensions: span 11m (36ft 1in); length
7.6m (24ft 11in); height 2.95m (9ft 8in)

Weight: 1240kg (2733.7lb) loaded

Armament: 1 x 8mm (0.315in) fixed
Schwarzlose MG and 1 x 8mm (0.315in)
flexible Schwarzlose MG and 6 x 12kg
(26.5lb) bombs

Specifications

Crew: 2

Powerplant: 1 x 171.5kW (230hp)
Hiero engine

Maximum speed: 175km/h (108.7mph)

Endurance: n/a

Service ceiling: 6850m (22,474ft)

Dimensions: span 11m (36ft 1in); length
7.6m (24ft 11in); height 2.95m (9ft 8in)

Weight: 1240kg (2733.7lb) loaded

Armament: 1 x 8mm (0.315in) fixed
Schwarzlose MG and 1 x 8mm (0.315in)
flexible Schwarzlose MG and 6 x 12kg
(26.5lb) bombs

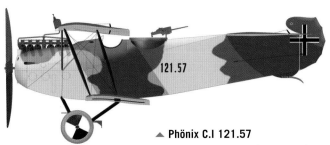

◢ Phönix C.I 121.57

Flik 57/Rb / San Godega di Urbano, Italian Front / October 1918

This Phönix C.I is shown in a later camouflage scheme. The pattern is that now
visible on an original Aviatik (Berg) D.I in the Vienna Technical Museum, but
analysis of paint samples from this airplane indicates the possibility the shades
originally may have been light and dark grey. The unique tail design gave the
observer an excellent field of fire.

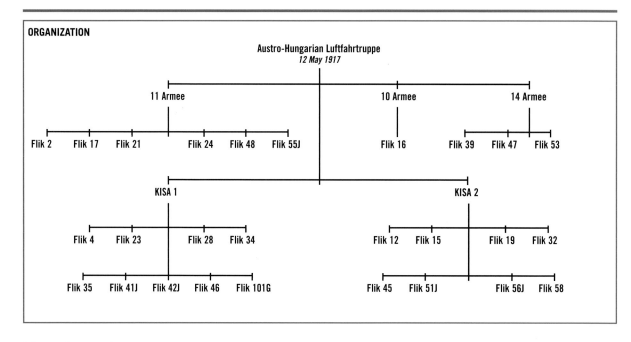

ORGANIZATION

Austro-Hungarian Luftfahrtruppe
12 May 1917

11 Armee

Flik 2   Flik 17   Flik 21   Flik 24   Flik 48   Flik 55J

10 Armee   **14 Armee**

Flik 16   Flik 39   Flik 47   Flik 53

KISA 1

Flik 4   Flik 23   Flik 28   Flik 34

KISA 2

Flik 12   Flik 15   Flik 19   Flik 32

Flik 35   Flik 41J   Flik 42J   Flik 46   Flik 101G

Flik 45   Flik 51J   Flik 56J   Flik 58

Photo Single-Seaters

The bulky glass plates initially used for photography during the war usually required two-seat airplanes so the observer could handle the plates and camera. However, by late 1916, Italian fighter opposition was making it more difficult for two-seaters to accomplish their missions. *Oblt* Dr Fritz Dubowsky, a photo specialist, conceived the idea of using fast, single-seat fighters for photo-reconnaissance. With film in short supply, Dubowsky developed a cassette that held a dozen large glass plates for the camera mounted behind the pilot that was controlled by two levers. By mid-1917, and growing in 1918, the *Luftfahrtruppe* initiated photo-fighter flights to obtain the critical intelligence needed over Italian lines. The Brandenburg D.I was the first type to be modified, followed by the Phönix D.I, Aviatik (Berg) D.I and Albatros D.III(Oef) fighters. Single-

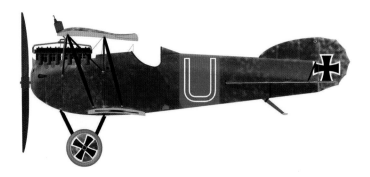

▲ **Phönix D.I**

Flik 14J / Feltre, Italian Front / Summer 1918

The Phönix D.I was developed from the unfortunate Brandenburg D.I through a series of prototypes. The Phönix D.I was a sturdy fighter with excellent handling characteristics. This one was flown from Feltre Aerodrome by *Stabsfeldwebel* Karl Urban, an ace with five victories. The letter 'U', the first letter in Urban's name, was his personal marking; the red band is the *Flik 14J* unit marking.

Specifications

Crew: 1	Dimensions: span 9.8m (32ft 1.8in); length
Powerplant: 1 x 149kW (200hp) Hiero engine	6.75m (22ft 1.7in); height 2.65m (8ft 8in)
Maximum speed: 178km/h (110.6mph)	Weight: 951kg (2096.6lb) loaded
Endurance: n/a	Armament: 2 x 8mm (0.315in) Schwarzlose MGs
Service ceiling: About 5500m (18,044ft)	

AUSTRO-HUNGARIAN UNITS, THE BATTLE OF PIAVE, 15 JUNE 1918		
Group	Division	Unit
10. Armee	Divisionskompagnien	17, 23, 27, 54, 72
	Jagdkompagnie	3
	Photoeinsitzer-kompagnien	10, 27
6. Armee	Divisionskompagnien	2, 4, 26, 28, 38, 40, 52, 53, 46, 59, 65, 67, 70
	Jagdkompagnien	30, 42, 56, 68, 72, 74
	Photokompagnien	14, 15
Isonzo Armee	Divisionskompagnien	12, 17, 22, 32, 34, 35, 37, 44, 50, 58, 62, 69, 71
	Jagdkompagnien	41, 43, 51, 61, 63, 46, 49
11. Armee	Divisionskompagnien	16, 21, 24, 31, 36, 39, 45, 48, 66
	Jagdkompagnien	9, 14, 55, 60
	Photokompagnien	11, 15
Pola	Fliegerkompagnien	101, 102, 103, 104, 105G

AUSTRO-HUNGARIAN UNITS, 18 OCTOBER 1918		
Group	Division	Unit
10. Armee	Fliegerkompagnien	2, 11, 16, 66
	Jagdkompagnien	14, 30, 53, 60
	Schlachtkompagnie	8
	Photokompagnie	39
Belluno	Fliegerkompagnien	4, 38, 57, 70
	Korpskompagnien	28, 52
	Schlachtkompagnien	26, 27, 59, 65, 67
	Photokompagnie	40
	Jagdkompagnien	42, 56, 68, 72, 74
Isonzo Armee	Fliegerkompagnien	5, 19, 22, 32, 35, 44, 49, 50, 58, 71
	Photokompagnien	12, 37, 46
	Schlachtkompagnien	34, 69
	Jagdkompagnien	41, 43, 51, 61, 63
11. Armee	Fliegerkompagnien	15, 24, 36, 45, 48
	Korpskompagnie	21
	Photokompagnie	31
	Jagdkompagnien	9, 20, 55
Pola	Fliegerkompagnien	101G, 102G, 103G, 104G, 105G

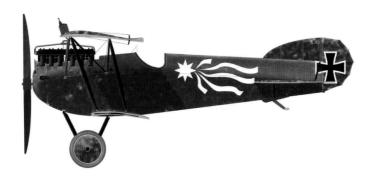

▲ **Phönix D.II**

Flik 55/J / Pergine, Italian Front / July 1918

The Phönix D.II was developed from the D.I to give even better manoeuvrability and performance by reducing weight and modifying the control surfaces. This one was flown by *Oblt* Hans Leiner from Pergine Aerodrome in July 1918; the stylized comet is Leiner's personal marking.

Specifications

Crew: 1

Powerplant: 1 x 149kW (200hp) Hiero engine

Maximum speed: 178km/h (110.6mph)

Endurance: n/a

Service ceiling: About 5500m (18,044ft)

Dimensions: span 9.8m (32ft 1.8in); length 6.75m (22ft 1.7in); height 2.65m (8ft 8in)

Weight: 900kg (1984lb) loaded

Armament: 2 x 8mm (0.315in) Schwarzlose MGs

Specifications

Crew: 1

Powerplant: 1 x 171.5kW (230hp) Hiero
  engine

Maximum speed: 185km/h (114.9mph)

Endurance: n/a

Service ceiling: About 6000m (19,685ft)

Dimensions: span 9.8m (32ft 1.8in); length
  6.75m (22ft 1.7in); height 2.65m (8ft 8in)

Weight: n/a

Armament: 2 x 8mm (0.315in) Schwarzlose MGs

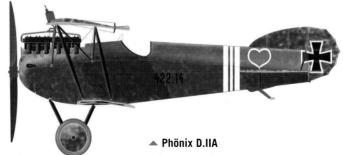

▲ Phönix D.IIA

Flik 55/J / Pergine, Italian Front / June 1918

Adding a more powerful engine to the Phönix D.II created the Phönix D.IIa, giving better speed and climb rate. This one was flown by *Feldwebel* Alexander Kasza, an ace with eight victories, from Pergine Aerodrome in July 1918. The three white bands are Kasza's personal marking. The red heart is said to have been added after the death of Kasza's close friend Josef Kiss, an ace with 19 victories.

▼ SPAD VII

91a Squadriglia / Italian Front

This SPAD VII was flown by *Tenente* Fulco Ruffo di Calabria, Italy's fifth-ranking ace with 20 victories. The skull and crossed bones were Calabria's personal insignia. The SPAD VII was lighter and more manoeuvrable than the faster, more heavily-armed SPAD XIII.

Specifications

Crew: 1

Powerplant: 1 x 134kW (180hp) Hispano-
  Suiza 8Ab V8 in-line piston engine

Maximum speed: 212km/h (132mph)

Endurance: 1 hour 30 mins

Service ceiling: 6553m (21,499ft)

Dimensions: span 7.82m (25ft 8in);
  length 6.08m (19ft 11in); height 2.20m
  (7ft 3in)

Weight: 705kg (1554lb) max take-off

Armament: 1 x 7.7mm (.3in) MG)

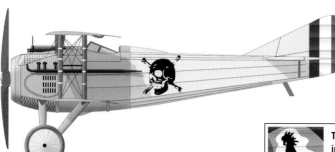

 The stallion rampant was Baracca's personal insignia. Enzo Ferrari received permission from Baracca's mother to use the insignia on his race cars and it is now the symbol of the Ferrari company.

Specifications

Crew: 1

Powerplant: 1 x 164kW (220hp) Hispano-
  Suiza 8Be eight-cylinder Vee engine

Maximum speed: 218km/h (135.5mph)

Range: 400km (250 miles) (estimated)

Endurance: 1 hour 40 mins

Service ceiling: 6800m (22,310ft)

Dimensions: span 8.08m (26ft 6in); length
  6.25m (20ft 6in); height 2.60m (8ft 6in)

Weight: 856.5kg (1888lb) max take-off

Armament: 2 x 7.7mm (.303in) Vickers
  water-cooled MGs

▲ SPAD S.XIII

91a Squadriglia / Italian Front / Spring 1918

This SPAD XIII was flown by *Maggiore* Francesco Baracca, Italy's leading ace with 34 victories. The sturdy SPAD XIII was faster than opposing Austro-Hungarian fighters. In fact, the SPAD XIII was used by the leading aces of France and the United States as well as Italy.

Specifications

Crew: 1

Powerplant: 1 x 167.8kW (225hp) Daimler
engine

Maximum speed: 202km/h (125.5mph)

Endurance: n/a

Service ceiling: About 5500m (18,045ft)

Dimensions: span 9.0m (29ft 6.3in); length
7.43m (24ft 4in); height 2.64m
(8ft 7in)

Weight: 995kg (2193lb) max take-off

Armament: 2 x 8mm (0.315in) Schwarzlose MGs

▲ **Albatros D.III (Oef)**

Flik 3/J / Romagnano, Italian Front / August 1918

Albatros D.III(Oef) 253.116 was flown by 10-victory ace *Oblt* Friedrich Navratil,
commanding officer of *Flik 3/J*. The marking is his personal marking. The 253
series powered by the 168kW (225hp) Daimler was the ultimate Albatros D.III and
its pilots considered it fully competitive with all Allied fighters.

▲ **Albatros D.III (Oef)**

Flik 41/J / Sesana, Italian Front / February–March 1918

Albatros D.III(Oef) 153.10 is one of the airplanes flown by *Hptm* Godwin
Brumowski, the leading Austro-Hungarian ace with 35 victories.

Specifications

Crew: 1

Powerplant: 1 x 129.18kW (200hp)
Daimler engine

Maximum speed: 188km/h (117mph)

Endurance: n/a

Service ceiling: About 5500m (18,045ft)

Dimensions: span 9.0m (29ft 6.3in); length
7.35m (24ft 1in); height 2.80m (9ft 2in)

Weight: 987kg (2176lb) max take-off

Armament: 2 x 8mm (0.315in) Schwarzlose MGs

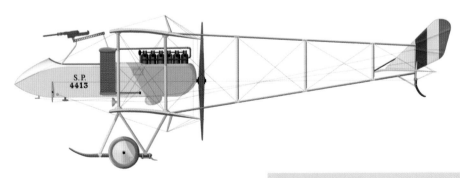

▲ **Savoia-Pomilio SP2**

Squadriglia Unknown / Italian Front / 1917

Despite its obsolete configuration, the SP2 was a reliable airplane generally liked
by its crews. As with most Allied pushers, it served long past the time it should
have been replaced by more modern designs.

Specifications

Crew: 2

Powerplant: 1 x 193.9kW (260hp)
Fiat A.12 engine

Maximum speed: 136km/h (84.5mph)

Endurance: 4 hours

Service ceiling: About 4000m (13,123ft)

Dimensions: span 16.7m (54ft 9.4in); length
10.7m (35ft 1in); height 3.55m (11ft 7.7in)

Weight: 1700kg (3748lb) max take-off

Armament: 1 x 6.5mm (0.256in) flexible Fiat-
Revelli MG

ALLIED AIRCRAFT ON THE MACEDONIAN FRONT, JUNE 1918				
Type	British	French	Italian	Total
Corps Reconnaissance:	26	130	13	169
Single-Seat Fighters	15	205	11	231
Day Bombing	0	18	0	18
Short-Range Night Bombing	0	10	0	10
Total	41	363	24	428

ALLIED AIRCRAFT ON THE ITALIAN FRONT, JUNE 1918			
Type	British	Italian	Total
Corps Reconnaissance	201	24	225
Single-Seat Fighters	223	72	295
2-Seat Fighter Reconnaissance	0	8	8
Day Bombing	45	0	45
Long-Range Night Bombing	8	0	8
Total	477	104	581

LEADING AUSTRO-HUNGARIAN ACES	
Ace	Score
Hptm Godwin Brumowski	35
Offz Julius Arigi	32
Oblt Benno Fiala	28
Oblt Frank Linke-Crawford †	27
Lt Josef Kiss †	19
Ltn Franz Gräser †	18
Fldwb Eugen Bönsch	16
Sfdwb Stefan Fejes	16
Oblt Ernst Strohschneider †	15

Note: † indicates killed in the war.

LEADING ITALIAN ACES	
Ace	Score
Maj Francesco Baracca †	34
Ten Silvio Scaroni	26
Ten Col. Pier Piccio	24
Ten Flavio Baracchini	21
Capt Fulco Ruffo di Calabria	20
Ten Ferruccio Ranza	17
Sgt Marziale Cerutti	17

Note: † indicates killed in the war.

seat conversions of the Aviatik (Berg) C.I were similarly modified.

French and British assistance

During Italy's great Caporetto defeat in late 1917, in which German units participated, Italy lost many airplanes, many aircrew and with them air superiority. During the disastrous retreat the Italian air force gave its best, recklessly attacking enemy ground troops to stop the advance despite heavy losses to ground fire. Many airfields were overrun by enemy troops resulting in the loss of many airplanes on the ground. Italy requested Allied assistance and some French and British air units were quickly sent along with many French-built Hanriot and SPAD fighters. The British supplied three fighter squadrons equipped with Sopwith Camels, one RE.8 reconnaissance squadron, and one flight, later a

Specifications

Crew: 2

Powerplant: 1 x 186kW (250hp) Fiat A.12 engine

Maximum speed: 185km/h (114.9mph)

Endurance: 3–4 hours

Service ceiling: 5000m (16,404ft)

Dimensions: span 11.64m (38ft 2.3in); length 8.94m (29ft 4in); height 3.35m (11ft)

Weight: 1577kg (3747lb) max take-off

Armament: 1 x 6.5mm (0.256in) fixed Fiat-Revelli MG, 1 x 6.5mm (0.256in) flexible Fiat-Revelli MG; 6 x 26kg (57lb) bombs

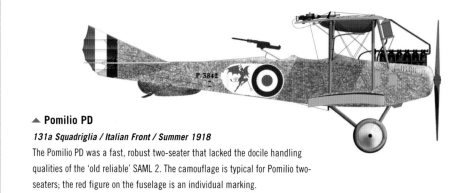

▲ **Pomilio PD**

131a Squadriglia / Italian Front / Summer 1918

The Pomilio PD was a fast, robust two-seater that lacked the docile handling qualities of the 'old reliable' SAML 2. The camouflage is typical for Pomilio two-seaters; the red figure on the fuselage is an individual marking.

▲ **Pomilio PE**

112a Squadriglia / Castenedolo, Italy / 1918

The more streamlined Pomilio PE was even faster than its predecessor the PD though its handling qualities were no better. This example flew from Castemedolo Aerodrome in 1918. The unusual presentation of the fuselage cockade was a unit style.

Specifications

Crew: 2

Powerplant: 1 x 223.7kW (300hp) Fiat A.12bis engine

Maximum speed: 194km/h (120.5mph)

Endurance: 3–5 hours

Service ceiling: 5100m (16,732ft)

Dimensions: span 11.64m (38ft 2.3in); length 8.94m (29ft 4in); height 3.35m (11ft)

Weight: 1537kg (3388.5lb) max take-off

Armament: 1 x 6.5mm (0.256in) fixed Fiat-Revelli MG, 1 x 6.5mm (0.256in) flexible Fiat-Revelli MG; 6 x 26kg (57lb) bombs

Specifications

Crew: 2

Powerplant: 1 x 212.5kW (285hp) Fiat A.12

Maximum speed: 186.5km/h (115.9mph)

Endurance: 4 hours

Service ceiling: More than 5000m (16,404ft)

Dimensions: span 13.32m (43ft 8.4in); length 9.07m (29ft 9in); height 3.15m (10ft 4in)

Weight: 1480kg (3263lb) max take-off

Armament: 2 x 6.5mm (0.256in) Fiat-Revelli MGs (1 fixed and 1 flexible)

▲ **SIA 7b1**

35a Squadriglia / Padova, Italy / January 1918

The SIA 7B was a disaster for the Italian air service. Handsome, powerful and fast, it was structurally weak and a number disintegrated in flight, forcing its withdrawal from service. The number 35 on the fuselage indicates the *squadriglia*.

▲ **SVA 10**

87a Squadriglia / San Pelagio, Italian Front / August 1918

The SVA series were strong, fast, reliable airplanes used for long-distance reconnaissance and day bombing. This SVA 10 was specially modified with pilot *Capt* Natale Palli in back (note the fairing between cockpits for the modified throttle) to enable the poet D'Annunzio to accompany the spectacular propaganda leaflet raid on Vienna on 9 August 1918. All eight aircraft returned safely from this remarkable long-distance flight over enemy territory.

Specifications SVA-10/IF

Crew: 2

Powerplant: 1 x 153kW (205hp) SPA 6A engine

Maximum speed: 200km/h (124.3mph)

Endurance: 7 hours (normally 3 hours 10 mins)

Service ceiling: 4800m (15,748ft)

Dimensions: span 9.243m (30ft 4in); length 8.10m (26ft 7in); height 2.72m (8ft 11in)

Weight: 1065g (2348lb) max take-off

Armament: None (normally 2 x 7.7mm (0.303in) MGs (1 fixed forward-firing, 1 flexible rearward-firing); plus light bomb load

The Lion of St Mark emblem was the insignia of the *87a Squadriglia* 'Serenissima'. The version on this airplane varies somewhat from that normally used by this squadriglia.

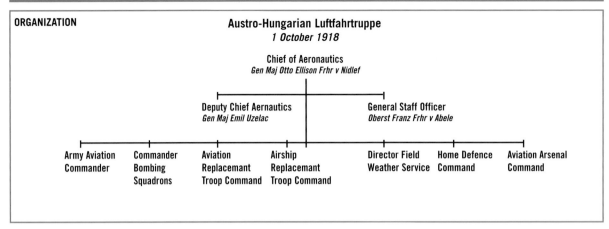

ORGANIZATION

Austro-Hungarian Luftfahrtruppe
1 October 1918

Chief of Aeronautics
Gen Maj Otto Ellison Frhr v Nidlef

Deputy Chief Aernautics
Gen Maj Emil Uzelac

General Staff Officer
Oberst Franz Frhr v Abele

Army Aviation Commander

Commander Bombing Squadrons

Aviation Replacemant Troop Command

Airship Replacemant Troop Command

Director Field Weather Service

Home Defence Command

Aviation Arsenal Command

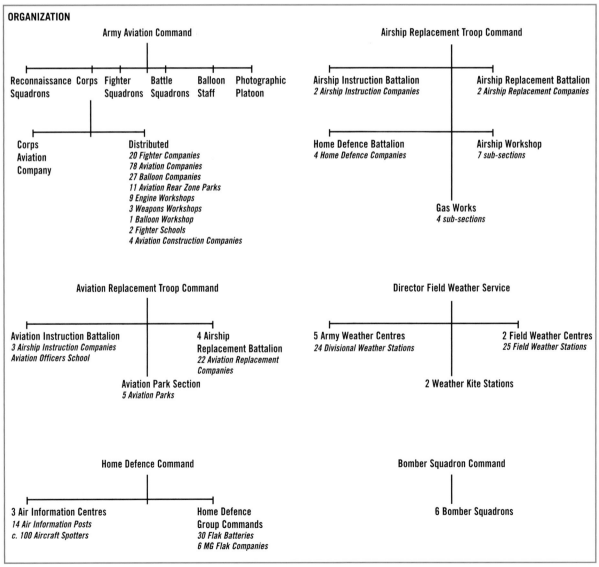

ORGANIZATION

Army Aviation Command

Reconnaissance Squadrons

Corps

Fighter Squadrons

Battle Squadrons

Balloon Staff

Photographic Platoon

Corps Aviation Company

Distributed
20 Fighter Companies
78 Aviation Companies
27 Balloon Companies
11 Aviation Rear Zone Parks
9 Engine Workshops
3 Weapons Workshops
1 Balloon Workshop
2 Fighter Schools
4 Aviation Construction Companies

Airship Replacement Troop Command

Airship Instruction Battalion
2 Airship Instruction Companies

Airship Replacement Battalion
2 Airship Replacement Companies

Home Defence Battalion
4 Home Defence Companies

Airship Workshop
7 sub-sections

Gas Works
4 sub-sections

Aviation Replacement Troop Command

Aviation Instruction Battalion
3 Airship Instruction Companies
Aviation Officers School

4 Airship Replacement Battalion
22 Aviation Replacement Companies

Aviation Park Section
5 Aviation Parks

Director Field Weather Service

5 Army Weather Centres
24 Divisional Weather Stations

2 Field Weather Centres
25 Field Weather Stations

2 Weather Kite Stations

Home Defence Command

3 Air Information Centres
14 Air Information Posts
c. 100 Aircraft Spotters

Home Defence Group Commands
30 Flak Batteries
6 MG Flak Companies

Bomber Squadron Command

6 Bomber Squadrons

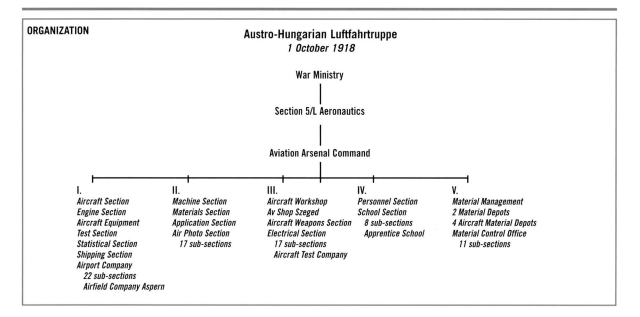

ORGANIZATION

Austro-Hungarian Luftfahrtruppe
1 October 1918

War Ministry

Section 5/L Aeronautics

Aviation Arsenal Command

I.	II.	III.	IV.	V.
Aircraft Section	*Machine Section*	*Aircraft Workshop*	*Personnel Section*	*Material Management*
Engine Section	*Materials Section*	*Av Shop Szeged*	*School Section*	*2 Material Depots*
Aircraft Equipment	*Application Section*	*Aircraft Weapons Section*	*8 sub-sections*	*4 Aircraft Material Depots*
Test Section	*Air Photo Section*	*Electrical Section*	*Apprentice School*	*Material Control Office*
Statistical Section	*17 sub-sections*	*17 sub-sections*		*11 sub-sections*
Shipping Section		*Aircraft Test Company*		
Airport Company				
22 sub-sections				
Airfield Company Aspern				

squadron, of Bristol F.2B two-seat fighters. The French provided reconnaissance squadrons with A.R. biplanes and some fighter squadrons. The British and French help stabilized the situation until Italy could re-group and re-equip her air service. By the Battle of the Piave in June 1918 the Italians had regained air superiority, which they held until the Armistice.

The final Italian offensive, known as the Battle of Vittorio Veneto, started on 24 October 1918 and resulted in the collapse of the Austro-Hungarian forces. During the war both sides fought bravely and with enormous skill, but the greater industrial potential of Italy generally gave her air superiority, and in the end Italy prevailed.

The skull was the personal marking of the pilot, *Tenente* Alberto Bortolozzo. The *260a Squadriglia* was stationed at Venice at this time.

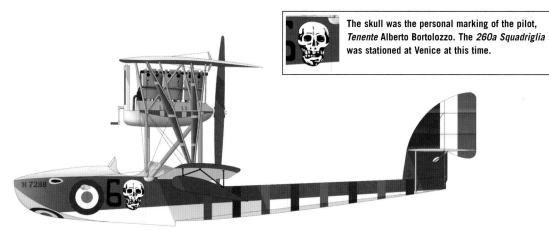

▲ **Macchi M.5**

260a Squadriglia / Venice, Italy / Summer 1918

The Macchi M.5 flying boat fighter was faster than the Nieuport fighters it replaced and was safer to fly over the Adriatic.

Specifications

Crew: 1

Powerplant: 1 x 119kW (160hp) Isotta-Fraschini V.4B inline piston engine

Maximum speed: 181km/h (112.4mph)

Range: 500km (310.7 miles)

Service ceiling: 3900m (12,795ft)

Dimensions: span 11.9m (39ft 0.5in); length 8.08m (26ft 6in); height 2.85m (9ft 4.5in)

Weight: 990kg (2183lb) max take-off

Armament: 2 x 7.7mm (0.303in) Vickers MGs

Chapter 7

The Middle East

Far from the decisive Western Front, the Middle East campaigns were dominated by fighting between armies with limited aerial support. However, aerial reconnaissance by the few airplanes available proved invaluable to success on the ground. Despite courageous fighting and some notable victories, the Ottoman Empire's lack of industry and primitive transportation infrastructure doomed it in a struggle with advanced industrial nations like Britain and France because an over-stretched Germany was unable to provide sufficient help to redress the imbalance.

◀ **Air war in a distant land**

Ltn Emil Meinecke poses beside his Halberstadt D.V fighter after a hard combat with British aircraft. Meinecke flew with the fighter element of Ottoman *Flieger Abteilung* 6 at Chanak (now Cannakale) in the Dardanelles and achieved six victories to become an ace.

An interesting backwater
1914–1918

With no aviation industry of its own, the Ottoman Empire was completely dependent on her German ally for airplanes.

FROM AN AVIATION perspective the Middle East was an interesting backwater during the war. The Ottoman Empire had very limited transportation and industrial capacity and was unable to manufacture either airplanes or aero-engines, so was totally dependent on Germany. Preoccupied with the decisive Western Front and faced with long, insecure supply lines to the Ottoman Empire, Germany was unable to provide much help. A major motivation for Britain to attack the Ottoman Empire was its strategic location, which blocked an easy southern sea route to supply Russia and also threatened the important Suez Canal.

Gallipoli

Britain and France sought an opportunity to force open a supply route to Russia through the Dardanelles and to drive the Ottoman Empire out of the war. First they attempted to force passage using a number of older battleships and supporting vessels. However, Turkish forts, mobile artillery and mines defended the narrow way through. During the initial attack on 18 March 1915 the Allies, silencing the main batteries in the forts, came close to success but could not destroy the lighter, mobile batteries. Then five ships struck mines, and the naval attack was broken off. The Allies next decided to invade up the Gallipoli peninsula. The resulting campaign was one of the most frustrating and disastrous of the war for the Allies, who were forced to withdraw starting in December after heartbreaking losses.

When the Allies arrived off Gallipoli they brought the first airplanes with them, and both British and French forces used under-powered floatplanes for reconnaissance. The hot weather reduced air density and thus lift, further limiting the performance of these early airplanes. On 17 February 1915 a Wight seaplane from the seaplane tender HMS *Ark Royal* made the first reconnaissance of the Dardanelles and dropped a bomb, and two days later aircraft from *Ark Royal* directed the fire of warships against Turkish forts at the entrance to the Dardanelles. On 15 March the French seaplane carrier *Foudre* arrived with her 74kW (100hp) Nieuport VI floatplanes, which had figured so importantly in defeating the Turkish advance on the Suez Canal in early 1915. The Turks had no aerial reconnaissance for their attack, giving the Allies a crucial advantage. *Foudre* operated her Nieuports until departing on 23 May.

On 24 March No. 3 Squadron, RNAS, arrived with 18 airplanes and made its first reconnaissance on the 28th. On 9 April the first British balloon ship, the *Manica*, arrived. The balloons were intended to spot for the fleet's heavy guns, and proved very effective in helping British warships drive off the Turkish battleship *Turgud Reis* several times on 25 April, the day of the troop landings. On 9 June another balloon ship, the *Hector*, arrived, and a third, the *Canning*, arrived in early October.

On 4 May French escadrille M.F.98T (T for Tenedos) was ready for action with eight Maurice Farmans flying from Tenedos with No. 3. On 12 June the British seaplane carrier HMS *Ben-my-Chree* arrived in the area bringing five additional seaplanes.

The first victory in the arena came on 22 June when a British Voisin downed a German airplane over Gallipoli. On 12 August Flt Cmdr Edmunds, flying a Short 184 seaplane, made the first successful aerial torpedo attack, sinking a Turkish steamer. Later it was determined the ship had been beached after previously being hit by a submarine torpedo.

Edmunds' Short could barely stagger into the air with its heavy load. On 17 August two more Turkish ships in the Dardanelles were torpedoed by the Short seaplanes, one by Edmunds. The other torpedo was launched by the Short while it was in the water; after releasing its torpedo the Short was finally able to take off. By the end of August No. 2 Squadron RNAS had arrived with 22 airplanes; six Morane Parasols, six BE.2c and six Caudron biplanes, and four Bristol Scouts. Later Nieuport 10 and 12 two-seaters arrived.

On 16 September Turkish troops downed an RFC Caudron with rifle fire; this was the first Allied airplane lost to enemy action in this arena. About this time at least one British non-rigid airship began anti-submarine patrols in the area.

During the campaign the Allied navies dominated the sea and cut off Ottoman supplies and reinforcements via ships. The Allied airmen regularly bombed Ottoman supply lines on land and were a serious threat; had they been more numerous and capable, they could have been decisive. However, the technology of the time was inadequate.

When Bulgaria entered the war allied with Germany and the Ottoman Empire, a direct rail line

◢ Short 184

HMS Ben-my-Chree / Gallipoli Front / August 1915

Flying this Short 184, F/Cdr C.H.K. Edmonds made the world's first successful aerial torpedo attack against a ship on 12 August 1915 in the Dardanelles. This historic mission was staged from the seaplane tender HMS *Ben-my-Chree*. The seaplane sports early national markings and the serial number on the rudder.

Specifications

Crew: 2

Powerplant: 1 x 194kW (260hp) Sunbeam Maori Vee piston engine

Maximum speed: 142km/h (88mph)

Endurance: 2 hours 45 mins

Service ceiling: 2745m (9000ft)

Dimensions: span 19.36m (63ft 6in); length 12.38m (40ft 7in); height 4.11m (13ft 6in)

Weight: 2433kg (5363lb) max take-off

Armament: 1 x 7.92mm (.303in) Lewis MG; plus 2 x 35.6cm (14in) torpedo or up to 236kg (520lb) of bombs

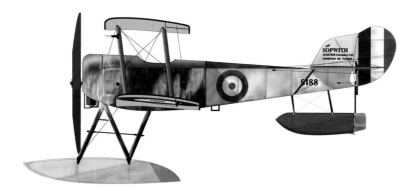

◢ Sopwith Baby

HMS Ben-my-Chree / Gallipoli Front / Summer 1915

This Sopwith Baby was another seaplane from the seaplane tender HMS *Ben-my-Chree* in the Dardanelles. The Baby was used for reconnaissance. The seaplane's finish is heavily weathered; there are no unit or personal markings.

Specifications

Crew: 1

Powerplant: 1 x 82kW (110hp) Clerget engine

Maximum speed: 148km/h (92mph)

Endurance: 2 hours 15 mins

Service ceiling: Unknown

Dimensions: span 7.82m (25ft 8in); length 6.96m (22ft 10in); height 3.05m (10ft)

Weight: 717kg (1580lb) max take-off

Armament: 1 x 7.62mm (.303in) Lewis MG

between Germany and Turkey became available. To severe it, in 1915 British aircraft made repeated attacks on a critical bridge over Maritza River. Airplanes and seaplanes of No. 2 and 3 Squadrons made five raids on the bridge in November and 1 in December. On the 19 November attack Lt Bell-Davies, flying a converted Nieuport 10, won the Victoria Cross for rescuing Flt Lt G.G. Smiley after Smiley's Farman was downed by ground fire.

Ottoman Air Service

At the time of the Ottoman Empire's entry into the war on 29 October 1914, the Empire had no air service or airplanes at all, and soon requested German help because the ability to perform air reconnaissance was essential. Germany, though pressed, promised 24 Rumpler and Albatros two-seaters with 89kW (120hp) engines, together with 12 pilots and 32 mechanics, all German civilians. *Oblt* Erich Serno, an experienced pilot, placed in charge, was released from the Prussian Army and attached to the German military mission in Constantinople. Upon arriving there in January 1915, Serno found that his real mission was considerably more challenging than he had been told: he was to create and command an Ottoman air service. By Imperial decree of the Sultan, Serno was taken into the Turkish army as a *Hauptmann* and named commander of the Ottoman *Fliegertruppe*. His task was daunting;

aviation supplies and equipment were not available, and machine tools were very difficult to obtain. Even hand tools were so scarce that some had to be purchased at the bazaar. Furthermore, with no aviation industry, local artisans had to be recruited and trained on airplane maintenance and repair.

Meanwhile, just getting the airplanes and related equipment and supplies to Turkey was difficult; the only routes were through then-neutral Bulgaria (which sided with Germany) or Romania (which sided with Russia), and considerable subterfuge was needed. The first three aircraft shipped were confiscated en route in Bulgaria, as was one of the next shipment of five, but the remaining four aircraft arrived in March 1915, soon after the Allies bombarded the forts at the Dardanelles.

The first ex-German airplane arrived at the Dardanelles on 17 March 1915 and the next day made its first reconnaissance flight with Serno at the controls and *Kapitän-Leutnant* Schnieder, second staff officer to the admiral, as observer. Climbing to the airplane's ceiling of 1600m (2500ft), they flew over ancient Troy on their way to survey the large Allied fleet. Under anti-aircraft fire from the fleet they saw the ships form up to force their way into the straits. Grasping the implications, after reconnoitering the fleet they returned to base, then got on horseback to carry the news to Admiral von

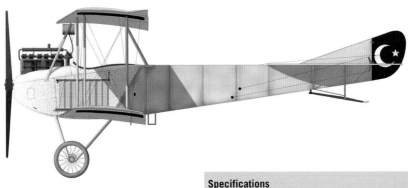

▲ **LVG B.I**

Unknown Ottoman Unit / Turkey / 1916

This unarmed LVG B.I in early Ottoman markings was used for reconnaissance. The B.I was a safe, sturdy two-seater of modest performance.

Specifications

Crew: 2	Service ceiling: About 2500m (8202ft)
Powerplant: 1 x 74.57kW (100hp)	Dimensions: span 14.5m (47ft 7in); length 9m
Mercedes D.I engine	(29ft 6in); height n/a
Maximum speed: 90km/h (55.9mph)	Weight: 1132kg (2496lb) max take-off
Endurance: n/a	Armament: Light bombs

Usedom. The defences were immediately alerted and were able to repel the Allied assault. Soon two more airplanes were assigned to the Dardenelles, combining with the first airplane to form the *Dardanelles Fliegerabteilung*. The German civilians were enlisted in the Turkish army, the pilots as *Leutnants*, the mechanics as NCOs. During the campaign the unit flew reconnaissance missions far out into the Mediterranean to the islands of Tenedos, Imbros and even Lemnos in their landplanes.

German airplanes continued to trickle down to Turkey and a *Wasserfliegerabteilung* of three seaplanes was formed at the Dardanelles. These underpowered seaplanes had a ceiling of 1000m (3300ft) in the hot

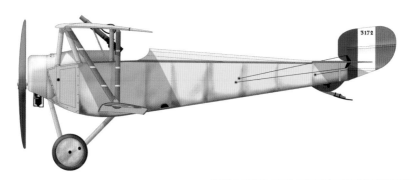

▲ Nieuport 10

No. 3 Squadron, RNAS / Tenedos, Bulgarian Front / December 1915

This Nieuport 10 was flown by F/Cdr R. Bell-Davies from Tenedos in December 1915 and is the airplane he was flying when he landed and rescued a fellow airman during a bombing raid; Bell-Davies was awarded the Victoria Cross for his actions. There are no personal or unit markings, but there is a serial number on the rudder.

Specifications

Crew: 1–2	Service ceiling: About 4000m (13,123ft)
Powerplant: 1 x 59.65kW (80hp)	Dimensions: span 7.92m (25ft 12in); length
Le Rhône engine	7.05m (23ft 2in); height 2.67m (8ft 9in)
Maximum speed: 146km/h (91.3mph)	Weight: 660kg (1452lb) max take-off
Endurance: 3 hours	Armament: 1–2 x 7.7mm (.303in) Lewis MGs

▲ Bristol M.1C

No. 72 Squadron, RAF / Mesopotamia / Spring 1918

Due to prejudice against the monoplane, the fast, manoeuvrable Bristol M.1C was used only for training and in the Middle East. The markings are a personal or Flight Commander marking, not a unit marking. The short range of the M.1C precluded its use as an escort fighter.

Specifications

Crew: 1	Dimensions: span 9.37m (30ft 9in); length
Powerplant: 1 x 82kW (110hp) Le Rhône 9J	6.22m (20ft 5in); height 2.13m (7ft)
rotary piston engine	Weight: 608kg (1340lb) max take-off
Maximum speed: 170km/h (106mph)	Armament: 1 x 7.7mm (.303in) fixed Vickers
Endurance: 1 hour 45 mins	MG
Service ceiling: 6400m (21,000ft)	

▲ **Halberstadt D.V**

Unknown Unit / Middle East / 1917

The sturdy, manoeuvrable Halberstadt D.V was one of the few fighters available to the Central Powers in the Middle East. Like most Ottoman airplanes this one has the Ottoman insignia but no personal or unit markings.

Specifications

Crew: 1	Service ceiling: 4500m (14,764ft)
Powerplant: 1 x 89.5kW (120hp)	Dimensions: span 8.8m (28ft 10in); length
Argus As.II engine	7.30m (23ft 11in); height 2.66m (8ft 9in)
Maximum speed: 160km/h (99.4mph)	Weight: 812kg (1790lb) max take-off
Endurance: 2 hours	Armament: 1 x 7.92mm (.313in) MG

climate and soon had to fly at night because at such a low altitude they gathered too many holes from enemy rifle fire. They made repeated bombing attacks on enemy airfields and camps on Imbros and Tenedos with 10kg (22lb) Constantinople-made bombs. Finally, on 26 October 1915 the German and Austro-Hungarian troops fighting in Serbia joined up with Bulgarian troops, now their allies, and direct communication with Turkey via rail was established, greatly easing the supply of airplanes and parts.

Some of the first machines supplied via the new route were armed Gotha WD.2 seaplanes. In addition to longer, more effective reconnaissance missions, the WD.2s were able to perform armed anti-submarine patrols over the Sea of Marmara. British submarines, which heretofore had not been attacked there, were now subject to bombing and their operations were significantly hindered, though none were sunk or seriously damaged by the attacks.

In the late stages of the Gallipoli campaign four German fighter pilots arrived with their Fokker *Eindeckers*; Buddecke shot down four airplanes, Meinecke two, Schüz two and Muhra one, to give the Allies a hard departure. In the autumn of 1915 Russian naval forces started laying mines around the Bosporus, leading to assignment of seaplanes there for scouting and locating mines.

By early 1916 No. 30 Squadron RFC had been wiped out through attrition during the British advance into Mesopotamia (now Iraq) while the Turks had no aircraft there; in the Suez the British had No. 14 and No. 17 Squadrons RFC while the Turks had no aircraft there; and the British had four seaplane tenders operating off the Turkish Mediterranean coast. The scarcity of Turkish airplanes now changed thanks to increased supplies from Germany, and new Ottoman units, all with Turkish and German personnel, to fly them.

One of the first urgent requirements was to get airplanes to Baghdad for reconnaissance against the British forces advancing on the city. The primitive transportation facilities in the Ottoman Empire were always a critical problem, and never more than now. Moving the nine airplanes to Baghdad from Constantinople took an arduous nine weeks via ox carts, horse wagons, narrow-gauge railways and river rafts. Fuel and other supplies took the same route. Once the airplanes arrived, they performed reconnaissance sorties enabling plans to be made that resulted in a defeat for the British army, which temporarily relieved the threat.

German Pascha Units

In February 1915 Turkey was defeated in an attack on the Suez Canal, but in 1916 another attempt was to be made, but with the aid of aerial reconnaissance. At the request of the Turkish government, Germany sent the so-called Pascha *Fliegerabteilung 300*, a German

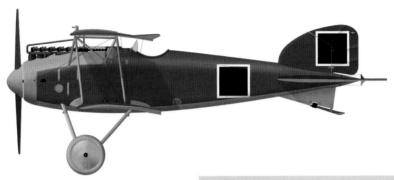

▲ **Albatros D.II**

Unknown Unit / Middle East / 1917

The Albatros D.II also made it to the Middle East in small numbers and was a faster, more powerful and heavily armed opponent for Allied airplanes than the Halberstadt. This one has the Ottoman insignia but no personal or unit markings.

Specifications

Crew: 1	Service ceiling: 5181.6m (17,000ft)
Powerplant: 1 x 119kW (160hp)	Dimensions: span 8.5m (27ft 11in); length
Mercedes D.III engine	7.40m (24ft 3in) height 2.95m (9ft 6in)
Maximum speed: 175km/h (109.4mph)	Weight: 888kg (1954lb) max take-off
Endurance: 1 hour 30 mins	Armament: 2 x 7.92mm (.313in) MGs

unit, with six Rumpler C.I reconnaissance planes and two Pfalz E.II single-seat fighters. After a two-month journey, they arrived at the flying field prepared for them in Beersheba in southern Palestine in early March 1916 and immediately began reconnaissance missions. On 7 March British seaplanes from HMS *Ben-my-Chree* discovered and photographed the preparations there. Shortly after arrival at Beersheba, Hans Henkel flew his Rumpler over Jerusalem to encourage the population, the first time airplanes had ever flown over this ancient city. Two Rumplers deployed to El Arish on the Mediterranean coast and began flying reconnaissance missions, providing the only information on enemy dispositions. Armed with their reports, in late April the Turkish forces attacked British troops east of the canal, capturing a large number of prisoners. The airplanes reached the Suez Canal, reconnoitering and dropping light bombs on enemy installations. However, detailed reconnaissance showed that British troops had fortified a line east of the canal so strongly that a decisive Turkish attack could not succeed.

One notable long-distance reconnaissance flight by *Fliegerabteilung 300* was a reconnaissance to Cairo in November 1916. The airplane dropped bombs on the railway station, and took photographs of the Pyramids during its flight. In contrast to this flight, desert flying typically offered few prominent landmarks and navigation was very difficult. On the

other hand, the empty landscape made it easy to detect trenches, strong points and marching troops.

The Tide Turns

On 10 January 1916 Russian General Yudenich launched an offensive in the Caucasus that inflicted enormous losses on the Turkish Army. One initial Russian advantage was a much larger number of airplanes for reconnaissance (in December 1916 the whole Turkish Army only had 72 airplanes). Turkish reinforcements had to be moved to defend against this devastating offensive. Only the collapse of the Russian Army after the abdication of the Tsar in March 1917 saved the Turkish Army from destruction that year. This was the turning point in the war in the Middle East, and from then on the Turks were on the defensive. Despite the reprieve the Turks received from the chaos in Russia, the British took Baghdad on 11 March 1917, and this area was the focus of air operations for most of the year until the British offensive in Palestine.

Meanwhile, on 9 July 1917 a twin-engine British Handley Page O/100 bombed Constantinople with a dozen 51kg (112lb) bombs, having arrived at Mudros the previous day from Britain. On the night of 2/3 September the Handley Page bombed Adrianople while flown by Jack Alcock, who in 1919 was first to fly across the Atlantic (with Arthur W. Brown). On the same night the *Wasserfliegerabteilung* bombed

Mudros. On their return to Mudros, Alcock and crew were disgruntled to find there was no breakfast to be had because the German bombing wiped out the kitchens. On a later raid Alcock's plane had engine failure and he was taken prisoner.

More Pascha Units arrive

In October 1917 the Pascha II German units, *Fliegerabteilungen 301, 302, 303* and *304b*, arrived in Aleppo and were immediately sent straight to Palestine. Each *Abteilung* had two Albatros D.III fighters and a small number of AEG C.IV reconnaissance planes. The AEG C.IV was a robust airplane with tubular steel airframe covered in fabric. Although the steel airframe was easy to repair in Germany, welding rigs were extremely scarce in Turkey, making repairs much more difficult than foreseen. A fighter unit sent to Palestine went by several designations, starting as *Jasta 55*, then known as *Jasta F*, and finally *Jasta 1F*. The fighters attached to *Fliegerabteilungen 300* were sometimes known as *Jasta 300*. By early in the summer of 1918 there were seven Pascha units on the Palestine Front (*Fliegerabteilungen 300–305* and *Jasta 1F*), but only five remained by the end of July and only three (*Fliegerabteilungen 303, 304b* and *305*) by the end of August. By October the remnants of the seven Pascha units, probably plus two or three Ottoman units, had been combined into one unnumbered provisional unit. By November this unit was reduced to two airplanes.

Meanwhile, more modern airplanes, including Halberstadt fighters, Albatros D.II and D.III fighters (equipped with two radiators for the heat) and C.III reconnaissance planes, Gotha WD.12 seaplanes, and AEG C.IV reconnaissance planes had been delivered to the Ottoman air service. In early 1918 20 Albatros D.V fighters were delivered, but these had more than usual structural defects and after two fatal crashes due to wing failure (one the *Staffelführer*), they were grounded.

German aviation reinforcements were countered by delivery of RE.8 and SPAD 7 aircraft to the British in even greater numbers, plus such rare types as the DH.1A, Bristol M.1C and Vickers F.B.19. Finally DH.9s and SE.5A and Bristol F.2B fighters arrived. Flown by 40th (Army) Wing (No. 1 Squadron, Australian Flying Corps, and No. 111, No. 144 and No. 145 Squadrons, RAF) and 5th (Corps) Wing (No. 14, No. 113, and No. 142 Squadrons, RAF) in Palestine, these aircraft outnumbered the Turkish and German airplanes and gave Britain both quantitative and qualitative air superiority.

The Collapse

Despite Allied aviation superiority, the low density of their airplanes over the front enabled German and Turkish units to engage in bombing, artillery spotting and long-range reconnaissance around Palestine. Eight German reconnaissance airplanes arrived in May 1918; these were a combination of LVG C.V and Rumpler C.IV two-seaters that

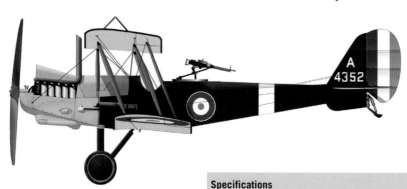

▲ **Royal Aircraft Factory RE.8**

No. 30 Squadron, RFC/RAF / Mesopotamia / 1918

Modest aerial opposition in the Middle East made the RE.8 a useful type. The white band was the unofficial No. 30 Squadron marking.

Specifications

Crew: 2

Powerplant: 1 x 112kW (150hp)
   RAF 4a12-cylinder Vee piston engine

Maximum speed: 164km/h (102mph)

Endurance: 4 hours 15 mins

Service ceiling: 4115m (13,500ft)

Dimensions: span 12.98m (42ft 7in); length
   6.38m (20ft 11in); height 2.9m (9ft 6in)

Weight: 1301kg (2869lb) max take-off

Armament: 1 x 7.62mm (.303in) forward-firing
   Vickers MG, 1 x 7.62mm (.303in) Lewis MG
   over rear cockpit; 102kg (224lb) bomb load

enabled continuation of reconnaissance missions even in the face of modern British fighters. The next month a final delivery of eight German fighters arrived; sources differ as to whether these were Albatros D.III or Pfalz D.IIIa machines. By the end of June the Turks were reduced to an average of 20 airplanes for the battles in East Jordan, 13 reconnaissance planes and seven fighters. While there was frequent air combat with losses on both sides, much of the attrition was caused by accidents and by mechanical breakdown and wear and tear. By July the British, aided by a great numerical advantage, held complete air superiority over the Palestine battlefield and in August German flying units were running out of airplanes.

On 19 September 1918 the British launched the decisive Battle of Megiddo and the Turkish front was finally broken. The Jenin airfield was singled out for special attention; a Handley-Page O/400 (C.9681 of No. 1 Squadron, AFC) bombed the field, and No. 111 Squadron RAF in their SE.5As kept continuous air patrols over it and strafed it to prevent reconnaissance missions from taking off.

British forces advanced through the gap and, supported by RAF air attacks on retreating Turkish troops, routed the Turkish army. On 20 September British cavalry, still useful in this arena, suddenly overran the airfield of the Pascha units at Jenin, capturing several German aircraft, including a DFW C.V that had only recently arrived in the final shipment of German airplanes.

ALLIED AIRCRAFT ON THE MIDDLE EAST, JUNE 1918			
Type	British	Italian	Total
Corps Reconnaissance	190	9	199
Single-Seat Fighters	49	15	64
2-Seat Fighter Reconnaissance	24	8	32
Day Bombing	6	4	10
Total	269	36	305

The Valley of Death

The AFC and RAF had been watching five strategic hill passes that the Ottoman army would have no other option but to retreat through. Then on 21 September the RAF and AFC caught the Turks making their way through Wadi Fari'a and devastated them with nearly six hours of continuous bombing and strafing attacks, causing immense casualties and complete panic. The airmen called the wadi 'The Valley of Death'. Ultimately, these attacks broke the morale of the Ottoman troops. As for the airmen, they were both proud of their accomplishment and sickened by the slaughter. Although the remaining DFW C.Vs and their crews gave good service, it was far too late to change the outcome of the ground battle, and on 1 November the Turks signed an armistice.

In total Germany supplied approximately 230 airplanes to the Ottoman air service in addition to about 155 airplanes supplied to the German Pascha units that served in arena.

▲ **Bristol F.2B**

No.1 Squadron, AFC / Palestine / 1918

Possessing excellent performance, reliability and armament, the Bristol F.2B two-seat fighter was probably the most effective combat airplane in the Middle East. The white area was painted to reflect the intense desert sun.

Specifications

Crew: 2

Powerplant: 1 x 205kW (275hp) Rolls-Royce Falcon III V-12 engine

Maximum speed: 182km/h (113mph)

Endurance: 3 hours

Service ceiling: 6096m (20,000ft)

Dimensions: span 11.96m (39ft 3in); length 7.90m (25ft 11in); height 2.97m (9ft 9in)

Weight: 1261kg (2779lb) loaded

Armament: 1 x 7.7mm (.303in) Vickers MG, 1–2 x 7.7mm (.303in) flexible Lewis MG

Chapter 8

Air Combat Comes of Age

'Bloody April', in 1917, was the high water mark of German air superiority. In April the RFC lost 319 aircrew killed or missing during 29,500 operational flight hours. In May, the RFC lost 187 aircrew flying 39,500 hours, and in June RFC losses fell to 165 aircrew during 35,500 flying hours. While fighting was still heavy, the crisis was past. The Allies gradually regained air superiority and held it to the end of the war.

◀ **Manfred von Richthofen (right) and his younger brother Lothar von Richthofen**
Both von Richthofen brothers are wearing their Pour le Mérites (Germany's highest award, nicknamed the Blue Max) in this photograph taken at *Jasta 11*. Manfred, the famous 'Red Baron,' was the war's leading ace with 80 victories. Starting later, Lothar achieved an impressive 40 victories. Lothar's fighting style was much more emotional than his older brother's and it got him into more trouble; he was wounded in action several times but, unlike Manfred, survived the war.

New types reach the front
MAY 1917–NOVEMBER 1918

With inexhaustible resources, the Allies developed new airplanes and produced them in huge numbers, thereby achieving air superiority until the Armistice.

Several things prevented the Germans from achieving air supremacy and destroying the RFC. Certainly one was the RFC's numerical advantage. Made possible by the courage and sacrifice of the airmen, the RFC simply swamped the Germans with numbers. The RFC paid the price in blood to maintain intensive air operations in the face of German technical superiority. The Germans simply could not stop so many courageous airmen from penetrating over German lines despite their losses.

Letting the customer into the store

Another factor was the German embrace of the strategic defensive. As the German fighter pilots put it, this meant 'letting the customer come into the store'. If Germany had possessed the numbers of aircraft needed, they could have gone on the offensive like the British and devastated the RFC. But the German numerical inferiority made that impractical. The strategic defensive was forced on Germany by

the Allied advantage in airplane production bolstered by the distant blockade strategy of the Royal Navy. Although the Germans had technical superiority from late 1916 through to April 1917, they were unable to translate that into air supremacy.

New Allied fighters

Crucial to the RFC's recovery was the increased delivery of airplanes, especially new, fourth-generation types that replaced the obsolete airplanes that had suffered so heavily in the first few months of 1917. The Bristol F.2A, which debuted in April, has already been discussed, but even more important were the new British single-seat fighters, the new SE.5a that started arriving at the Front in April and Sopwith Camel that followed in June. Both types were strong, manoeuvrable and armed with two machine guns.

The SE.5, powered by the 112kW (150hp) Hispano-Suiza V-8, arrived first with the deployment

▲ **Albatros D.V**

Jasta 32b / Western Front / Spring 1918

A mediocre fighter, the D.V certainly looked good; early examples had a head rest. This one was flown by *Ltn* Rudolf Windisch, an ace who scored 22 victories and later became *Jastaführer* of *Jasta 66*. He was downed in French lines on 27 May 1918 and his fate is unknown; unusually he was awarded the Pour le Mérite after his capture. The black tail is the *Jasta* marking; the rest are personal markings.

Specifications

Crew: 1

Powerplant: 1 x 119kW (160hp) Mercedes D.III inline piston engine

Maximum speed: 170km/h (105.6mph)

Endurance: 2 hours

Service ceiling: 5700m (18,700ft)

Dimensions: span 9.05m (29ft 7in); length 7.33m (24ft); height 2.70m (8ft 10in)

Weight: 915kg (2017lb) max take-off

Armament: 2 x 7.92mm (0.313in) LMG 08/15 MGs

of the newly formed No. 56 Squadron in April, and was quickly replaced by the slightly modified SE.5a fitted with the more powerful 150kW (200hp) version of the Hispano-Suiza. Combining a synchronized Vickers with an over-wing Lewis, the SE.5a was a robust fighter that was faster than the Albatros and could out-climb it. The Sopwith Camel, one of the iconic airplanes of World War I, was a scrapper. The Camel had two synchronized Vickers machine guns mounted in a distinctive hump behind the engine, resulting in its name. The Camel had better speed and climb than its predecessor the Pup, and was the first Sopwith design that had proper engineering analysis of its structure to ensure adequate strength. The Camel was robust and very manoeuvrable, but had eccentric flying

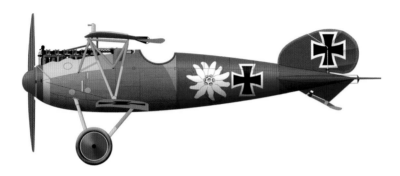

▲ Albatros D.V

Jasta 5 / Boistrancourt, Western Front / January 1918

Despite its shortcomings, the D.V was produced in large numbers for lack of a better alternative. This D.V was flown by Paul Baumer from Boistrancourt in January 1918. Baumer went on to score 43 victories, 20 in September 1918 alone, and was awarded the Pour le Mérite. The green tail with red trim is the *Jasta* marking; the Edelweiss is Baumer's personal marking.

Specifications

Crew: 1

Powerplant: 1 x 119kW (160hp) Mercedes D.III inline piston engine

Maximum speed: 170km/h (105.6mph)

Endurance: 2 hours

Service ceiling: 5700m (18,700ft)

Dimensions: span 9.05m (29ft 7in); length 7.33m (24ft); height 2.70m (8ft 10in)

Weight: 915kg (2017lb) max take-off

Armament: 2 x 7.92mm (0.313in) LMG 08/15 MGs

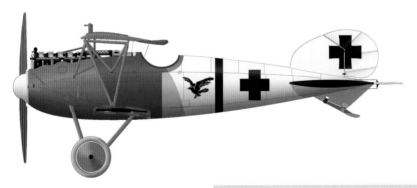

▲ Albatros D.VA

Jasta 18 / Western Front / Summer 1918

The Albatros D.Va was a lightened development of the D.III. Its performance was essentially the same as the D.III. The structural changes weakened the lower wing attachment to the fuselage, resulting in failures in flight that killed some unfortunate pilots and limited its effectiveness. *Jasta 18* used the raven as a unit insignia as the *Staffelführer's* name was August Raben (*raben* is German for raven).

Specifications

Crew: 1

Powerplant: 1 x 134kW (180hp) Mercedes D.IIIa inline piston engine

Maximum speed: 180km/h (112mph)

Endurance: 2 hours

Service ceiling: 5700m (18,700ft)

Dimensions: span 9.05m (29ft 7in); length 7.33m (24ft); height 2.70m (8ft 10in)

Weight: 937kg (2066lb) max take-off

Armament: 2 x 7.92mm (0.313in) LMG 08/15 MGs

characteristics. Many pilots were killed in flying accidents while training on the Camel, but those who survived to master it found it a great dogfighter.

The French took advantage of the new, more powerful Hispano-Suiza engine to develop the SPAD XIII from the earlier SPAD VII. With increased power the new SPAD was able to mount two synchronized Vickers machine guns instead of the one used by the SPAD VII. Introduced in April 1917, the SPAD XIII became one of the great fighters of the war. Produced in massive numbers, it was exported to Italy and also became the standard fighter used by the United States. The similar SPAD XII was produced in modest numbers; it differed from the SPAD XIII primarily in its armament, which was one machine gun plus a hand-loaded, single-shot 37mm cannon

▲ Sopwith Camel

10(N) Squadron, RNAS / Western Front / late 1917

The Sopwith Camel arrived at the Front in June 1917 and immediately proved its value as a dogfighter. It was the first British fighter at the Front with two synchronized machine guns and the first Sopwith design to feature a structure that had been analyzed for strength by engineers. The white bars are the unit marking; the letter 'B' indicates 'B' Flight, 'CLEADA' is a personal marking.

Specifications

Crew: 1	Dimensions: span 8.53m (28ft);
Powerplant: 1 x 97kW (130hp) Clerget 9-	length 5.72m (18ft 9in); height 2.58m
cylinder air-cooled rotary piston engine	(8ft 6in)
Maximum speed: 188km/h (117mph)	Weight: 1453kg (3203lb) max take-off
Endurance: 2hr 30 mins	Armament: 2 x 7.7mm (.303in) Vickers MGs
Service ceiling: 5790m (19,000ft)	

▲ RE.8

No. 21 Squadron, RFC / Droglandt, Western Front / late 1917

The RE.8 replaced the hapless BE.2 series at the Front. Its revised seating and armament were a great improvement. Unfortunately, it retained the BE.2's excessively stable design, which was wonderful for normal flight but a handicap when engaged by fighters. The white dumbbell was the unit marking.

Specifications

Crew: 2	length 8.49m (27ft 10.5in); height 3.46m
Powerplant: 1 x 104kW (140hp) RAF 4a	(11ft 4.5in)
12-cylinder Vee piston engine	Weight: 2869kg (6325lb) max take-off
Maximum speed: 158km/h (98mph)	Armament: 1 x 7.62mm (0.303in) forward-
Endurance: 4 hours 30 mins	firing Vickers MG, 1–2 x 7.62mm (0.303in)
Service ceiling: 3353m (11,000ft)	Lewis MG over rear cockpit; 102kg (224lb)
Dimensions: span 12.98m (42ft 7in);	bomb load

firing through the propeller hub. One hit from the cannon could bring down an opponent, but hand-loading the gun during air combat was impractical and most pilots preferred the SPAD XIII.

The SPAD XVII was a development of the SPAD XIII with the new 224kW (300hp) Hispano-Suiza engine; about 20 were delivered to the Storks late in the war, but the increased power provided almost no performance increase, showing the basic airframe was at the end of its development potential.

The best British fighter of the war?

In early 1918 the Sopwith Dolphin appeared. Like the SE.5a, it was powered by the 149kW (200hp)

▲ **SE.5a**

No. 40 Squadron, RFC / Western Front / Winter 1917–18

The SE.5 arrived at the Front in April 1917 with No. 56 Squadron and was soon replaced by the more powerful SE.5a, one of the best fighters of the war. The SE.5a was strong, stable and faster than nearly all its opponents. This airplane was powered by a Hispano-Suiza. The rudder pennant indicates a flight leader.

Specifications

Crew: 1	Dimensions: span 8.11m (26ft 7.4in); length
Powerplant: 1 x 149kW (200hp) Hispano-Suiza	6.38m (20ft 11in); height 2.89m (9ft 6in)
8a 8-cylinder inline piston engine	Weight: 1047kg (2308lb) max take-off
Maximum speed: 217km/h (135mph)	Armament: 1 x 7.7mm (0.313in) Vickers MG,
Endurance: 2 hours 30 mins	1 x 7.7mm (0.313in) Lewis MG; 4 x 11.3kg
Service ceiling: 6705.5m (22,000ft)	(25lb) bombs

Specifications

Crew: 1	Dimensions: span 8.11m (26ft 7.4in); length
Powerplant: 1 x 149kW (200hp) Wolseley Viper	6.38m (20ft 11in); height 2.89m (9ft 6in)
inline piston engine	Weight: 880kg (1940lb) max take-off
Maximum speed: 222km/h (137.8mph)	Armament: 1 x 7.7mm (0.313in) Vickers MG,
Endurance: 2 hours 30 mins	1 x 7.7mm (0.313in) Lewis MG; 4 x 11.3kg
Service ceiling: 6705.5m (22,000ft)	(25lb) bombs

The white letter 'U' on the fuselage indicates this aircraft is assigned to 'C' Flight. The two white bands around the rear fuselage are the squadron marking.

▲ **SE.5a**

No. 60 Squadron, RAF / Western Front / Summer 1918

Not as manoeuvrable as its stablemate the Camel, the SE.5a was faster, easier to fly and had much safer handling characteristics. SE.5a units suffered noticeably fewer losses than Camel units. This airplane was powered by a Wolseley Viper with shortened exhaust. The rudder pennant indicates a flight leader.

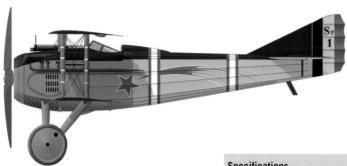

▲ SPAD VII

5eme Escadrille / Les Moeres, Belgium / Winter 1917–18

Derived from the two-seat 'pulpit' SA series, the SPAD VII was one of the great fighters of the war and was used by Britain, Belgium, Italy and Russia in addition to France. This one was flown by 10-victory Belgian ace *S/Lt* Edmond Thieffry.

Specifications

Crew: 1	Dimensions: span 7.82m (25ft 8in);
Powerplant: 1 x 134kW (180hp) Hispano-Suiza	length 6.08m (19ft 11in); height 2.20m
8Ab V8 in-line piston engine	(7ft 3in)
Maximum speed: 212km/h (132mph)	Weight: 705kg (1554lb) max take-off
Endurance: 1 hour 30 mins	Armament: 1 x 7.7mm (.3in) Vickers MG
Service ceiling: 6553m (21,499ft)	

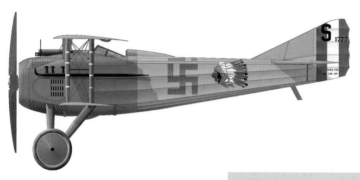

▲ SPAD VII

Escadrille SPA 124 (Lafayette Escadrille) / Western Front / October 1917

Powered by the innovative Hispano-Suiza V-8 engine, SPAD fighters were fast, strong and had good manoeuvrability and handling qualities. The Indian head was the unit insignia; the swastika was a personal insignia. Didier Masson was the original pilot; it was then used for a time by 16-victory ace Raoul Lufbery.

Specifications

Crew: 1	Dimensions: span 7.82m (25ft 8in);
Powerplant: 1 x 134kW (180hp) Hispano-Suiza	length 6.08m (19ft 11in); height 2.20m
8Ab V8 in-line piston engine	(7ft 3in)
Maximum speed: 212km/h (132mph)	Weight: 705kg (1554lb) max take-off
Endurance: 1 hour 30 mins	Armament: 1 x 7.7mm (.3in) Vickers MG
Service ceiling: 6553m (21,499ft)	

Hispano-Suiza, but in an attempt to maximize the pilot's field of view, the upper wing was staggered back so the pilot's head was in the middle of the upper wing middle section. The back stagger gave the Dolphin an unusual appearance. Conceived as a multi-gun fighter, the Dolphin had two fixed Vickers like the Camel, but also had one or two fixed Lewis guns firing upwards over the propeller arc. To save weight and improve performance, normally only one Lewis was fitted in combat, and some pilots flew with no Lewis guns at all. At high altitude the Dolphin out-performed the SE.5a and was probably the best British fighter of the war, but the pilots' lack of

enthusiasm for the unusual configuration, which looked dangerous in case of a nose-over on landing, limited it to a small number of squadrons.

The new Albatros D.V disappoints

While the Allies were introducing new types to combat that were good enough to serve until the end of the war, the Germans made the mistake of deciding to standardize on the Albatros. The Albatros D.V and D.Va, conceived as lightened versions of the D.III, arrived at the Front in May. The D.V had an elegantly streamlined fuselage of lighter construction combined with the same engine, armament, and

▲ **SPAD VII**

No.19 Squadron, RFC / Western Front / March 1917

The main shortcoming of the SPAD VII as a fighter was its single synchronized machine gun. The black dumbbell marking was the unofficial unit insignia.

Specifications

Crew: 1

Powerplant: 1 x 134kW (180hp) Hispano-
Suiza 8Ab V8 in-line piston engine

Maximum speed: 212km/h (132mph)

Range: 350km (217 miles)

Service ceiling: 6550m (21,500ft)

Dimensions: span 7.82m (25ft 8in);
length 6.08m (19ft 11in); height 2.20m
(7ft 3in)

Weight: 705kg (1554lb) max take-off

Armament: 1 x 7.7mm (.3in) MG

Specifications

Crew: 1

Powerplant: 1 x 164kW (220hp) Hispano-
Suiza 8Ab V-8 engine

Maximum speed: 203km/h (126mph)

Endurance: 1 hour 45 mins

Service ceiling: 6850m (22,474ft)

Dimensions: span 8.00m (26ft 3in); length
6.40m (21ft); height 2.55m (8ft 4in)

Weight: 883kg (1947lb) loaded

Armament: 1 x 7.7mm (.303in) Vickers MG
and 1 x 12-round 37mm (1.46in) S.A.M.C
cannon

▲ **SPAD XII**

Escadrille SPA 38 / Western Front / 1918

The SPAD XII was a more powerful development of the SPAD VII. The main change was the addition of a hand-loaded, single-shot 37mm cannon that fired through the propeller hub. A few pilots, who appreciated its devastating effect and could accept its limitations, preferred this plane. This one was flown by Lt Georges Madon, the fourth-ranking French ace with 41 victories. Madon commanded SPA 38 and painted his airplane red so the other pilots could keep track of it in combat – the same reason the Red Baron painted his fighters red.

▲ **SPAD XIII**

Escadrille SPA 3 / Western Front / September 1917

Like the SPAD XII, the SPAD XIII was a slightly enlarged, more powerful development of the SPAD VII. The difference was the SPAD XIII mounted two synchronized machine guns, an arrangement much more practical for most pilots than the single-shot cannon of the SPAD XII. This airplane was flown by Capt Georges Guynemer, the second-ranking French ace with 53 victories. The stork was the unit insignia.

Specifications

Crew: 1

Powerplant: 1 x 164kW (220hp) Hispano-Suiza
8Be eight-cylinder Vee engine

Maximum speed: 218km/h (135.5mph)

Endurance: 1 hour 40 mins

Service ceiling: 6800m (22,310ft)

Dimensions: span span 8.08m (26ft 6in);
length 6.25m (20ft 6in); height 2.60m
(8ft 6in)

Weight: 856.5kg (1888lb) max take-off

Armament: 2 x 7.7mm (.303in) Vickers MGs

▲ **SPAD XIII**

Escadrille SPA 103 / Western Front / Autumn 1918

One of the fastest fighters of the war, the robust SPAD XIII was widely used by France, Italy and the new USAS. This one was flown by Capt René Fonck, the leading Allied ace with 75 victories. The stork was the unit insignia.

Specifications

Crew: 1

Powerplant: 1 x 164kW (220hp) Hispano-
   Suiza 8Be eight-cylinder Vee engine

Maximum speed: 218km/h (135.5mph)

Endurance: 1 hour 40 mins

Service ceiling: 6800m (22,310ft)

Dimensions: span span 8.08m (26ft 6in);
   length 6.25m (20ft 6in); height 2.60m
   (8ft 6in)

Weight: 856.5kg (1888lb) max take-off

Armament: 2 x 7.7mm (.303in) Vickers MGs

Specifications

Crew: 2

Powerplant: 1 x 280kW (375hp) Rolls-Royce
   Eagle VIII engine

Maximum speed: 230km/h (143mph)

Endurance: 3 hours 45 mins

Service ceiling: 7010m (23,000ft)

Dimensions: span 12.92m (42ft 4in);
   length 9.2m (30ft 2in); height 3.35m
   (11ft)

Weight: 1575kg (3472lb) max take-off

Armament: 1 x 7.7mm (0.303in) Vickers
   fixed MG, 1–2 x 7.7mm (0.303in) Lewis
   flexible guns; 2 x 104kg (230lb) bomb load

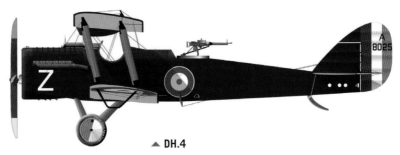

▲ **DH.4**

No. 202 Squadron, RAF / Western Front / 1918

The DH.4 was a classic design that excelled as a long-range reconnaissance airplane, day bomber and even as a Zeppelin interceptor. The 'Z' indicates a 'C' Flight airplane; there were no unit markings.

▲ **DH.4**

No. 57 Squadron, RAF / Western Front / October 1917

A variety of engines were used in the DH.4, but the 280kW (375hp) Rolls-Royce Eagle the DH.4 made the fastest airplane on the Western Front – remarkable for such a large two-seater. This airplane was downed on 2 October 1917 by *Ltn* Walther Kleffel of *Jasta 18* for his only victory. Lt C.G. Crane was taken prisoner and 2/Lt. A.L. Inglis was killed in action. The white circle was the unit marking.

Specifications

Crew: 2

Powerplant: 1 x 186kW (275hp) Rolls-Royce
   Eagle VI engine

Maximum speed: 191.5km/h (119mph)

Endurance: 3 hours 45 mins

Service ceiling: 5486m (18,000ft)

Dimensions: span 12.93m (42ft 4.5in); length
   9.19m (30ft 2in); height 3.175m (10ft 5in)

Weight: 1503kg (3313lb) max take-off

Armament: 1 x 7.7mm (0.303in) fixed Vickers
   MG; 1–2 7.7mm (0.303in) flexible Lewis MGs;
   1 x 104kg (230lb)

flying surfaces as the D.III. With so much in common, the performance improvement over the D.III could only be minor. But the lightened structure was not as strong, and structural failures of the lower wing became a serious problem. The sesquiplane wing cellule copied from the Nieuport was barely suitable for the D.III, and the lighter, weaker structure of the D.V/D.Va was not strong enough to stand up to the demands of intense air combat. Failures of the lower wing joint with the fuselage started to occur, frequently with fatal results. The structure was modified several times to strengthen it but the problem was never completely solved. Though the structure was strong enough statically, there was a problem with wing vibration and twisting about the single spar at high speed and high 'G' loading because of combat manoeuvres. However, this was not understood at the time.

As a result the German pilots were inhibited from making the most of their new airplanes in combat just as the Allies introduced superior types, and Germany lost air superiority to the Allies for the rest of the war. The elegant Pfalz D.III entered combat in September, but was similar to the Albatros in engine, armament and configuration, so offered negligible performance improvement. At least the Pfalz was stronger; although the Pfalz engineers adapted the Nieuport's sesquiplane wing cellule, they used two spars in the lower wing, which minimized the twisting of the wing during combat manoeuvres, so structural failures were no longer a problem.

In contrast to fighter design, Germany did better with the important two-seat reconnaissance airplanes. For much of the war the Allies used technically inferior two-seaters. The British relied for far too long on the overly stable BE.2 series, which was further handicapped by its mediocre performance and awkward armament and seating arrangement. The observer sat between the wings in front of the pilot, which limited both his visibility and field of fire of his machine gun. The RE.8, which replaced the BE.2, had a more powerful engine for better performance, and the observer was moved to the back with a rotating turret that gave him a greatly improved field of fire. Additionally, the RE.8 pilot now had a fixed, synchronized machine gun, which had been lacking in the BE.2. Unfortunately, the RE.8 had too much in common with the BE.2, especially too much stability, and the improvement in combat capability

was not as much as was needed. The new, improved RE.8, while not as vulnerable as the BE.2, continued to suffer heavily when intercepted by fighters. The Armstrong-Whitworth F.K.8 was a better two-seat reconnaissance plane but served in smaller numbers than the RE.8.

New French reconnaissance aircraft

Developments in early French two-seat reconnaissance planes were hampered primarily because the French relied on the obsolete pusher configuration far too long. The pusher configuration had two inherent limitations, which are obvious at a glance. One was the aerodynamic drag from the profusion of bracing struts and wires connecting the tail that limited speed and climb. The other was the limited field of fire of the observer's gun behind and below the airplane, making these slow targets even more vulnerable to fighter attack. The limited field of fire was a significant vulnerability from the time of the Fokker *Eindecker* – the Albatros made these obsolete airplanes deathtraps in air combat.

Like the British, the French belatedly started replacing their out-of-date reconnaissance pushers with mediocre replacements like the A.R.1 and Sopwith Strutter. While the Strutter was a very good airplane when introduced in 1916, the French did not get their copies to the Front in numbers until 1917, a full year later, which meant the Strutter was already obsolescent when it entered French service.

In 1917 the final generation of French two-seaters reached the Front. First was the SPAD XI, which debuted in September. Developed from the smaller SPAD VII as a two-seat fighter, the SPAD XI inherited the fighter's good looks, good speed for a larger airplane, and robust structure. Unfortunately, it did not inherit the good manoeuvrability and handling characteristics of its predecessor. While strong and fast, the SPAD XI was prone to stalling and spinning without apparent provocation, and therefore was not especially popular with its crews. Not suitable for its designed role as a two-seat fighter, it was used as a reconnaissance plane, where it made a useful replacement for the A.R.1/A.R.2 and Sopwith Strutter. The pressing need for its engine for SPAD fighters limited its production, and finally its 164kW (220hp) Hispano-Suiza was replaced with the 179kW (240hp) Lorraine to create the nearly identical SPAD XVI. The boost in power from the

▲ Armstrong Whitworth FK.8

No. 2 Squadron, RFC / Western Front / Summer 1917

The sturdy FK.8 was used for reconnaissance and artillery spotting alongside the RE.8 and, a better airplane in nearly all respects, was more popular with its crews. It was also used for night bombing and even in Home Defence units. The white triangle was the squadron marking at the time.

Specifications

Crew: 2

Powerplant: 1 x 119kW (160hp)
  Beardmore engine

Maximum speed: 158km/h (98mph)

Endurance: 3 hours

Service ceiling: 3690m (13,000ft)

Dimensions: span 13.26m (43ft 6in); length
  9.58m (31ft 5in); height 3.33m (10ft 11in)

Weight: 1275kg (2811lb) max take-off

Armament: 1 x 7.7mm (0.303in) Vickers MG,
  1–2 x 7.7mm (0.303in) Lewis MGs; 8 x 11.4kg
  (25lb) bombs

Queenie II was the aircraft of Sgt F. Dismore and 1/AM C. Hare. It was flown to Hondschoote to allow French airmen a close view after mistaken French attacks.

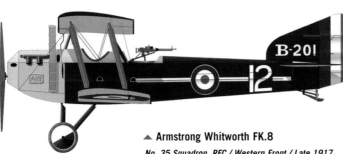

▲ Armstrong Whitworth FK.8

No. 35 Squadron, RFC / Western Front / Late 1917

This was the first FK.8 to use the V-strut undercarriage from the Bristol F.2B that eventually became standard on the FK.8. The white fuselage stripe was the unit insignia at this time; on 22 March 1918 it was ordered removed.

Specifications

Crew: 2

Powerplant: 1 x 119kW (160hp)
  Beardmore engine

Maximum speed: 158km/h (98mph)

Endurance: 3 hours

Service ceiling: 3690m (13,000ft)

Dimensions: span 13.26m (43ft 6in); length
  9.58m (31ft 5in); height 3.33m (10ft 11in)

Weight: 1275kg (2811lb) max take-off

Armament: 1 x 7.7mm (0.303in) Vickers MG,
  1–2 x 7.7mm (0.303in) Lewis MGs;
  8 x 11.4kg (25lb) bombs

Specifications

Crew: 2

Powerplant: 1 x 149kW (200hp) Benz Bz.IV
  inline piston engine

Maximum speed: 155km/h (97mph)

Endurance: 3hours 30 mins

Service ceiling: 5000m (16,405ft)

Dimensions: span 13.27m (43ft 6.5in);
  length 7.88m (25ft 10in);
  height 3.25m (10ft 8in)

Weight: 1430kg (3153lb) max take-off

Armament: 1 x 7.92mm (.312in) LMG08/15
  forward-firing MG, 1 x 7.92mm (0.312in)
  Parabellum MG

▲ DFW C.V

Flieger Abteilung (A) 239 / Western Front / Summer 1918

The tough, reliable and manoeuvrable DFW C.V was a difficult opponent for Allied fighters until the end of the war. The great ace Major J.B. McCudden, VC, paid tribute to one DFW 'at last I broke off the combat, for the Hun was too good for me and had shot me about a lot. Had I persisted he certainly would have got me, for there was not a trick he did not know, so I gave that liver-coloured DFW best.' 'Gretel' and 'Lo' were personal markings.

▲ Nieuport 24bis

Escadrille N 62 / Western Front / Autumn 1916

The Nieuport sesquiplane design was nearing the end of its development potential when the Nieuport 24 was introduced. Still retaining the excellent manoeuvrability characteristic of Nieuports, it was obsolescent compared to the Camel and SE.5a. *Zigomar 5* was the personal insignia of Lt Paul Tarascon and the Gallic rooster was the escadrille insignia.

Specifications

Crew: 1
Powerplant: 1 x 96.9kW (130hp)
 Le Rhône 9Jb engine
Maximum speed: 170km/h (105.6mph)
Range: 250km (155 miles)

Service ceiling: 6900m (22,638ft)
Dimensions: span 8.25m (27ft .8in); length
 5.87m (19ft 3in); height 2.4m (7ft 10.4in)
Weight: 547kg (1206lb) max take-off
Armament: 1 x 7.7mm (0.303in) fixed Vickers MG

Specifications

Crew: 1
Powerplant: 1 x 96.9kW (130hp)
 Le Rhône 9Jb engine
Maximum speed: 172km/h (106.9mph)
Range: 250km (155 miles)
Service ceiling: 6850m (22,474ft)
Dimensions: span 8.2m (26ft 11in); length
 5.85m (19ft 2in); height 2.42m (7ft 11in)
Weight: 535kg (1179lb) loaded
Armament: 1 x 7.7mm (0.303in) Lewis MG

▲ Nieuport 27

No. 1 Squadron, RFC / Western Front / Autumn 1917

The Nieuport 27 was the final sesquiplane Nieuport to achieve production and soldiered on until replaced by more modern fighters. The 'H' indicates it was assigned to 'B' Flight and the black vertical bar behind the cockade was the squadron marking.

▲ Pfalz D.III

Jasta 21s / Villers le Chèvre, Western Front / December 1917

Powered by the same engine as the Albatros and featuring the same armament and airframe technology, the Pfalz D.III had essentially the same performance. However, the Pfalz was much stronger and was a useful supplement to the Albatros. This one was flown by *Ltn d.R.* Fritz Höhn, a 21-victory ace; the stripes are his personal markings.

Specifications

Crew: 1
Powerplant: 1 x 119W (160hp) Mercedes
 D.IIIa inline piston engine
Maximum speed: 180km/h (112mph)
Endurance: 2 hours
Service ceiling: 6000m (19,685ft)
Dimensions: span 9.4m (30ft 10in); length
 6.95m (22ft 9 ¹/₂in); height 2.67m (8ft 9in)
Weight: 923kg (2035lb) max take-off
Armament: 2 x 7.92mm (0.313in) fixed
 forward-firing LMG 08/15 MGs

Lorraine did nothing to solve manoeuvrability and handling problems, nor did it boost performance due to greater weight, but at least the SPAD XVI was available in numbers.

Designed from the outset as a two-seat reconnaissance plane, the Salmson 2A2 was one of the truly great World War I airplanes. Powered by a 172kW (230hp) Salmson Canton-Unné water-cooled radial engine, the Salmson 2A2 was strong, fast, manoeuvrable and reliable, and carried a good payload. Arriving at the Front in December, it served in 55 French escadrilles and became the main reconnaissance type with the USAS. Popular with its crews, it was faster than the Albatros D.V and Pfalz D.III and could also, remarkably, out-climb them.

The Breguet 14 was another of the great warplanes of World War I. Produced as the Breguet 14B2 day bomber, in 1918 it equipped all French day-bomber units. It was also widely used as the Breguet 14A2 reconnaissance plane, equipping 59 French units and

▲ LVG C.V

Flieger Abteilung (A) 253 / Western Front / Spring 1918

The LVG company soon tired of producing the DFW C.V under licence and hired its designer away from DFW. Unsurprisingly, the resulting LVG C.V resembled the earlier DFW. Like the DFW C.V the LVG C.V was a tough, reliable, manoeuvrable airplane that served with distinction until war's end. The crescent moon on the fuselage was the personal marking of *Ltn* Teske, who had flown with the Turks.

Specifications

Crew: 2

Powerplant: 1 x 149kW (200hp) Benz Bz.IV engine

Maximum speed: 170km/h (155.3mph)

Endurance: 3 hours 30 mins

Service ceiling: 5029m (16,500ft)

Dimensions: span 13.6m (44ft 7in); length 8.07m (26ft 5.7in); height 3.36m (11ft .25in)

Weight: 1505kg (3318lb) max take-off

Armament: 1 x 7.92mm (0.313in) fixed and 1 x 7.92mm (0.313in) flexible MG

▲ LVG C.VI

Unknown Unit / Western Front / Summer 1918

The LVG C.VI was a lighter, more compact development of the C.V that replaced the C.V in production in 1918 and gave similar excellent service. The black and white markings are thought to be unit markings but the unit is unknown. The '12' on the fin is its tactical number within the unit.

Specifications

Crew: 2

Powerplant: 1 x 149kW (200hp) Benz Bz.IV engine

Maximum speed: 170km/h (155.3mph)

Endurance: 3 hours 30 mins

Service ceiling: 6507m (21,350ft)

Dimensions: span 13m (42ft 8in); length 7.45m (24ft 5in); height 2.8m (9ft 2in)

Weight: 1309kg (2886lb) max take-off

Armament: 1 x 7.92mm (0.313in) fixed and 1 x 7.92mm (0.313in) flexible MG

also serving with Belgium and the USAS. Like the Salmson, the Breguet 14 was strong, fast, handled well and carried a heavy payload.

New German reconnaissance aircraft

The Germans introduced two-seat tractor biplanes with the gunner in back with a flexible machine gun in the middle of 1915, and in 1916 introduced a new, more powerful generation of two-seaters that were faster, more manoeuvrable and armed with a fixed, synchronized gun for the pilot as well as the observer's flexible gun. From that time onwards, in the hands of a capable crew, the German two-seater represented a formidable opponent, and many experienced fighter pilots viewed them as being even more dangerous than fighters.

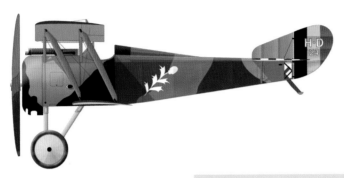

▲ Hanriot HD.1

9eme Escadrille / Les Moeres, Western Front / Summer 1918

The Hanriot HD.1 was stronger than the Nieuports and equally manoeuvrable, making it the aircraft of choice of the Belgian and Italian air services. France passed it up, preferring the more powerful SPADs. This French-built example was flown by S/Lt Willy Coppens, who with 37 victories, most balloons, was Belgium's leading ace. The thistle was the escadrille marking.

Specifications

Crew: 1

Powerplant: 1 x 89kW (120hp) Le Rhône 9Jb
9-cylinder rotary piston engine

Maximum speed: 186km/h (116mph)

Range: 2hr 30 mins

Service ceiling: 6000m (19,700ft)

Dimensions: span 8.7m (28ft 6in); length
5.85m (19ft 2in); height 2.94m (9ft 7.7in)

Weight: 605kg (1334lb) max take-off

Armament: 1 x 7.7mm (.303in) Vickers MG

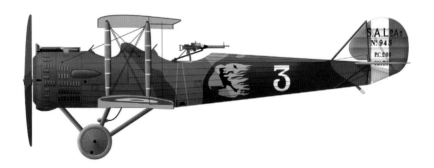

▲ Salmson 2A2

Escadrille SAL 18 / Western Front

The Salmson 2A2 offered the performance, reliability and good handling qualities France had been looking for in a reconnaissance airplane. Once it became available it quickly replaced the obsolete A.R.s and Sopwith Strutters. The fuselage marking is the unit insignia and the airplane's tactical number within the escadrille is behind the unit insignia.

Specifications

Crew: 2

Powerplant: 1 x 171.5kW (230hp)
Salmson 9Za engine

Maximum speed: 188km/h (117mph)

Range: 500km (310.7 miles)

Service ceiling: 6250m (20,505ft)

Dimensions: span 11.75m (38ft 6.6in); length
8.50m (27ft 10.6in); height 2.90m (9ft 6in)

Weight: 1290kg (2844lb) max take-off

Armament: 1 x 7.7mm (0.303in) fixed Vickers
MG and 2 x 7.7mm (0.303in) flexible Lewis
MGs

GERMAN ARMED, PHOTO-RECONNAISSANCE BIPLANES, 1917–18						
	1917		1918			
Manufacturer and Type	31 Oct	31 Dec	28 Feb	30 Apr	30 Jun	31 Aug
Rumpler Rubild	11	64	51	45	39	99
Rumpler Rubild Mb	–	–	–	50	43	78
Total	11	64	51	95	82	177

The Albatros company produced a number of good two-seater designs. The C.I, the first Albatros with armament, was introduced in Spring 1915, followed later by the more powerful C.III with a fixed gun for the pilot. The C.V, designed for long-range photo-reconnaissance and introduced in the summer of 1916, featured the classic streamlined wood fuselage that characterized the Albatros fighters. It was faster than Allied fighters of the time and could out-climb them, and enjoyed a lengthy career until the new generation of Allied fighters arrived in spring 1917. The Albatros C.VII was a good general-purpose two-seater, but the later C.X and C.XII, although elegant, offered disappointing performance and were mostly relegated to the less demanding Eastern Front.

The DFW C.V was one of the first German two-seaters powered by the 149kW (200hp) Benz fitted to so many reconnaissance designs. Reaching the Front in the fall of 1916, the DFW C.V was a tough, manoeuvrable airplane with good flying characteristics that was a dangerous opponent for Allied fighters until the Armistice. Produced under licence by many manufacturers, 3955 were built, making it the most produced German warplane.

The Aviatik company, after building many sturdy two-seaters that saw widespread service through early 1917, competed with the DFW with its own C.II. After 75 were produced, Aviatik was forced to build the superior DFW under licence. LVG two-seaters were also numerous in the early war period, but LVG too was required to build the DFW C.V when it failed to produce its own competitive design. LVG was unhappy about producing another company's design under license, so it fired its designer and hired the designer of the DFW C.V, who went on to design the similar, but improved, LVG C.V and C.VI, which were so common in 1918.

The 119kW (160hp) Rumpler C.I and 149kW (200hp) Rumpler C.III were solid, widely used two-seaters, but the improved 194kW (260hp) Rumpler C.IV introduced early in 1917 became famous as one of the great long-range reconnaissance planes of the war. As summarized in an adjacent table, the basic C.IV airframe underwent modifications that improved its performance and reconnaissance capabilities. Allied fighters were seldom able to intercept the high-flying Rumplers, whose crews endured flights up to six hours long in open, unheated cockpits and exposed to temperatures down to -50°C (-58°F) to complete their missions.

With their C.V the Halberstadt company built the best German short-range reconnaissance plane, an enlarged version of their CL.IV two-seat fighter.

▲ **Halberstadt C.V**

Unknown Unit / Western Front / Autumn 1918

The Halberstadt C.V was an enlarged development of the CL.IV and was the best German short-range reconnaissance and artillery spotting type during the war's final months. This DFW-built example is in factory finish except for the large tactical number '5' on the fuselage for identification within its unit.

Specifications

Crew: 2

Powerplant: 1 x 149/164kW (200/220hp) Benz Bz.IVü engine

Maximum speed: 290km/h (180mph)

Endurance: 3 hours 30 mins

Service ceiling: n/a

Dimensions: span 13.62m (44ft 8in); length 6.92m (22ft 8in); height 3.36m (11ft .28in)

Weight: 1360kg (2998lb) max take-off

Armament: 1 x 7.92mm (0.313in) fixed MG and 1 x 7.92mm (0.313in) flexible MG

RUMPLER AIRCRAFT USING C.IV AIRFRAME		
Designation	Engine	Notes
Rumpler C.IV	194kW/260hp Mercedes D.IVa 183kW/245hp Maybach Mb.IVa 194kW/260hp Basse & Selve BuS.IVa	Developed from earlier C.III, many different equipment installations
Rumpler C.IV(Pfal)	194kW/260hp Mercedes D.IVa	Originally designated Pfalz C.I, license-built C.IV with ailerons on all four wings
Rumpler C.V	183kW/245hp Maybach Mb.IVa	Fitted with bomb racks, different (smaller?) aux tank
Rumpler C.VI	194kW/260hp Mercedes D.IVa	Equipped with Messter strip camera; later re-designated Rubild, different (larger?) auxiliary fuel tank
Rumpler C.VII	183kW/245hp Maybach Mb.IVa	
Rumpler C.VIII	134kW/180hp Argus As.III	Operational trainer not used in combat
Rumpler C.IX	183kW/245hp Maybach Mb.IVa	Large long-range fuel tank
Rubild	194kW/260hp Mercedes D.IVa	New designation for C.VI
Rubild(Bayru) BuS	194kW/260hp Basse & Selve BuS.IVa	Rubild with Basse & Selve BuS.IVa
Rubild Mb	183kW/245hp Maybach Mb.IVa	Rubild with Maybach Mb.IVa

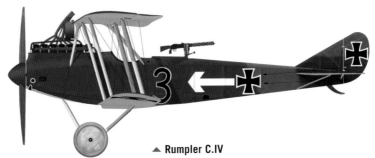

Specifications
Crew: 2
Powerplant: 1 x 194kW (260hp) Mercedes
 D.IVa engine
Maximum speed: 175km/h (108.3mph)
Endurance: 4–7 hours
Service ceiling: About 7000m (22,966ft)
Dimensions: span 12.66m (41ft 6in); length
 8.4m (27ft 6.7in); height n/a
Weight: 1630kg (3594lb) max take-off
Armament: 1 x 7.92mm (0.313in) fixed and
 1 x 7.92mm (0.313in) flexible MG

▲ **Rumpler C.IV**
Flieger Abteilung 7 / Western Front / late 1917
The elegant Rumpler C.IV offered exceptional ceiling and good speed at high altitude and was the best German long-range reconnaissance plane. This is an early version with propeller spinner. Later versions actually had less drag without the spinner. The white arrow is the unit marking; the '3' is its tactical number. Small eyes and mouth personalize it with a face.

▲ **Rumpler C.IV**
Flieger Abteilung (A) 235 / Western Front / late 1917
See the table above for a summary of the many variations of the Rumpler C.IV that served at the Front. It was rarely intercepted at altitude by Allied fighters, who generally could not catch it or even reach its altitude. No unit markings are visible; the '5' is its tactical number within the unit.

Specifications
Crew: 2
Powerplant: 1 x 194kW (260hp) Mercedes
 D.IVa engine
Maximum speed: 175km/h (108.3mph)
Endurance: 4–7 hours
Service ceiling: About 7000m (22,966ft)
Dimensions: span 12.66m (41ft 6in); length
 8.4m (27ft 6.7in); height n/a
Weight: 1630kg (3594lb) max take-off
Armament: 1 x 7.92mm (0.313in) fixed and
 1 x 7.92mm (0.313in) flexible MG

Specifications

Crew: 1
Powerplant: 1 x 119kW (160hp)
  Mercedes D.III engine
Maximum speed: 190km/h (118mph)
Endurance: 2 hours
Service ceiling: About 6000m (19,685ft)
Dimensions: span 9.4m (30ft 10in); length
  6.4m (21ft); height 2.6m (8ft 6in)
Weight: 845kg (1863lb) max take-off
Armament: 2 x 7.92mm (0.313in) MGs

▲ Roland D.VIA

Unknown Jasta / Western Front / Summer 1918

After the disappointing Roland D.II and D.III fighters, the next Roland design to
see combat was the D.VIA. Limited by the same engine and armament as the
earlier Albatros D.V, the D.VIA was stronger, more manoeuvrable and slightly
faster. The D.VIB had more power and improved performance. The D.VI was only
used in small numbers due to the arrival of the superior Fokker D.VII.

▲ SPAD XI

4eme Escadrille / Belgium / October 1918

The SPAD XI was developed from the SPAD VII as a two-seat fighter. Although it
had good speed and strength, it had marginal handling and manoeuvrability and
so was used for reconnaissance. This is a Belgian example that carried King
Albert I as observer on several flights piloted by *Sous-Lieutenant* Henri Crombez.

Specifications

Crew: 2
Powerplant: 1 x 164kW (220hp) Hispano-
  Suiza 8Bc engine
Maximum speed: 195.5km/h (121.5mph)
Endurance: 2 hours 15 mins
Service ceiling: 6300m (20,669ft)
Dimensions: span 11.24m (36ft 10in);
  length 7.80m (25ft 7in); height 2.50m
  (8ft 2in)
Weight: 1035kg (2321lb) max take-off
Armament: 1 x 7.7mm (0.303in) fixed
  Vickers, 1–2 x 7.7mm (0.303in) flexible
  Lewis MGs, plus 70kg (154lb) of bombs

▲ SPAD XVI

Escadrille SPA 21 / Western Front / Summer 1918

A re-engined SPAD XI, the SPAD XVI was widely used for reconnaissance by
France, but its poor handling characteristics (it would stall and spin with
little provocation like the SPAD XI) made it equally unpopular with its crews.
One went to Belgium and six to the USAS. The dramatic fuselage marking is
the escadrille insignia.

Specifications

Crew: 2
Powerplant: 1 x 179kW (240hp) Lorraine
  8Bb engine
Maximum speed: 180km/h (112mph)
Range: n/a
Service ceiling: About 5000m (16,404ft)
Dimensions: span 11.21m (36ft 9in); length
  7.84m (25ft 8.6in); height 2.84m (9ft 4in)
Weight: 1140kg (2513lb) max take-off
Armament: 1 x 7.7mm (0.303in) fixed
  Vickers MG and 1–2 x 7.7mm (0.303in)
  flexible Lewis MGs, plus 70kg (154lb)

▲ Sopwith Dolphin
No. 23 Squadron, RAF / Western Front / Summer 1918

The Sopwith Dolphin was Britain's first multi-gun fighter. Like the earlier Camel it had two fixed, synchronized Vickers machine guns; many operational examples also carried a single Lewis gun firing over the propeller arc. The pilot was Lt J. Pearson, the circle was the unit insignia and the 'U' indicates 'C' Flight.

Specifications

Crew: 1

Powerplant: 1 x 149kW (200hp) Hispano-
  Suiza engine

Maximum speed: 195.5km/h (121.5mph)

Endurance: n/a

Service ceiling: 6096m (20,000ft)

Dimensions: span 9.9m (32ft 6in); length
  6.785m (22ft 3in); height 2.59m (8ft 6in)

Weight: 1959kg (4319lb) max take-off

Armament: 2 x 7.7mm (0.303in) fixed Vickers
  and 1 x 7.7mm (0.303in) Lewis MGs

▲ Sopwith Dolphin
No. 79 Squadron, RAF / Western Front / Summer 1918

Not as popular as the SE.5a because of its pilot accommodations, the Dolphin had better performance at high altitude. The white squares behind the cockpit were the squadron marking: the 'T' indicates a spare aircraft not assigned to a specific flight.

Specifications

Crew: 1

Powerplant: 1 x 149kW (200hp) Hispano-
  Suiza engine

Maximum speed: 195.5km/h (121.5mph)

Endurance: n/a

Service ceiling: 6096m (20,000ft)

Dimensions: span 9.9m (32ft 6in); length
  6.785m (22ft 3in); height 2.59m (8ft 6in)

Weight: 1959kg (4319lb) max take-off

Armament: 2 x 7.7mm (0.303in) fixed Vickers
  and 1 x 7.7mm (0.303in) Lewis MGs

▲ SE.5a
No. 56 Squadron, RFC / Vert Galant, Western Front / Late 1917

This SE.5a was flown by Capt J.T.B. McCudden, VC, 'B' Flight commander. McCudden had 57 victories and was likely the top-ranking British ace; unlike some other top British aces, nearly all his victories were confirmed by wreckage of the German airplane claimed. The spinner was from an LVG C.V McCudden downed, and the cockpit combing was modified.

Specifications

Crew: 1

Powerplant: 1 x 149kW (200hp) Hispano-Suiza
  8a 8-cylinder inline piston engine

Maximum speed: 217km/h (135mph)

Endurance: 2 hours 30 mins

Service ceiling: 6706m (22,000ft)

Dimensions: span 8.11m (26ft 7in); length
  6.38m (20ft 11in); height 2.89m (9ft 6in)

Weight: 1047kg (2308lb) max take-off

Armament: 1 x 7.62mm (0.303in) fixed
  forward-firing Vickers MG, 1 x 7.7mm
  (0.313in) Lewis MG; 4 x 11.3kg (25lb) bombs

The triplane craze
SPRING 1917–SPRING 1918

In the spring of 1917 the new Sopwith Triplane was the only Allied fighter that could beat the Albatros, creating a year-long triplane craze in Germany.

ONE DEVELOPMENT DEAD-END that deserves special mention can best be described as the triplane craze. Many different configurations were tried in aviation's infancy, when the most effective architecture was not obvious. For sound structural and aerodynamic reasons, most airplanes before and during the war were either monoplanes or biplanes. However, in early 1917 Sopwith introduced a triplane development of their agile Pup fighter. The Sopwith Triplane retained the single gun and general lines of the Pup, but had a more powerful, 82kW (110hp) rotary coupled with a new triplane wing cellule. Somewhat fragile and few in numbers, the Sopwith Triplane still came as a nasty shock to the dominant Albatros pilots because it alone of the Allied fighters of the time could out-climb the Albatros while also out-manoeuvring it and matching

it for speed. Despite the overall German superiority during the spring of 1917, the Sopwith Triplane caused the Germans to think that perhaps the triplane had some inherent superiority to the biplane. To the contrary, the biplane configuration is inherently a better compromise between strength, weight, and aerodynamic drag than the triplane, which has too much drag.

Engineering resources wasted

However, the light, agile Sopwith Triplane had hit a lucky peak of triplane potential, and the result was the triplane craze, though it was confined almost entirely to Germany and Austria. German authorities, followed by the Austrians, requested their manufacturers to develop triplane fighters, resulting in a plethora of new designs that never reached the

▲ **Sopwith Triplane**

No. 10(N) Squadron, RNAS / Droglandt, Western Front / Summer 1917
Developed from the beloved Pup, the Sopwith Triplane was one of the few Allied fighters able to best the Albatros D.III in early 1917. It had good climb and manoeuvrability, but with only a single gun was under-armed. Nevertheless, its performance created a triplane craze in Germany. 'Black Maria' was one of 62-victory ace Lt Col Raymond Collishaw's airplanes and one of a handful with two guns. The black nose, fin and wheel covers are the markings of 'B' Flight.

Specifications

Crew: 1

Powerplant: 1 x 97kW (130hp) Clerget 9B 9-
 cylinder rotary piston engine

Maximum speed: 188km/h (117mph)

Endurance: 2 hours 45 mins

Service ceiling: 6250m (20,500ft)

Dimensions: span 8.08m (26ft 6in); length
 5.74m (18ft 10in); height 3.2m (10ft 6in)

Weight: 699kg (1541lb) max take-off

Armament: 1–2 x 7.62mm (0.303in) fixed
 forward-firing Vickers MGs

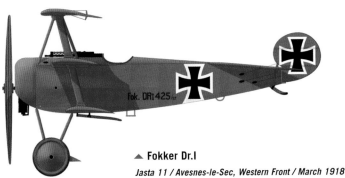

Specifications

Crew: 1

Powerplant: 1 x 82kW (110hp) Oberusel Ur.II
9-cylinder rotary piston engine

Maximum speed: 185km/h (115mph)

Endurance: 1hr 30 mins

Service ceiling: 6100m (20,015ft)

Dimensions: span 7.19m (23ft 7in); length
5.77m (18ft 11in); height 2.95m (9ft 8in)

Weight: 586kg (1291lb) max take-off

Armament: 2 x 7.92mm (0.313in) fixed
forward-firing LMG 08/15 MGs

▲ **Fokker Dr.I**

Jasta 11 / Avesnes-le-Sec, Western Front / March 1918

Possibly the most famous airplane of the war, this is the fighter that Manfred von
Richthofen, the famous Red Baron, was flying at the time of his death. It is shown
with its original 'iron cross' insignia, which was changed to the straight-sided
'Balken Cross' style before the Red Baron's fatal flight on 21 April 1918.

Specifications

Crew: 1

Powerplant: 1 x 82kW (110hp) Oberusel Ur.II
9-cylinder rotary piston engine

Maximum speed: 185km/h (115mph)

Endurance: 1hr 30 mins

Service ceiling: 6100m (20,015ft)

Dimensions: span 7.19m (23ft 7in); length
5.77m (18ft 11in); height 2.95m (9ft 8in)

Weight: 586kg (1291lb) max take-off

Armament: 2 x 7.92mm (0.313in) fixed
forward-firing LMG 08/15 MGs

▲ **Fokker Dr.I**

Jasta 11 / Avesnes-le-Sec, Western Front / March 1918

The Fokker Triplane shared nothing with the Sopwith other than its basic configuration. It
was a supreme dogfighter that could out-manoeuvre and out-climb all opponents, but
was too slow. This one was flown by Lothar von Richthofen, the Red Baron's younger
brother and a 40-victory ace. The yellow was Lothar's personal color; red was the *Jasta*
color. Like his brother, Lothar won the Pour le Mérite.

▲ **Fokker Dr.I**

Jasta 19 / Balâtre, Western Front / Spring 1918

This Fokker Triplane was flown by six-victory ace *Ltn* Rudolf Rienau in Spring
1918. The black and yellow tailplane and white cowl are the *Jasta* markings;
the white stripe around the fuselage is Rienau's personal marking.

Specifications

Crew: 1

Powerplant: 1 x 82kW (110hp) Oberusel Ur.II
9-cylinder rotary piston engine

Maximum speed: 185km/h (115mph)

Endurance: 1hr 30 mins

Service ceiling: 6100m (20,015ft)

Dimensions: span 7.19m (23ft 7in); length
5.77m (18ft 11in); height 2.95m (9ft 8in)

Weight: 586kg (1291lb) max take-off

Armament: 2 x 7.92mm (0.313in) fixed
forward-firing LMG 08/15 MGs

Front and wasted a great deal of engineering resources in the process. Only two German triplane fighters reached production. One was the Pfalz Dr.I (Dr for *dridecker*, or triplane); only 10 were built and while there are photographs of it at *Jasta 73*, its appearance in combat is not confirmed. The other was the Fokker Triplane, made famous as the airplane the Red Baron was flying when he was killed.

In many ways the Fokker Triplane is a paradox. It came at a time when the Albatros, Roland and Pfalz fighters were inferior to their Allied opponents, so was welcomed warmly by the German pilots. It was

GERMAN ARMED, SINGLE-ENGINE TRIPLANES, 1917–18							
	1917			1918			
Manufacturer and Type	31 Aug	31 Oct	31 Dec	28 Feb	30 Apr	30 Jun	31 Aug
Fokker Dr.I	2	17	35	143	171	118	65
Pfalz Dr.I	–	–	–	–	9	7	1
Total	2	17	35	143	180	125	66

initially beset with some structural failures, but the problems were soon rectified and, despite being slow, the Fokker Triplane became the aircraft of choice of

Specifications

Crew: 1

Powerplant: 1 x 119kW (160hp) Siemens-
    Halske Sh.III

Maximum speed: n/a

Endurance: 2 hours

Service ceiling: 7000m (22,966ft)

Dimensions: span 8.5m (27ft 10.6in);
    length 5.5m (18ft 0.5in); height 2.70m
    (8ft 10in)

Weight: 705kg (1554lb) max take-off

Armament: 2 x 7.92mm (.312in)
    LMG 08/15 MGs

▲ **Pfalz Dr.I**

Jasta 73 / Mars sous Bouroq, Western Front / Spring 1918

The Pfalz Dr.I was the only other German triplane fighter placed in production, but only 10 were produced because it offered little advantage over the Fokker and development of its Siemens-Halske engine was not complete. The Pfalz D.VIII was a faster, more successful biplane derivative of the Dr.I. This aircraft is in plain Pfalz factory finish and standard national markings without unit or personal marks.

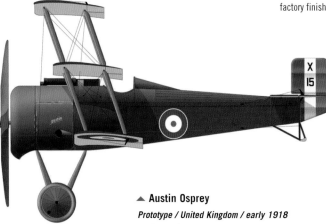

▲ **Austin Osprey**

Prototype / United Kingdom / early 1918

The Austin Osprey was a British triplane fighter that offered no advantages over the Sopwith Snipe, which was chosen for production instead. The Osprey was limited to prototype status despite its good performance.

Specifications

Crew: 1

Powerplant: 1 x 171.5kW (230hp)
    B.R.2 engine

Maximum speed: 118.5km/h (73.6mph)

Endurance: About 2 hours 30 mins

Service ceiling: 5791m (19.000ft)

Dimensions: span 7m (23ft); length 5.36m
    (17ft 7in); height 3.25m (10ft 8in)

Weight: 856kg (1888lb) max take-off

Armament: 2 x 7.7mm (0.303in) Vickers MGs

FRENCH AVIATION MILITAIRE, AUGUST 1917	
Type	Strength
Fighters	
Nieuport 11 / 16 / 17 / 24	336
SPAD 7 / 12 / 13	465
Subtotal Fighters	801
Bombers	
Voisin 5 / 8	86
Breguet 4 / 5 / 12	68
Breguet 14 B2	24
Caproni 3 (License built)	16
Sopwith 1½ Strutter	142
Paul Schmitt P.S.7	43
Subtotal Bombers	379
Reconnaissance	
Farman MF.11	1
Farman F.40 series	152
Caudron G.3 / 4 / 6	283
Caudron R.4	53
Nieuport 14	16
Morane-Saulnier P	61
A.R.1 / A.R.2	216
Sopwith 1½ Strutter	234
Letord 1 / 2 / 4 / 5	89
Salmson S.M.1	26
Other	1
Subtotal Reconnaissance	1,132
Total	2,312

FRENCH AVIATION MILITAIRE, 1 NOVEMBER 1917	
Type	Strength
Fighters	
Nieuport 16 / 17 / 24	310
SPAD 7 / 13	444
Subtotal Fighters	754
Bombers	
Farman F.40 series	15
Voisin 8	102
Breguet 4 / 5	47
Breguet 14 B2	77
Caproni 3 (License-built)	12
Sopwith 1½ Strutter	157
Paul Schmitt P.S.7	31
Subtotal Bombers	441
Reconnaissance	
Farman F.40 series	51
Caudron G.4 / G.6	153
Nieuport 12	4
Morane-Saulnier P / T	33
A.R.1 / A.R.2	313
Breguet 14 A2	77
Sopwith 1½ Strutter	351
SPAD 11	78
Letord 1 / 2 / 4 / 5	121
Salmson S.M.1	26
Subtotal Reconnaissance	1,207
Total	2,402

▲ **Armstrong Whitworth FK.10**

Prototype / United Kingdom / early 1917

The FK.10 quadraplane was another exploration into the realm of too many wings. Too many wings create too much drag; the biplane was a better design choice. Only four prototypes of this two-seater were built; none served operationally.

Specifications

Crew: 2

Powerplant: 1 x 96.9kW (130hp) Clerget rotary piston engine

Maximum speed: 135km/h (84mph)

Endurance: 2 hours 30 minutes

Service ceiling: 10,000m (32,808ft)

Dimensions: span 8.48m (27ft 10in); length 6.78m (22ft 3in); height 3.51m (11ft 6in)

Weight: 916kg (2019lb) max take-off

Armament: 1 x 7.7mm (0.303in) forward-firing Vickers MG, 1 x 7.7mm (0.303in) rearward-firing Lewis MG

German aces. On the positive side, it had exceptional climb and manoeuvrability ideally suited to close-in, high-G manoeuvring combat, or dog-fighting as it was called. It had the standard two synchronized machine guns and, once the quality control problems were solved, was a sturdy airplane. Despite the claims of some critics, it was not a copy of the Sopwith, sharing nothing in common with that airplane's design other than its triplane configuration. While it needed more speed to be a first-class fighter, at least it out-performed its

opponents in both climb and manoeuvrability, whereas the Albatros was now inferior in all respects.

Eventually, the higher drag of the triplane forced designers to abandon the configuration. The Sopwith Triplane was replaced by the biplane Camel, which did not really out-perform it but was much sturdier and had two guns. The Fokker Triplane was developed into the faster Fokker D.VI biplane. But the D.VII, with a more powerful water-cooled Mercedes or BMW engine, was a more potent fighter and D.VI production was limited.

Production and strategy
SPRING 1916–1918

The Allies' decisive advantages in resources made a quick German victory on the battlefield essential. However, their failure to achieve that put the Germans on the strategic defensive.

WARS ARE NOT WON just on the battlefield; they are also won or lost in the factories. The quantity and quality of the weapons are critical to success, and industrial capacity of the combatants is key. Manpower resources are also critical if conflict turns into a war of attrition, which it so often does.

The table of prewar industrial potential of the key combatants (below) makes clear that, while Germany and Austria were initially competitive with Britain and France in industrial production, they were greatly out-numbered in population. This made it imperative for Germany to gain a quick, decisive victory on the battlefield to win the war, and this was the goal of their Schlieffen Plan. When the Germans failed to win this quick victory, the war became one of attrition in which the Allies had a decisive

manpower advantage. Moreover, the Royal Navy, supreme at sea, implemented a distant blockade that starved Germany of resources, both raw materials and food. This element of the war was the decisive factor that lead to Germany's eventual defeat.

The imbalance of resources and industrial capacity also revealed itself in the war that was fought in the air. The table of aviation production by combatant (see opposite) illustrates why Germany had to go on the strategic defensive in the air as well as on the ground. Allied production was far greater than that of Germany and Austria, especially in the critical category of aero-engines.

Aviation success story

Of the great powers, France's aviation production effort was by far the most successful despite the occupation of much of France by the German army. In particular, French production of aero-engines was critical to the Allied war effort. France supplied both aero-engines and completed aircraft to every Allied country to supplement their own production. However, the French contribution is even greater than indicated by the table. In addition to direct imports, Russia was extremely dependent on France for licence production of French airplanes and aero-engines. Likewise, Britain and especially Italy built many French engines and airplanes under licence.

POPULATION AND TONS OF STEEL BY COMBATANT (MILLIONS)		
Country	Population (plus Colonies)	Steel Production (tons)
Austria-Hungary	51.4	2.6
Germany	66.3	17.0
Sub-total Central Powers	**117.7**	**19.6**
France	90.1	4.3
United Kingdom	422.7	10.0
Sub-total Allies	**512.8**	**14.3**

Russia produced far more aircraft than engines, and that was common; aero-engines were much more difficult to produce than wood and fabric airframes. Lack of aero-engines was also a critical problem in Britain, and French engines made up the difference. Furthermore, until 1918 French airplane production exceeded that of Britain. Britain designed some excellent aircraft, but could seldom deploy them in the desired numbers due to limited aero-engine production. America did not enter the war until early 1917 and her production was primarily training planes. America's production of the powerful Liberty engine was late in the war and most of the engines did not reach Europe before the Armistice. Furthermore, nearly all American aircraft used in combat were purchased from France.

German aviation production, especially aero-engines, was limited by the scarcity of raw materials as a result of the Royal Navy's distant blockade. Early in the stalemate on the Western Front, the Germans were forced onto the strategic defensive. While the British implemented an aerial offensive, the German fighters waited over their own lines to intercept them, conserving their resources. This policy, together with prevailing westerly winds, meant most air combats took place on the German side of the lines. Allied airmen surviving the downing of their airplanes were captured while surviving German airmen went back to their units. Moreover, scarce resources lead to some design decisions that are otherwise difficult to understand. For example, the armoured German J-type airplanes were all fitted with the 149kW (200hp) Benz engine, resulting in an underpowered aircraft with only modest performance and, during routine operations, compromised safety in flight. More powerful engines were available, but they were needed for other airplanes. Scarce resources were also a major factor in German engine production strategy. Once reliable and fairly powerful six-cylinder engines were in mass production, Germany devoted more effort to refining airframes and neglected engine development. In contrast, the French, with far more resources at their disposal, continually focused on development of more powerful engines.

The general problem of inadequate engine production was a major reason why the vast majority of World War I airplanes used a single engine. Another limitation was inadequate performance if an engine failed. By modern standards, the airplanes

AVIATION PRODUCTION		
Country	Airplanes	Aero Engines
Austria-Hungary	5,286	4,902
Germany	50,296	43,486
Sub-total Central Powers	**55,582**	**48,388**
France	51,700	92,386
Italy	11,986	14,849
Russia	5,607	1,511
United Kingdom	52,027	41,034
United States	10,980	32,420
Sub-total Allies	**132,300**	**182,200**
Total	**187,882**	**230,588**

were all underpowered, and twin-engine types generally could not maintain altitude on the power of only one engine. The loss of power from an engine failure was not the only problem; all propellers were of fixed pitch, meaning they could not be 'feathered' in the event the engine failed. (To feather a propeller means to rotate the blades so they face sideways to the wind for reduced drag and to stop rotation. Inability to feather the propeller means it continues to 'windmill' after engine failure, resulting in aerodynamic drag similar to that of a parachute of the same diameter.) Faced with engine failure due to combat damage or mechanical fault, a World War I twin-engine airplane could only descend gradually until it landed. The pilot's joke is that the engine that continues running takes you to the scene of the accident. Even most modern light twin-engine airplanes have modest performance after an engine failure despite their ability to feather the propeller.

▲ **Jasta 12 at Toulis Aerodrome 15 March 1918**
Fokker Triplane and Albatros fighters line up in front of their tent hangars.
Triplanes were replacing the outdated Albatros fighters of Jasta 12 at this time.

The *Amerika Program*
APRIL 1917–1918

After America entered the war, Germany implemented the *Amerika Program* to double aviation production and provide a technically superior fighter. Lack of resources was its undoing.

THE RESOURCE-STARVED German aviation industry was already unable to match Allied rates of production before America had even entered World War I. After America declared war, Germany implemented the *Amerika Program* to tackle the problem. The Germans strived to double production of their combat airplanes and fuel, but this was a goal never achieved due to lack of resources.

Though they failed to reach their production goals, Germany was successful in doubling the number of *Jastas* from 40 to 80, although the *Jastas* were seldom at authorized strength. Finally, in the final month of the war, the *KESTs* (*Kampeinsitzer Staffeln*) were re-designated *Jastas 81–90*.

The *Amerika Program* aimed to:
- Increase aircraft production from 1000 to 2000 airplanes per month.
- Increase aero-engine production from 1250 to 2500 aero-engines per month.
- Increase aircraft machine-gun production to 1500 per month.
- Increase aviation fuel output from 5500 tonnes (6000 tons) to 10,900 tonnes (12,000 tons) per month.
- Obtain 24,000 suitable recruits for the air service.
- Make a special effort to obtain technical superiority in aircraft, especially a new fighter plane and high-performance aero-engine.

German fighter competitions
1918

The German fighter competitions were instrumental in helping Germany regain technical parity with Allied fighters in the war's final months as exemplified by the potent Fokker D.VII.

A CRITICAL ASPECT OF the *Amerika Program* was the development of a new fighter plane and a high-performance engine, which were needed in order to counter-balance numerical inferiority with technical superiority. German fighter development had stagnated after the Albatros fighters established technical superiority during the autumn of 1916 through the spring of 1917.

That soon changed as the Allies introduced the Sopwith Camel, SE.5a and SPAD XIII late in the spring of 1917. These new fighters were technically superior to the Albatros D.III, and introduction of the Albatros D.V at the same time changed nothing because it was no improvement over the D.III. German fighter pilots became increasingly critical of the technical inferiority of their aircraft; even the Red Baron complained bitterly. However, von Richthofen

had the influence to do something about this situation, and he used it. He wrote a friend at *Idflieg* (the German Inspectorate of Aviation Troops) and explained the problem in detail. Von Richthofen suggested a formal fighter competition open to all manufacturers. The pressing need, combined with a sound idea and the backing of the most famous German ace, lead to the first German fighter competition, which was held in January 1918. In the event, these fighter competitions proved to be instrumental in enabling Germany to reach technical parity with the Allies in the last months of the war.

The first winner
The Fokker D.VII won the first competition and entered service in April/May 1918. Although sharing its engine and armament with the Albatros, Pfalz and

other German designs, the Fokker D.VII introduced some important structural and aerodynamic innovations, which significantly improved its effectiveness. By far the most important was its wooden wing, which was built around a box spar. It was thick and had a rounded-off leading edge, providing high lift and exceptional stalling characteristics. This made the D.VII manoeuvrable and easy to pilot, even enabling it to fly 'hanging on its prop' without stalling. These exceptional handling qualities enabled average pilots to become good pilots and made aces out of good pilots.

Thick wing yet low drag

Other designers had always used thin airfoils because they had less drag than the Fokker wing. But the strong Fokker wing did not need the extensive system of bracing wires thin airfoils needed. The combined drag of thin airfoils with their bracing wires was greater than the drag of the thick Fokker wing, which needed no bracing wires. This factor was the key to the Fokker's improved speed and climb.

Because of stagnant engine development, the Fokker D.VII was first powered by the same 119kW (160hp) Mercedes engine used in the Albatros scouts in August 1916. It was not until the new BMW engine finally arrived in June/July that the Fokker D.VII grew into the premier fighter of the war. The BMW engine was similar to the familiar 119kW (160hp) Mercedes D.III engine but developed its 138kW (185hp) at 2000m (6500ft) altitude because it was over-compressed (it could not be run at full throttle until reaching the thinner air at this altitude without detonation and engine damage). This design gave it more power at high altitude, so Mercedes countered with the 134kW (180hp) D.IIIa and finally the 149kW (200hp) D.IIIaü, the latter being over-compressed like the BMW. Both engines were used in the D.VII, with the D.IIIaü performing nearly as well as the BMW. The BMW-powered Fokker D.VII became a legend in its own time, but its arrival came too late and there were too few of them to win the air war for Germany.

The Pfalz company, based in Bavaria, built airplanes throughout the war, initially including licence-built copies of the Morane-Saulnier L, and later original fighter designs. The Pfalz D.III was a good, solid fighter that only lacked the power to be competitive with Allied fighters. The Pfalz D.XII,

which resembled the Fokker D.VII, went into service in the summer of 1918 but problems with its frontal, car-type radiator delayed its arrival by a couple of months. By the time the D.XII arrived the Fokker D.VII had earned a huge reputation and was in great demand by the pilots, many of whom wanted no other plane. The D.XII was another good, solid Pfalz design that never made a name for itself, overshadowed as it was by the competition.

Two other aircraft powered by an innovative counter-rotary engine also made a good impression at the First Fighter Competition and saw operational service that was primarily limited by engine availability. These were the Pfalz D.VIII and Siemens-Schuckert D.III, both powered by the 119kW (160hp) Siemens-Halske Sh.III rotary. In this unique engine the cylinders rotated in one direction while the propeller rotated in the other, giving a relative speed between them of 1800rpm with a propeller speed of only 900rpm. Compared to a typical rotary of 1400rpm, this enabled the Sh.III to produce more power while enabling use of a larger, slower-turning and more efficient propeller, giving the fighters good speed and exceptional climb. The SSW D.III was used in small numbers before being replaced by the similar D.IV, which was faster thanks to the reduced drag from its smaller wing. The Pfalz D.VIII was not as manoeuvrable as the SSW fighters but had similar climb. Therefore it was mostly assigned to the KESTs (*Kampeinsitzer Staffeln*) stationed behind the lines to intercept Allied day bombers on missions well behind the lines.

Yet another two fighters that showed promise at the competition were the Fokker D.VI and Roland D.VI. These were built in small numbers to evaluate them at the front.

The competition idea was such a good one that Germany held two additional fighter competitions, the next in July 1918 and the third in October 1918. The July competition lead to the creation of the Fokker E.V/D.VIII parasol monoplane fighter, which entered service in August. The Fokker V.29, a parasol monoplane derivative of the Fokker D.VII, was the main winner of the last competition along with the Rumpler D.I high-altitude fighter. The V.29 would have replaced the D.VII on the production lines had the war lasted longer.

The competition idea was extended to two-seaters, and this was held in the summer of 1918.

Operation Michael
MARCH 1918

The German Spring Offensive of 1918, named Operation Michael, represented Germany's last realistic chance to win the war. Its failure spelled inevitable defeat.

ONCE AMERICA ENTERED the fray, her huge population and industrial potential meant the end was in sight for Germany. But it would take time to manifest that potential on the battlefront, and Germany remained determined to defeat her enemies before American help could arrive in quantity. The overall strategy was to first defeat a staggering Russia in the East, then quickly move those troops to the Western Front for a final, decisive offensive.

The first part of the strategy went well. In 1917 the Russian Empire collapsed in chaos and in the fall a peace treaty was signed, enabling Germany to move large forces from East to West. The aim of Operation Michael, also known to the German troops as the *Kaiserschlacht* (Kaiser's battle), was to split apart the Allied armies and finally achieve victory.

To support Operation Michael the German *Luftstreitkräfte* (Air Force) was enlarged as much as possible, relying on the impact of the *Amerika Program* for this strengthening. However, the *Amerika Program* never reached its goals. Not only were the Germans unable to achieve the desired

JGI–IV			
Unit	Date Established	Component Jastas	First CO
JGI	24 June 1917	4, 6, 10, 11	*Rittm* M. von Richthofen
JGII	2 Feb 1918	12, 13, 15, 19	*Hptm* A. von Tutschek
JGIII	2 Feb 1918	2, 26, 27, 36	*Oblt* B. Loerzer
JGIV	10 Oct 1918	23b, 32b, 34b, 35b	*Hptm* E. von Schleich

production quantities, they were unable to obtain technical superiority. The excellent Fokker D.VII only arrived at the front in late April/early May, after Operation Michael had already stalled and failed.

Part of strengthening the *Luftstreitkräfte* was organizational. After reviewing the success of JG.I, Richthofen's 'Flying Circus' (so called because the planes were painted garishly for easy identification

▲ **Fokker D.VII(OAW)**

Jasta 12 / Western Front / Summer 1918

The Fokker D.VII quickly proved itself at the Front and was soon being built by several manufacturers under licence; this one was produced by OAW (*Ostdeutsche Albatros Werke*). The blue fuselage was the *JG II* shade; the white nose was the unit marking of *Jasta 12* and the white fuselage band was the personal marking of the unknown pilot.

Specifications

Crew: 1

Powerplant: 1 x 134kW (180hp) Mercedes D.IIIa engine

Maximum speed: 190km/h (118mph)

Endurance: 2 hours

Service ceiling: 7000m (22,965ft)

Dimensions: span 8.7m (29ft 1in); length 6.95m (22ft 8in); height 2.95m (9ft 6in)

Weight: 880kg (1940lb) max take-off

Armament: 2 x 7.92mm (0.313in) LMG 08/15 MGs

during dogfights), since its formation in the summer of 1917, two more *Jagdgeschwaders* were formed in early February 1918 to provide air superiority over the front as Operation Michael was launched. To strengthen these formations, as many of the component *Jastas* (or fighter squadrons), were equipped with the Fokker Triplane as possible. The airplane Germany truly needed, the BMW-powered Fokker D.VII, was not yet available, but the Fokker Triplane was the next best choice. Despite being slow, at least the Triplane was able to out-climb and out-

manoeuvre all opponents. However, the Albatros and Pfalz scouts that were also available were inferior to modern Allied fighters in all performance aspects.

Initially Operation Michael went well, and the German fighters managed to achieve air superiority over the battle area. But the Allies, who were encouraged by the knowledge of massive American reinforcements on their way, were eventually able to stop the attack despite sustaining heavy losses. With that, any realistic German hope for victory vanished and the war's outcome was no longer in doubt.

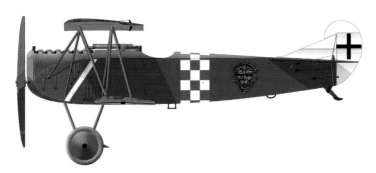

▲ **Fokker D.VII(OAW)**

Jasta 13 / Western Front / Summer 1918

Innovative structural and aerodynamic design combined to give the D.VII good speed and climb and exceptional manoeuvrability and handling qualities. When powered by the over-compressed BMW like this one of *Ltn* Franz Büchner, a 40-victory ace and Pour le Mérite winner, it was the premier fighter of the war. The blue fuselage was the JG II shade; the green nose was the unit marking of *Jasta 13* and the fuselage band and lion's head were Büchner's personal markings.

Specifications

Crew: 1

Powerplant: 1 x 138kW (185hp) B.M.W. IIIa 6-
  cylinder inline piston engine

Maximum speed: 205km/h (127mph)

Endurance: 2 hours

Service ceiling: 6980m (22,900ft)

Dimensions: span 8.7m (29ft 1in); length
  6.95m (22ft 8in); height 2.95m (9ft 6in)

Weight: 880kg (1940lb) max take-off

Armament: 1–2 x 7.92mm (0.313in) LMG
  08/15 MGs

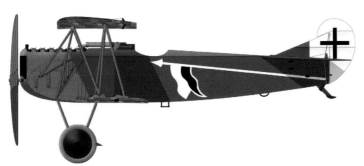

▲ **Fokker D.VII**

Jasta 15 / Western Front / Summer 1918

The steel tube fuselage and thick airfoil section of the D.VII set the pace for airplane development postwar. The blue fuselage was the JG II shade; the red nose was the unit marking of *Jasta 15*. The Uhlan lance with black and white pennant was the personal marking of the pilot, *Vzfw* Gustav Klaudet, and symbolized his cavalry service. Klaudet was an ace with six victories.

Specifications

Crew: 1

Powerplant: 1 x 145kW (195hp) Mercedes IIIaü
  6-cylinder inline piston engine

Maximum speed: 200km/h (124mph)

Endurance: 2 hours

Service ceiling: 7000m (22,965ft)

Dimensions: span 8.7m (29ft 1in); length
  6.95m (22ft 8in); height 2.95m (9ft 6in)

Weight: 880kg (1940lb) max take-off

Armament: 2 x 7.92mm (0.313in)
  LMG 08/15 MGs

TOTAL GERMAN ORDER OF BATTLE, 21 MARCH 1918	
Type	Strength
Flieger Abteilungen	153
Schlachtstaffeln	38
Jagdstaffeln	81
Bombengeschwadern	7

OPERATION MICHAEL GERMAN ORDER OF BATTLE, START DATE	
Type	Strength
Flieger Abteilungen	49
Schlachtstaffeln	27
Jagdstaffeln	35
Bombengeschwadern	4

The white brand of the 4th Dragoons (a combination of 4 D) was the personal marking of *Ltn* Oliver von Beaulieu-Marconnay, 25-victory ace and 19-year-old *Jastaführer* of *Jasta 19*.

OPERATION MICHAEL GERMAN ORDER OF BATTLE, 31 MARCH 1918	
Type	Strength
Flieger Abteilungen	55
Schlachtstaffeln	27
Jagdstaffeln	42
Bombengeschwadern	4

▲ **Fokker D.VII**

Jasta 19 / Western Front / Summer 1918

When powered by the over-compressed BMW.III engine that gave its rated power at 2000m (6560ft), the D.VII could out-climb all opponents, had a higher ceiling and finally gave the Germans a fighter with speed competitive with the SE.5a and SPAD XIII. The blue fuselage was the *JG II* shade; the yellow nose was the unit shade of *Jasta 19*. The white brand of the 4th Dragoons was the personal marking of *Ltn* Oliver von Beaulieu-Marconnay, at 20 the youngest recipient of the Pour le Mérite, which he received while dying from wounds in the hospital. He scored 25 victories and became *Jastaführer* of *Jasta 19* while still just 19 years old.

Specifications

Crew: 1

Powerplant: 1 x 138kW (185hp) B.M.W. IIIa 6-cylinder inline piston engine

Maximum speed: 205km/h (127mph)

Endurance: 2 hours

Service ceiling: 6980m (22,900ft)

Dimensions: span 8.7m (29ft 1in); length 6.95m (22ft 8in); height 2.95m (9ft 6in)

Weight: 880kg (1940lb) max take-off

Armament: 2 x 7.92mm (0.313in) LMG 08/15 MGs

Ground attack
1914–1918

The Allies relied on standard fighters for ground attack, but the Germans developed two distinct classes of specialized designs, the CL-class two-seat fighters and J-class armoured airplanes.

THE RANGE AND WEAPONS PAYLOAD of World War I airplanes remained limited, so during the war the airplane made its greatest contribution as the primary means of reconnaissance. However, from the beginning of the war airplanes had been used to attack ground targets. As airplanes became faster and

better armed, and pilots became more experienced, the impact of these attacks increased. As ground attack became more effective, different ideas and technology emerged on how best to exploit it.

The British, in keeping with their concept of the continuous air offensive, preferred fighter planes in general and used them for ground attack as well as air combat. The table outlining the composition of the various air services in August 1918 (*see* p170) shows the majority of the British inventory being made up of fighters and bombers, and not observation planes.

The makeup of the French air service was closer to the German model than the British because both Germany and France placed great value on reconnaissance. The Germans were on the defensive, so they had a greater proportion of fighters than France, while France had more bombers. The Austrians had proportionally more fighters because they too were on the defensive.

German ground-attack units

When hard pressed the Germans used fighters for ground attack, but generally preferred aircraft designed for that role and crews trained for it. Starting in 1917 the Germans deployed two new categories of combat aircraft designed to assist the troops by direct intervention on the battlefield. First to arrive, and produced in greatest numbers, were the CL-type, the designation standing for light C-type,

effectively a two-seat fighter. The CL types were designed to escort reconnaissance airplanes and for ground attack. As experience with these types grew, however, the Germans learned how to use them with greater impact. *Schlastas* (ground-attack units), were formed with six CL-types. The *Schlastas* were used at full strength during attacks and in critical defensive situations, and were highly effective. By 1918 they had become the true offensive units of the *Luftstreitkräfte*. The airplanes were equipped with the same engines that powered the Albatros and Pfalz fighters of the time, and the additional weight of the second crewman reduced their speed and climb compared to a single-seat fighter. On the other hand, the CL types could manoeuvre with single-seat fighters and were well armed with machine guns for both pilot and observer. Therefore, they were well able to defend themselves without need for escorts, and a wise Allied fighter pilot treated them with respect. Interestingly, experience with the CL-types and the Bristol Fighter lead the British, French and Americans to each plan on greatly expanding their two-seat fighter inventory in 1919 had the war lasted.

▲ **SE.5as of No. 1 Squadron RAF, July 1918**

No. 1 Squadron went to France in March 1915 with a variety of reconnaissance aircraft. By January 1917 the squadron was fully equipped with Nieuport scouts, and in January 1918 it re-equipped with SE.5as. The white ring behind the cockade was the squadron marking at the time of this photograph.

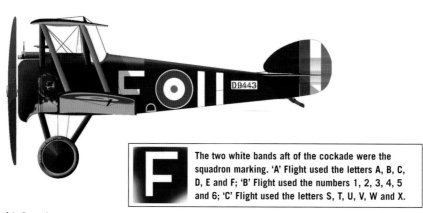

Specifications
Crew: 1
Powerplant: 1 x 97kW (130hp) Clerget 9-
   cylinder air-cooled rotary piston engine
Maximum speed: 1858km/h (115mph)
Endurance: 2hr 30 mins
Service ceiling: 5790m (19,000ft)
Dimensions: span 8.53m (28ft); length
   5.72m (18ft 9in); height 2.59m (8ft 6in)
Weight: 659kg (1453lb) max take-off
Armament: 2 x 7.7mm (.303in) Vickers MGs,
   plus four 11.35kg (25lb) bombs

The two white bands aft of the cockade were the squadron marking. 'A' Flight used the letters A, B, C, D, E and F; 'B' Flight used the numbers 1, 2, 3, 4, 5 and 6; 'C' Flight used the letters S, T, U, V, W and X.

▲ Sopwith Camel

No. 3 Squadron, RAF / Western Front / October–November 1917

The manoeuvrable Sopwith Camel earned a reputation as an excellent dogfighter. It was widely used for ground attack as well and often carried four 9kg (20lb) bombs for this task. The letter 'F' indicates this airplane was from 'A' Flight.

Specifications
Crew: 1
Powerplant: 1 x 82kW (110hp) Le Rhône
   rotary piston engine
Maximum speed: 177km/h (110mph)
Range: 2 hours 45 minutes
Service ceiling: 4875m (16,000ft)
Dimensions: span 7.82m (25ft 8in); length
   6.71m (22ft); height 2.78m (9ft 11.5in)
Weight: 677kg (1492lb) max take-off
Armament: 1 x 7.7mm (.303in) Vickers MG,
   4 x 11.3kg (25lb) bombs on underwing racks

▲ Airco DH.5

No. 41 Squadron, RFC / Western Front / October 1917

The Airco DH.5 was not competitive with German fighters and was therefore frequently used for ground attack. Its back-staggered upper wing gave the pilot excellent visibility forward but hindered visibility to the rear. The white bands either side of the cockade are the squadron markings; the 'F' indicates an airplane of 'A' Flight. Pilot 2/Lt F.S. Clarke was made prisoner of war on 29 October 1917 while flying this airplane.

▼ Halberstadt CL.II Schlasta

By 1918 the *Schlasta* was the offensive arm of the German air service. *Schlastas* had six airplanes and generally attacked at low level in line abreast to assist German troops during important attacks or vital defence situations. Most *Schlasta* airplanes were of the CL class and the robust, manoeuvrable Halberstadt CL.II was one of the types most widely used. These airplanes are from *Schlasta 24b*.

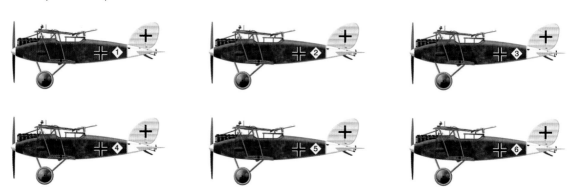

▲ Halberstadt CL.II

Schlasta 24b / Western Front / 1918

By mid-1917 the Germans had developed the CL-class as two-seat escort fighters and ground-attack airplanes. Resembling the earlier Halberstadt fighters from which it was developed, the CL.II was strong, manoeuvrable, and had good handling qualities. The communal cockpit enabled the crew to coordinate well together during combat.

Specifications

Crew: 2

Powerplant: 1 x 119kW (160hp) Mercedes
  D.III inline piston engine

Maximum speed: 165km/h (103mph)

Endurance: 3 hours

Service ceiling: 5090m (16,700ft)

Dimensions: span 10.77m (35ft 4in);
  length 7.30m (23ft 11.5in); height 2.70m
  (8ft 10in)

Weight: 1130kg (2493lb) max take-off

Armament: 1 x 7.92mm (0.312in) LMG
  08/15 fixed forward-firing MG, 1 x 7.92mm
  (0.312in) LMG 14 trainable MG

This airplane is in standard factory finish with two additions; the axe is a personal marking and the tactical number '5' means it is the fifth of six airplanes in the *Schlasta*.

▲ Halberstadt CL.IV

Unknown Schlasta / Western Front / 1918

The Halberstadt CL.IV was developed from the earlier CL.II to further enhance its already excellent manoeuvrability and entered service in Summer 1918. Their single-bay design make them look much like single-seat fighters, and the gunner could be a surprise for an attacking fighter pilot.

Specifications

Crew: 2

Powerplant: 1 x 119kW (160hp)
  Mercedes D.III engine

Maximum speed: 165km/h (102.5mph)

Endurance: 3 hours

Service ceiling: 5090m (16,700ft)

Dimensions: span 10.70m (35ft 1in); length
  6.5m (21ft 4in); height 2.70m (8ft 10in)

Weight: 1040kg (2293lb) max take-off

Armament: 1 x 7.92mm (0.313in) fixed MG and
  1 x 7.92mm (0.313in) flexible MG

Specifications

Crew: 2

Powerplant: 1 x 119kW (160hp) Isotta-
  Fraschini V.4B inline piston engine

Maximum speed: 165km/h (102.5mph)

Endurance: 3 hours

Service ceiling: 6000m (19,685ft)

Dimensions: span 11.7m (38ft 4.6in);
  length 7.58m (24ft 10in); height 2.8m
  (9ft 2in)

Weight: 1081kg (2383lb) max take-off

Armament: 1 x 7.7mm (0.303in) fixed and
  1 x 7.7mm (0.303in) flexible MG

▲ Hannover CL.III

Flieger Abteilung 7 / Western Front / 1918

The Hannover CL.II and CL.III were excellent companions to the Halberstadts. All were robust, reliable airplanes that could manoeuvre with Allied fighters and had the additional combat effectiveness of a 'sting' in the tail, making them tough opponents. The white arrow is the unit marking.

▲ AEG J.I

Flieger Abteilung 221 / Western Front / 1918

While all combatants experimented with armouring airplanes, only the Germans operated specialized armoured airplanes in quantity during the war. First to arrive at the Front was the AEG J.I, developed from the steel-tube-framed C.IV and featuring 5mm (0.2in) thick armour around the engine and cockpits. The J-type (armoured infantry airplane) was originally designed for infantry cooperation.

Specifications	
Crew: 2	Dimensions: span 13m (42ft 7.8in); length
Powerplant: 1 x 149kW (200hp)	7.2m (23ft 7.5in); height 3.3m (10ft 8in)
Benz Bz.IV engine	Weight: 1876kg (4136lb) max take-off
Maximum speed: 140km/h 87.5mph)	Armament: 1 x 7.92mm (0.313in) MG
Endurance: n/a	
Service ceiling: 3000m (9842ft)	

GERMAN ESCORT/GROUND ATTACK BIPLANES

Manufacturer and Type	1917	1918			
	31 Dec	28 Feb	30 Apr	30 Jun	31 Aug
Halberstadt					
CL.II	170	224	342	311	175
CL.IV	–	–	–	–	136
Hannover					
CL.II	162	295	249	72	31
CL.IIIa	–	–	109	159	233
CL.III	–	–	51	67	29
Total	332	519	751	609	604

GERMAN ARMOURED INFANTRY/GROUND ATTACK BIPLANES

Manufacturer and Type	1917				1918			
	30 Jun	31 Aug	31 Oct	31 Dec	28 Feb	30 Apr	30 Jun	31 Aug
AEG								
J.I	4	1	11	35	55	66	43	28
J.II	–	–	–	–	–	15	65	63
J.	3	–	–	–	–	–	–	–
Albatros								
J.I	–	–	–	37	42	33	51	16
J.II	–	–	–	–	–	–	–	19
Junkers								
J.I	–	1	1	4	16	25	25	60
Total	7	2	12	76	113	139	184	186

The second new category Germany introduced was the J-type, heavily armoured two-seaters designed for low-level cooperation with the infantry. Slow and under-powered, the J-types relied on their armour for protection against both ground fire and enemy fighters. All J-types enclosed the crew in armour, and all but the (quickly replaced) Albatros J.I enclosed the engine in armour as well.

Operational experience soon blurred the line between infantry cooperation and ground attack, and a pair of downward-firing machine guns was installed in most J-types. These were used to fire from low altitude into trenches, horse lines, machine-gun nests and gun batteries. The Allied preponderance in tanks led to the installation of flexible 20mm Becker cannon in a number of AEG J.II and Albatros J.I and J.II airplanes for tank busting, making them the distant ancestor of modern attack helicopters.

ALLIED AND CENTRAL POWERS AIR FORCES, AUGUST 1918

Air Service	Fighter	Observation	Bomber
France	34%	51%	15%
Great Britain	55%	23%	22%
Italy	46%	45%	9%
United States	46.5%	46.5%	7%
Germany	42%	50%	8%
Austria-Hungary	63%	28%	9%

▲ Junkers J.I

Flieger Abteilung (A) 217 / Western Front / 1918

The second armoured German type to arrive at the Front was the Junkers J.I. It won fame both as the most rugged J-type and the world's first production all-metal airplane. As far as is known, none were shot down by Allied fighters.

Specifications

Crew: 2

Powerplant: 1 x 149kW (200hp) Benz Bz.IV

6-cylinder inline piston engine

Maximum speed: 155km/h (97mph)

Endurance: n/a

Service ceiling: 3000m (9842.5ft)

Dimensions: span 15m (49ft 2.5in); length

9.06m (29ft 8.7in); height 3.47m

(11ft 4.6in)

Weight: 2176kg (3885lb) max take-off

Armament: 1 x 7.92mm (0.31in)

trainable MG

Specifications

Crew: 2

Powerplant: 1 x 149kW (200hp)

Benz Bz.IV engine

Maximum speed: 140km/h (87.5mph)

Endurance: n/a

Service ceiling: 3000m (9842ft)

Dimensions: span 13m (42ft 7.8in); length

7.86m (25ft 9.5in); height 3.3m (10ft 8in)

Weight: 1900kg (4189lb) max take-off

Armament: 1 x 7.92mm (0.313in) flexible

MG and 2 x 7.92mm (0.313in) fixed MGs,

plus optional 1 x 20mm (0.79in) MG

▲ AEG J.II

Unknown Unit / Western Front / Autumn 1918

The low-flying J-types soon discovered the value of strafing enemy troops. The AEG J.II featured two machine guns firing downwards at 45 degrees for strafing in addition to the gunner's flexible Parabellum. The AEG J.II was the most numerous J-type because it was effective and much easier to produce than the Junkers J.I. Its horn-balanced controls made it more manoeuvrable than the earlier AEG J.I.

▲ Albatros J.II

Unknown Unit / Western Front / Autumn 1918

The Albatros company also produced armoured ground-attack airplanes. Their J.I, which did not have the engine armoured, was quickly replaced in production by the J.II that fixed that problem. The J.II also had two fixed guns firing downwards in addition to the gunners' flexible gun, and some carried a 20mm Becker cannon for tank busting. Other than the armour, the Albatros J-types were made of wood, so they were not as resistant to ground fire as the AEG and Junkers.

Specifications

Crew: 2

Powerplant: 1 x 164kW (220hp)

Benz Bz.IV engine

Maximum speed: 140km/h (87.5mph)

Endurance: 2 hours 30 mins

Service ceiling: 1500m (4921ft)

Dimensions: span 14.1m (46ft 3in); length

8.44m (27ft 8in); height unknown

Weight: 1927kg (4248lb) max take-off

Armament: 1 x 7.92mm (0.313in) flexible MG

and 2 x 7.92mm (0.313in) fixed MGs, plus

optional 1 x 20mm (0.79in) MG

Tactical night bombing
1914–1918

Both sides undertook tactical night bombing throughout the war. By 1918 the Allies could also mount large day-bombing operations, but the Germans continued to rely on night bombing.

FROM THE EARLY MONTHS of the war the French engaged in night bombing, and were soon joined by the British and German air services. Both sides repeatedly attempted day bombing, but abandoned the idea because they sustained unacceptably high losses. It was not until the last year of the war that the Allies had enough air superiority to conduct extensive daylight bombing. The British IF focused on strategic industrial targets and, without fighter escorts, suffered accordingly. In 1918 the French were able to send well escorted formations of 60 to 100 bombers to tactical targets with acceptable losses to German fighters. The Germans simply did not have enough airplanes to engage in similar operations and focused their bombing efforts at night, where the chance of interception was much lower.

Throughout 1918 the British and French continued to bomb at night along with their daylight bombing operations. French night bombing was primarily carried out by Voisin 8 and 10 single-

GERMAN ARMED, LIGHT SINGLE–ENGINE BIPLANE NIGHT BOMBERS						
	1917		1918			
Manufacturer and Type	31 Oct	31 Dec	28 Feb	30 April	30 June	31 Aug
AEG N.I	2	31	37	19	7	4
Sablatnig N.I	–	–	–	–	2	9
Total	2	31	37	19	9	13

engine pushers, reliable airplanes that were much too vulnerable to fighters to venture out in daylight. The British did the same with the F.E.2 of similar configuration, and later used the large, twin-engine Handley-Page bombers as well.

While most Allied night bombers were single-engine pushers, Germany relied on twin-engine bombers like the Gotha G.V, Friedrichshafen G.III and AEG G.IV. These airplanes typically flew several missions (sometimes as many as six) each night, to compensate for their inferior numbers. Germany also

▲ **AEG G.IV**

Bogohl 8b, Staffel 27 / Bolchen, Western Front / Summer 1918

The AEG G.IV was one of the best night bombers of the war. Like other AEG designs its structure was made of welded steel tubing. This example is covered in night camouflage fabric; '27' is the *Staffel* number and '7' is its tactical number within the *Staffel*. It flew from Bolchen aerodrome in Summer 1918.

Specifications

Crew: 3

Powerplant: 2 x 194kW (260hp)
 Mercedes D.IVa inline engines

Maximum speed: 165km/h (103mph)

Endurance: 4–5 hours

Service ceiling: 4500m (14,765ft)

Dimensions: span 18.40m (60ft 3in); length
 9.7m (31ft 8in); height 3.9m (12ft 8in)

Weight: 3635kg (8014lb) max take-off

Armament: 2 x 7.92mm (0.312in) Parabellum
 MGs, plus 400kg (882lb) bomb load

used its regular C-class planes for night bombing, and experimented with specially designed single-engine night bombers of the N-class. The N-class airplanes had been modified from C-class planes, typically by enlarging the wings for more lift, to enable them to carry a heavier bomb load. Two types saw operational service, and only the AEG N.I was used in any numbers. It was not until the late summer of 1918

that the French introduced the Farman F.50 to operations, which finally gave them a sturdy twin-engine night bomber like those that had long been used by Germany.

German night bombers were so effective the Allies simply did not believe the small number available for surrender after the Armistice. This was a tribute to the men who flew them nightly on so many missions.

▲ AEG N.I

Unknown Unit / Western Front / 1918

Germany produced a small number of single-engine two-seaters modified for night bombing. The AEG N.I was developed from the C.IV with a larger wing to carry more bombs, and was the most numerous of these rare types. Germany preferred twin-engine airplanes for night bombing due to their heavier bomb load. There are no unit or personal markings; the interesting camouflage was frequently used on the larger AEG G.IV.

Specifications

Crew: 2

Powerplant: 1 x 112kW (150hp)
  Benz Bz.III engine

Maximum speed: n/a

Endurance: 4 hours

Service ceiling: 3000m (9842ft)

Dimensions: span 15.24m (50ft); length 7.2m
  (23ft 7.5in); height n/a

Weight: 1609kg (3547lb) max take-off

Armament: 1 x 7.92mm (0.313in) flexible MG,
  plus 6 x 50kg (110lb) bomb load

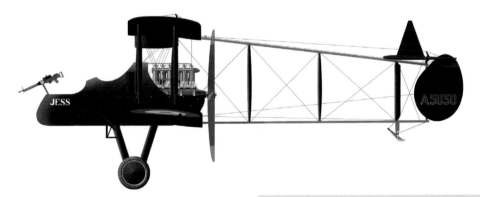

▲ RAF FE.2B

No. 100 Squadron, RAF (Independent Force) / Western Front / late 1918

The FE.2 series served in the RFC and RAF from early 1916 to the end of the war, serving longer at the Front than any other type of either side. Initially used for day fighting and reconnaissance, it was also effective to war's end as a night bomber despite its obsolete configuration. 'JESS' was a personal marking; there were no unit markings.

Specifications

Crew: 2

Powerplant: 1 x 119kW (160hp) Beardmore
  inline piston engine

Maximum speed: 147km/h (91.5mph)

Endurance: 4–5 hours

Service ceiling: 3353m (11,000ft)

Dimensions: span 14.55m (47ft 9in); length
  9.83m (32ft 3in); height 3.85m (12ft 7.5in)

Weight: 1378kg (3037lb) max take-off

Armament: 1 x 7.7mm (0.303in) Lewis MG,
  plus up to 136kg (300lb) of bombs

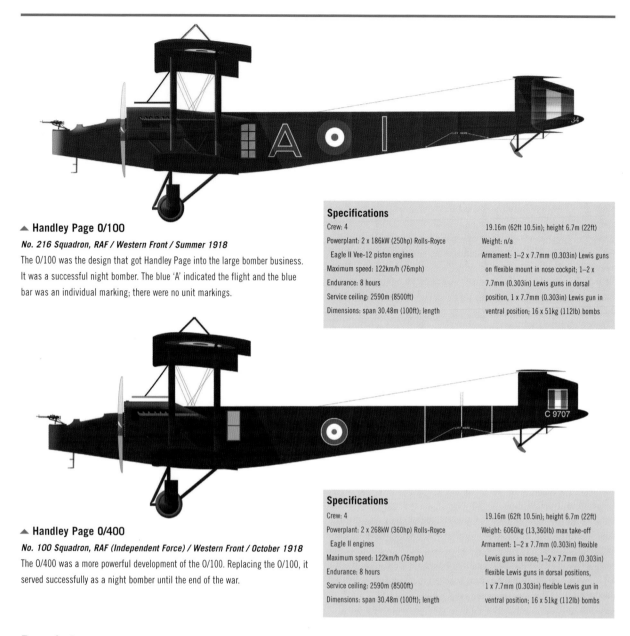

▲ **Handley Page 0/100**

No. 216 Squadron, RAF / Western Front / Summer 1918

The 0/100 was the design that got Handley Page into the large bomber business. It was a successful night bomber. The blue 'A' indicated the flight and the blue bar was an individual marking; there were no unit markings.

Specifications

Crew: 4

Powerplant: 2 x 186kW (250hp) Rolls-Royce
   Eagle II Vee-12 piston engines

Maximum speed: 122km/h (76mph)

Endurance: 8 hours

Service ceiling: 2590m (8500ft)

Dimensions: span 30.48m (100ft); length

19.16m (62ft 10.5in); height 6.7m (22ft)

Weight: n/a

Armament: 1–2 x 7.7mm (0.303in) Lewis guns
   on flexible mount in nose cockpit; 1–2 x
   7.7mm (0.303in) Lewis guns in dorsal
   position, 1 x 7.7mm (0.303in) Lewis gun in
   ventral position; 16 x 51kg (112lb) bombs

▲ **Handley Page 0/400**

No. 100 Squadron, RAF (Independent Force) / Western Front / October 1918

The 0/400 was a more powerful development of the 0/100. Replacing the 0/100, it served successfully as a night bomber until the end of the war.

Specifications

Crew: 4

Powerplant: 2 x 268kW (360hp) Rolls-Royce
   Eagle II engines

Maximum speed: 122km/h (76mph)

Endurance: 8 hours

Service ceiling: 2590m (8500ft)

Dimensions: span 30.48m (100ft); length

19.16m (62ft 10.5in); height 6.7m (22ft)

Weight: 6060kg (13,360lb) max take-off

Armament: 1–2 x 7.7mm (0.303in) flexible
   Lewis guns in nose; 1–2 x 7.7mm (0.303in)
   flexible Lewis guns in dorsal positions,
   1 x 7.7mm (0.303in) flexible Lewis gun in
   ventral position; 16 x 51kg (112lb) bombs

Parachutes

From the beginning of the war, balloon observers used parachutes to abandon their balloons when under attack. Unfortunately, the large size and heavy weight of those early parachutes prevented their use in the close confines of airplanes, which had limited payload. As the war ground on, both sides developed smaller, lighter parachutes. However, the British Guardian Angel parachute had many problems, and authorities decided not to issue them to airmen. One contention was that their use would encourage

aircrew to abandon damaged airplanes that could be brought back to base and repaired. Considering that it takes 20 years to create a pilot and a day or two to build an airplane, not to mention humanitarian concerns, this decision is astounding.

In 1918 the *Luftstreitkräfte* was the first air service to issue a standard parachute, the Heineke, to their pilots. A few of the new parachutes were issued to fighter pilots in 1917 for testing, but none were used in action. In April/May 1918 Germany started to

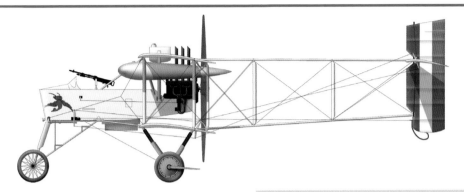

▲ Voisin 8

Escadrille VB 110 / Western Front / 1917

Once effective fighters were introduced, the Voisin pusher designs were too vulnerable for use as day bombers. However, development continued for use as night bombers. The Voisin 8 served as the main French night bomber in 1917. The bird on the nose (blue on some aircraft, black on others) is the unit insignia; there are no personal markings.

Specifications	
Crew: 2	Dimensions: span 18m (59ft .66in); length
Powerplant: 1 x 164kW (220hp)	10.35m (33ft 11.5in); height 3.95m
Peugeot 8Aa engine	(12ft 11.5in)
Maximum speed: 118km/h (73.3mph)	Weight: 1860kg (4102lb) max take-off
Range: 350km (217.5 miles)	Armament: 1 x 7.7mm (0.303in) MG, plus
Service ceiling: n/a	180kg (397lb) bomb load

▲ Voisin 10

Escadrille VB 109 / Western Front / 1918

The Voisin 10 was a development of the Voisin 8 with more power to carry a heavier bomb load. It served as the main French night bomber in 1918. The flying being carrying a lighted bomb was the unit insignia; there were no personal markings.

Specifications	
Crew: 2	Dimensions: span 17.90m (58ft 8.7in);
Powerplant: 1 x 209kW (280hp)	length 10.35m (33ft 11.5in); height 3.95m
Renault 12Fe engine	(12ft 11.5in)
Maximum speed: 135km/h (84mph)	Weight: 2200kg (4850lb) max take-off
Range: 350km (217.5 miles)	Armament: 1 x 7.7mm (0.303in) MG, plus
Service ceiling: n/a	300kg (661lb) bomb load

issue parachutes in quantity to *Jastas*, but pilots were mistrustful of them until several successful emergency descents had been made. On 27 June 1918 *Leutnant* Steinbrecher from *Jasta 46* became the first fighter pilot to successfully use a Heineke parachute to save his life when his Albatros D.Va was shot down in combat with a mix of Sopwith Camels and SE.5a fighters. On 29 June *Leutnant* Ernst Udet, *Jasta 4 Staffelführer*, was shot down by a Breguet 14 gunner while flying his Fokker D.VII and used his parachute to good advantage and was flying again the same day.

(Udet went on to become the second-ranking German ace with 62 confirmed victories.) Many other German pilots used a parachute in the last months of the war but Allied pilots often attacked and killed German pilots in their parachutes.

The Austrian *Luftfahrtruppe* also issued parachutes to some pilots in 1918. Remarkably, there is a photograph of the first successful use of a parachute by an Austro-Hungarian airman. On the morning of 22 August 1918 the technical officer of *Flik 42/J* gave each pilot in the alert section a new German Heineke

Sitzpolster parachute and relayed the CO's emphatic orders that the parachutes were to be worn. Five-victory ace Friedrich Hefty was one of those pilots, and dutifully donned his new parachute. Shortly afterwards the group was sent to intercept a group of Hanriot fighters. As Hefty turned into the attack, machine-gun fire ripped though his Albatros, which immediately burst into flames. Unable to extinguish the flames by side-slipping, Hefty considered using the parachute; the smell of his moustache singeing made his decision for him, and he bailed out. Hefty sprained his right ankle but was alive. The army group commander sent his congratulations and granted him a 500-crown bonus and two weeks leave for his ordeal.

Americans reach the front
SUMMER 1918

When America entered the war, her aviation industry was small and primitive, and nearly all airplanes flown by Americans in combat were purchased from France.

THE FIRST 'AMERICAN' aviation unit at the Front was the *Lafayette Escadrille*, an escadrille in the *Aviation Militaire* formed at the request of Americans sympathetic to France. Most pilots were American volunteers, although the commanders were French. The *Lafayette Escadrille* became a useful propaganda tool for the French, who were hoping to encourage America into the war on their side. This unit, officially know as N124 (later SPA124 when SPADs replaced their Nieuports), had a distinguished, if not stellar, war record. After America declared war, many months elapsed before American aviators arrived in France as part of the AEF (American Expeditionary Force). Most American pilots from the *Lafayette Escadrille* were transferred to the new USAS (United States Air Service) to spread their operational experience throughout the new air service.

Significantly, when the American aviation units were formed, nearly all their airplanes were bought from the French. The only American-built airplane to see combat on the Western Front was the Liberty Plane, powered by the new V-12 Liberty Engine. The Liberty Plane was a licence-built version of the British DH.4 of 1916. This was a good airplane, but the pilot and observer were separated by the main fuel tank, hampering their ability to coordinate during air combat, a serious tactical weakness. The DH.9 solved that problem and would have been a better basis for the Liberty Plane. The Liberty Engine for the Liberty Plane was designed, tested and placed in mass production in record time. At 298kW (400hp), it was one of the most powerful engines used in World War I and gave the Liberty Plane very good performance. During the war the Liberty Engine was adapted to a

▲ **SPAD XVI**

HQ USAS / Western Front / August 1918

The SPAD XVI was developed from the SPAD XI by replacing the 164kW (220hp) Hispano-Suiza, desperately needed for SPAD fighters, with the 179kW (240hp) Lorraine. Performance was no better despite the slight power increase, nor were poor handling qualities improved. This one was flown by Brig General 'Billy' Mitchell; the marking is his personal insignia.

Specifications

Crew: 2

Powerplant: 1 x 179kW (240hp) Lorraine 8Bb engine

Maximum speed: 180km/h (112mph)

Range: n/a

Service ceiling: About 5000m (16,404ft)

Dimensions: span 11.21m (36ft 9in); length 7.84m (25ft 8.6in); height 2.84m (9ft 4in)

Weight: 1140kg (2513lb) max take-off

Armament: 1 x 7.7mm (0.303in) fixed Vickers MG and 1–2 x 7.7mm (0.303in) flexible Lewis MGs, plus 70kg (154lb) of bombs

▼ Nieuport 28

27th Aero Squadron, USAS / Western Front / Summer 1918

France preferred SPAD fighters so the Nieuport 28 was available for sale to the newly arrived USAS, becoming the first fighter type flown by an American unit. Fast and manoeuvrable, it had structural defects and a few burst into flames because of broken fuel lines. The eagle is the unit insignia.

The screaming eagle was the insignia of the 27th Aero Squadron and was used on their Nieuport 28 and SPAD XIII fighters.

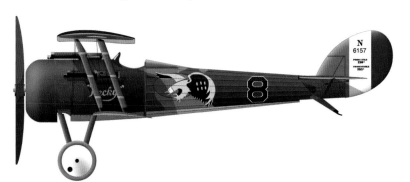

Specifications

Crew: 1

Powerplant: 1 x 119W (160hp) Gnome-Le Rhône 9N rotary piston engine

Maximum speed: 198km/h (123mph)

Range: 400km (248 miles)

Service ceiling: 5180m (16,995ft)

Dimensions: span 8.16m (26ft 9in); length 6.4m (21ft); height 2.50m (8ft 2in)

Weight: 698kg (1539lb) max take-off

Armament: 2 x 7.7mm (0.303in) fixed forward-firing Vickers MGs

Specifications

Crew: 2

Powerplant: 1 x 298kW (400hp) Packard Liberty V-12 inline piston engine

Maximum speed: 201km/h (124.7mph)

Endurance: 1 hour 50 mins

Service ceiling: 5180m (16,995ft)

Dimensions: span 12.95m (42ft 6in); length 9.19m (30ft 6in); height 3.14m (10ft 3.6in)

Weight: 1949kg (4297lb) max take-off

Armament: 2 x 7.7mm (0.303in) fixed Vickers MGs, 2 x 7.7mm (0.303in) flexible Lewis MGs; up to 146kg (322lb) of bombs

▲ DH.4 Liberty Plane

50th Aero Squadron, USAS / Western Front / Autumn 1918

The Liberty Plane was the DH.4 built under licence in the USA and fitted with the 298kW (400hp) Liberty V-12 engine. The Liberty Plane was the only American-built airplane to see service on the Western Front. Powerful and fast, it was popular as a reconnaissance plane, but crews preferred the more modern Breguet 14B2 for bombing. The Dutch cleaning woman was the squadron insignia.

▲ SPAD XI

1st Aero Squadron, USAS / Western Front / Summer 1918

Before receiving the excellent Salmson 2A2 the 1st Aero Squadron flew the SPAD XI for a time. The handling qualities of the handsome SPAD XI did not match its looks (it would stall and spin with little provocation) and crews were grateful to receive the Salmson to replace it. The American flag was the unit insignia.

Specifications

Crew: 2

Powerplant: 1 x 164kW (220hp) Hispano-Suiza 8Bc engine

Maximum speed: 185km/h (115mph)

Endurance: 2 hours 15 mins

Service ceiling: 6300m (20,669ft)

Dimensions: span 11.24m (36ft 10in); length 7.80m (25ft 7in); height 2.50m (8ft 2in)

Weight: 1035kg (2321lb) max take-off

Armament: 1 x 7.7mm (0.303in) fixed Vickers MG, 1–2 x 7.7mm (0.303in) flexible Lewis MGs, plus 70kg (154lb) of bombs

GERMAN ORDER OF BATTLE, 1 AUGUST 1918	
Unit Type	Establishment of Each Unit
56 Flieger Abteilungen (A)	6 C-type 2-seaters
37 Flieger Abteilungen	6 C-type 2-seaters
37 Flieger Abteilungen (A)	9 C-type 2-seaters
14 Flieger Abteilungen Lb	9 C-type 2-seaters
6 Reihenbildzüge	3 C-type 2-seaters with automatic cameras
81 Jagdstaffeln	13 D-type single-seat fighters
27 Bombenstaffeln	6 twin-engine G-type bombers and 3 C-type 2-seaters for daylight use
38 Schlachtstaffeln	6 CL-type 2-seaters
2 Riesenflugzeug Abteilungen	Actual strength 4-5 R-type heavy bombers

LEADING AMERICAN ACES	
Ace	Score
Capt E. Rickenbacker	26
Lt Frank Luke †	18
Maj Raoul Lufberry †	16
Capt Elliott Springs	16
Lt George Vaughn	13
Capt David Putnam †	13
Maj Reed Landis	12
Capt Eugene Kindley	12

Note: † indicates killed in the war.

number of different airplanes and overall was a major success. Even after the war, it was used in dozens of different airplanes. American production of the Liberty Plane was later severely criticized because both the airframe and engine failed to meet production goals but these goals were simply not realistic given the rudimentary state of the American aviation industry at that time. Compared to the accomplishments of other combatants, the Liberty Plane programme was a success, especially the Liberty Engine, which was comparable to the renowned British Rolls-Royce Eagle, yet could be built in much greater quantity.

As was to be expected, upon entering combat the American lack of experience showed, and the Americans suffering stinging losses at the hands of *JGII* and other experienced *Jastas*. But the survivors learned their lessons well and during the final weeks of the war developed into effective combat units.

Breakthrough on the ground

On 15 July the Germans launched their final offensive. As was the case with the earlier 1918 German offensives, it won some ground initially but was unable to achieve a breakthrough. On 18 July the Allies launched a counter-offensive, and on 8 August the British made a well concealed attack on the Somme with 456 tanks that broke the German lines. This was the beginning of the end. The German army, realizing that victory was now impossible, was demoralized.

German aviators also understood the fatal implications of the change in momentum on the ground yet air combat continued unabated. However, operations were now hindered by fuel shortages, grounding some combat planes and limiting the number of missions flown. Furthermore, German industry could no longer make up airplane losses.

▲ **Breguet 14A2**

9th Aero Squadron, USAS / Western Front / November 1918

This Breguet 14A2 was flown on night reconnaissance missions by 2nd Lt James Royer of the 9th Aero Squadron, USAS. The searchlights are the squadron insignia and the swastika was a personal insignia, a good luck symbol in several cultures before being used postwar as the symbol of the Nazi party.

Specifications

Crew: 2

Powerplant: 1 x 224kW (300hp) Renault 12Fcx inline piston engine

Maximum speed: 184km/h (114mph)

Endurance: 2 hours 45 mins

Service ceiling: 6100m (20,013ft)

Dimensions: span 14.86m (48ft 9in); length 8.87m (29ft 1in); height 3.3m (10ft 10in)

Weight: 1565kg (3450lb) max take-off

Armament: 1 x 7.7mm (0.303in) forward-firing Vickers MG; 2 x 7.7mm (0.303in) Lewis MGs; underwing racks with provision for up to 4x 120mm (4.7in) bombs

Specifications

Crew: 2

Powerplant: 1 x 171.5kW (230hp)
Salmson 9Za engine

Maximum speed: 188km/h (117mph)

Range: 500km (310.7 miles)

Service ceiling: 6250m (20,505ft)

Dimensions: span 11.75m (38ft 6.6in);
length 8.50m (27ft 10.6in); height 2.90m
(9ft 6in)

Weight: 1290kg (2844lb) max take-off

Armament: 1 x 7.7mm (0.303in) fixed
Vickers MG, 2 x 7.7mm (0.303in)
flexible Lewis MGs

▲ Salmson 2 A2

1st Aero Squadron, USAS / Western Front / Autumn 1918

The French-built Salmson 2A2 was used by American reconnaissance units, who liked its speed, climb, reliability and good handling and manoeuvrability. The American flag was the unit insignia.

▲ SPAD XIII

94th Aero Squadron, USAS / Western Front / September 1918

American fighter pilots were grateful when their Nieuports were replaced with the robust SPAD XIII. This one was flown by Capt Eddie Richenbacker of the 94th Aero Squadron, America's leading World War I ace with 26 victories, who was one of eighth aviators awarded the Medal of Honor for their war service. The 'Hat in the Ring' was the unit insignia; '1' was Richenbacker's airplane number.

Specifications

Crew: 1

Powerplant: 1 x 164kW (220hp) Hispano-
Suiza 8Bc V-8 engine

Maximum speed: 218km/h (135mph)

Endurance: 1hr 40 mins

Service ceiling: 6800m (22,310ft)

Dimensions: span span 8.08m (26ft 6in);
length 6.25m (20ft 6in); height 2.60m
(8ft 6in)

Weight: 856.5kg (1888lb) max take-off

Armament: 2 x 7.7mm (.303in) Vickers
water-cooled MGs

▲ SPAD XIII

27th Aero Squadron, USAS / Western Front / Autumn 1918

America's second-ranking ace was Lt Frank Luke of the 27th Aero Squadron, credited with 17 victories, who flew this SPAD XIII. Luke was awarded the Medal of Honor for his rapid victories. The eagle is the unit insignia; '2' was Luke's airplane number. The SPAD made such an impression on American pilots that old-fashioned combat airplanes are still sometimes called 'Spads'.

Specifications

Crew: 1

Powerplant: 1 x 164kW (220hp) Hispano-Suiza
8Bc V-8 engine

Maximum speed: 218km/h (135mph)

Endurance: 1hr 40 mins

Service ceiling: 6800m (22,310ft)

Dimensions: span span 8.08m (26ft 6in);
length 6.25m (20ft 6in); height 2.60m (8ft
6in)

Weight: 856.5kg (1888lb) max take-off

Armament: 2 x 7.7mm (.303in) Vickers
water-cooled MGs

Black September

SEPTEMBER 1918

Allied losses in September 1918, just weeks before the Armistice, were the highest of the war. German aviation remained ferociously intact, but it could not prevent defeat.

MUCH HAS BEEN WRITTEN about 'Bloody April', the month during 1917 when German air superiority was at its peak and the aggressive RFC fed obsolete airplanes flown by inexperienced airmen into the German mincing machine. RFC losses during that single month reached 245 airplanes and 319 airmen killed or missing plus 108 taken prisoner of war and 116 wounded. To that must be added French losses of 55 aircraft, 63 airmen killed or missing, 11 prisoners of war and 55 wounded.

Allied losses in September 1918, the month of the most intense air combat of the entire war, and only six weeks before the Armistice, were even worse. In September, at least 560 Allied aircraft were lost on the Western Front, most to German fighters. However, there were significant differences between the two months. 'Bloody April' was a painful defeat for the RFC, but 'Black September', despite its greater losses, was not. Allied forces were far larger in 1918, so the losses were proportionally smaller. Moreover, Allied airmen accomplished their missions despite their losses, their aircraft were technically equal to the German airplanes, their losses were being made good and their armies were advancing. The Germans, while having excellent pilots and airplanes, were outnumbered and on the defensive. And unlike the Allies, Germany was running out of resources, especially aviation fuel, and their losses were not being made good. Allied numbers continued to grow while German strength had reached a plateau.

Fierce fighting continued right up until the Armistice, but the outcome was no longer in any doubt. After the war the Germans insisted that they were 'undefeated in the air', and in a moral sense that was true. The *Luftstreitkräfte* was not driven from the skies, and German fighters fought to the end and continued to inflict losses on Allied formations that exceeded their own. However, Allied formations continued to expand their numerical superiority over the Germans and accomplished their missions despite German opposition. With technical and tactical parity, the growing imbalance of numbers could have only one outcome; defeat for the out-numbered.

Late Arrivals

Both sides continued to introduce new airplane types into service. The French were planning a major switch to two-seat fighters and had several new two-seat fighters ready for production, including the SPAD 20 and Hanriot HD.3. The single-seat Nieuport 29 fighter was also ready for production and restored Nieuport's reputation after the war.

The British were readying the excellent Martinsyde Buzzard fighter and introduced the Vickers Vimy and Handley Page V/1500 bombers just too late for combat. The Sopwith Snipe, the intended replacement for the Camel, combined a powerful 171kW (230hp) Bentley rotary with the outdated thin airfoil of the Camel. The Snipe was subject to prolonged development to make its handling qualities competitive with the thick-winged Fokker D.VII, and finally entered service in the last month of fighting. It had excellent climb and manoeuvrability, but the weight and drag of its complicated two-bay wing bracing meant it was not as fast as the Fokker, nor were its handling qualities quite as good. The Snipe was immortalized as the mount in which William Barker won the last aviation-related Victoria Cross of the war and became the standard RAF fighter after the war. Sopwith meanwhile was also planning the Dolphin II with the 224kW (300hp) Hispano-Suiza.

On the other side of the lines the Pfalz D.XV (finally a Pfalz that could match the Fokker D.VII), was at *Armeeflugparks* (Army Aircraft Parks) awaiting distribution to the *Jastas*. The fast, modern Junkers all-metal D.I fighter had just reached the Front, and the larger CL.I two-seat fighter was in production. Fokker also had two derivatives of its famous D.VII fighter ready for production. First was the V.29 parasol monoplane fighter; next was the C.I two-seat fighter that went on to a long and successful career

Specifications

Crew: 1

Powerplant: 1 x 145kW (195hp) Mercedes
 D.IIIaü engine

Maximum speed: 200km/h (124mph)

Endurance: 2 hours

Service ceiling: 7000m (22,965ft)

Dimensions: span 8.7m (29ft 1in); length
 6.95m (22ft 8in); height 2.95m (9ft 6in)

Weight: 880kg (1940lb) max take-off

Armament: 2 x 7.92mm (0.313in) LMG
 08/15 MGs

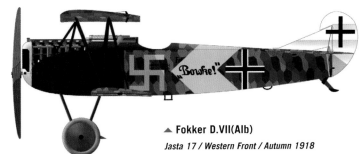

▲ Fokker D.VII(Alb)

Jasta 17 / Western Front / Autumn 1918

The Fokker D.VII was the fighter the Germans had been looking for since the Albatros D.V proved unable to match the new Allied fighters. The black nose with white radiator are the *Jasta 17* markings; the name and other markings are personal; the significance of 'Boroke' is unknown. It was flown by *Oblt* Hermann Pritsch, who scored one victory and was acting *Jastaführer* 29 May–12 June 1918.

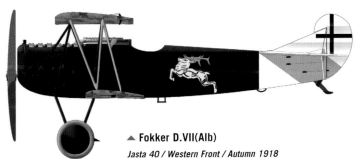

▲ Fokker D.VII(Alb)

Jasta 40 / Western Front / Autumn 1918

This D.VII was flown by *Ltn* Carl Degelow, *Staffelführer* of *Jasta 40*. An ace with 30 victories, on 9 November 1918 Degelow became the last airman to receive the Pour le Mérite. The black fuselage and white tail identified *Jasta 40*; the white stag was his personal emblem.

Specifications

Crew: 1

Powerplant: 1 x 138kW (185hp) BMW IIIa
 6-cylinder inline piston engine

Maximum speed: 205km/h (127mph)

Endurance: 2 hours

Service ceiling: 6980m (22,900ft)

Dimensions: span 8.7m (29ft 1in); length
 6.95m (22ft 8in); height 2.95m (9ft 6in)

Weight: 880kg (1940lb) max take-off

Armament: 2 x 7.92mm (0.313in) LMG
 08/15 MGs

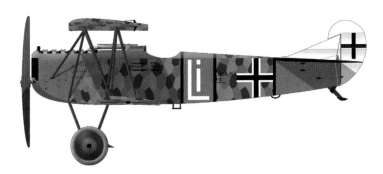

▲ Fokker D.VII(OAW)

Jasta 35b / Western Front / Autumn 1918

This elegant D.VII was flown by *Ltn d.R.* Rudolf Stark. The lilac designs on the fuselage were Stark's personal markings. Stark scored 11 victories and was the *Staffelführer* of *Jasta 35b* from 7 June 1918 to the end of the war. He wrote the well known book *Wings of War* first published in 1933. A replica of this airplane is in the USAF Museum at Wright-Patterson AFB.

Specifications

Crew: 1

Powerplant: 1 x 138kW (185hp) B.M.W. IIIa
 6-cylinder inline piston engine

Maximum speed: 205km/h (127mph)

Endurance: 2 hours

Service ceiling: 6980m (22,900ft)

Dimensions: span 8.7m (29ft 1in); length
 6.95m (22ft 8in); height 2.95m (9ft 6in)

Weight: 880kg (1940lb) max take-off

Armament: 1–2 x 7.92mm (0.313in) LMG
 08/15 MGs

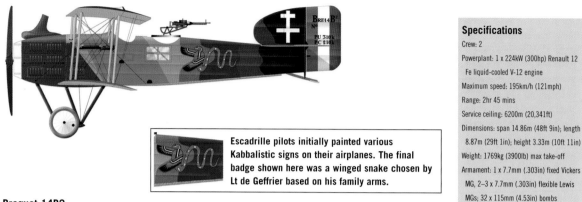

Specifications

Crew: 2

Powerplant: 1 x 224kW (300hp) Renault 12
Fe liquid-cooled V-12 engine

Maximum speed: 195km/h (121mph)

Range: 2hr 45 mins

Service ceiling: 6200m (20,341ft)

Dimensions: span 14.86m (48ft 9in); length
8.87m (29ft 1in); height 3.33m (10ft 11in)

Weight: 1769kg (3900lb) max take-off

Armament: 1 x 7.7mm (.303in) fixed Vickers
MG, 2–3 x 7.7mm (.303in) flexible Lewis
MGs; 32 x 115mm (4.53in) bombs

Escadrille pilots initially painted various Kabbalistic signs on their airplanes. The final badge shown here was a winged snake chosen by Lt de Geffrier based on his family arms.

▲ **Breguet 14B2**

Escadrille Br 107 / Western Front / 1918

The French Breguet 14B2 was the best day bomber of the war and was used in large formations during 1918. It was fast, reliable and carried a good bomb load. Crews especially appreciated its modern metal framework, which was safer than wood in a crash. The winged snake was the escadrille insignia.

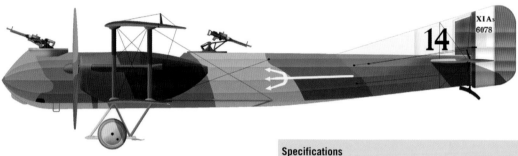

▲ **Caudron R.11**

Escadrille C 46 / Western Front / Summer 1918

During 1918 the three-seat Caudron R.11 flew along with Breguet 14 day bombers as close escort fighters, a role in which they were very effective. The R.11 was the most successful, and perhaps the only successful, multi-seat escort fighter. The white trident is the escadrille insignia; the tactical number is on the fin.

Specifications

Crew: 3

Powerplant: 2 x 160kW (215hp) Hispano-Suiza
8Bda engines

Maximum speed: 183km/h (114mph)

Range: 600km (373 miles)

Service ceiling: 5950m (19,521ft)

Dimensions: span 17.92m (58ft 9.5in);
length 11.22m (36ft 9.7in); height 2.8m
(9ft 2in)

Weight: 2165kg (4773lb) loaded

Armament: 5 x 7.7mm (.303in) flexible Lewis
MGs (2 in nose, 2 dorsal, 1 firing down)

Specifications

Crew: 1

Powerplant: 1 x 119kW (160hp) Siemens-
Halske Sh.III or IIIa rotary piston engine

Maximum speed: 180km/h (112mph)

Endurance: 2 hours

Service ceiling: 8000m (26,245ft)

Dimensions: span 8.4m (27ft 7.75in);
length 5.85m (19ft 2in); height 2.63m
(8ft 7.5in)

Weight: 740kg (1631lb) max take-off

Armament: 2 x 7.92mm (0.313in) fixed
forward-firing LMG 08/15 MGs

▲ **SSW D.III**

Jasta 4 / Western Front / Autumn 1918

The SSW D.III had exceptional climb and manoeuvrability, but its production was limited by engine availability. This one was flown by *Ltn* Ernst Udet, Germany's second-ranking ace with 62 victories. 'LO!', his fiancée's initials, was a personal marking, as was the red fuselage. Udet won the Pour le Mérite for his successes.

▲ SSW D.IV

Jasta 12 / Western Front / Autumn 1918

The SSW D.IV was developed from the D.III to offer greater speed at the expense of some loss of climb rate. However, climb and manoeuvrability remained outstanding and its pilots rated it as easily the best fighter at the Front. The blue fuselage indicated *JG II*, the white nose *Jasta 12*, and the white band was the unknown pilot's personal marking.

Specifications

Crew: 1

Powerplant: 1 x 119kW (160hp) Sh.III engine

Maximum speed: 190km/h (118mph)

Endurance: 2 hours

Service ceiling: 8000m (26,247ft)

Dimensions: span 8.35m (27ft 4.7in);
length 5.58m (18ft 3.6in); height 2.7m
(8ft 10in)

Weight: 735kg (1620lb) loaded

Armament: 2 x 7.92mm (0.313in) LMG
08/15 MGs

The face painted on *Fratz* and its name were both the personal markings of the pilot, *Ltn* Kurt Seit. Assigned to *Jasta 80b* on 4 June 1918, Seit scored five victories to become an ace.

Specifications

Crew: 1

Powerplant: 1 x 82kW (110hp) Oberursel
Ur.II engine

Maximum speed: 196km/h (122mph)

Endurance: About 1hr 30 mins

Service ceiling: n/a

Dimensions: span 7.2m (23ft 7in);
length 5.78m (18ft 11.5in); height 2.65m
(8ft 8in)

Weight: 588kg (1296lb) max take-off

Armament: 2 x 7.92mm (0.313in) MGs

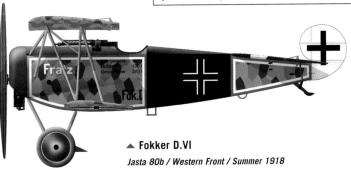

▲ Fokker D.VI

Jasta 80b / Western Front / Summer 1918

The little-known Fokker D.VI served in small numbers. Clearly related to the earlier Fokker Triplane and the contemporary D.VII, it was manoeuvrable and fast at low altitude, but needed more power. It was replaced in production by the more promising Fokker E.V monoplane fighter.

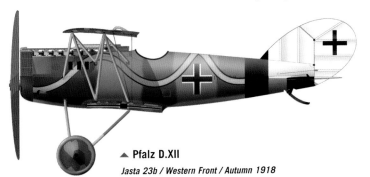

▲ Pfalz D.XII

Jasta 23b / Western Front / Autumn 1918

The Pfalz D.XII replaced the Pfalz D.III in production. Strong and fast, it was not as manoeuvrable as the Fokker D.VII and was never popular with pilots, all of whom wanted the legendary Fokker D.VII instead. The black and white tailplane was the unit marking; the yellow stripes were the pilot's personal markings.

Specifications

Crew: 1

Powerplant: 1 x 130.5kW (175hp) Mercedes
D.IIIa engine

Maximum speed: 180km/h (112mph)

Endurance: About 2 hours

Service ceiling: 5000m (16,404ft)

Dimensions: span 9m (29ft 6.3in); length
6.35m (20ft 10in); height 2.7m (8ft 10in)

Weight: 892kg (1966lb) max take-off

Armament: 2 x 7.92mm (0.312in)
Spandau MGs

GERMAN ORDER OF BATTLE, 11 NOVEMBER 1918	
Unit Type	Establishment
57 Flieger Abteilungen (A)	342 C-type 2-seaters
31 Flieger Abteilungen	186 C-type 2-seaters
37 Flieger Abteilungen (A)	333 C-type 2-seaters
10 Flieger Abteilungen Lb	90 C-type 2-seaters
5 Flieger Abteilungen (A) Lb	30 C-type 2-seaters
6 Flieger Abteilungen Pascha	36 C-type 2-seaters
6 Reihenbildzüge	3 C-type 2-seaters with automatic cameras
90 Jagdstaffeln	1134-1296 D-type single-seat fighters
8 Bombengeschwadern	162 twin-engine G-type bombers
38 Schlachtstaffeln	228 CL-type 2-seaters
2 Riesenflugzeug Abteilungen	6 R-type heavy bombers
56 Feldluftschiffer Abteilungen	
186 Ballonzüge	

FRENCH AVIATION MILITAIRE, 11 NOVEMBER 1918	
Type	Strength
Fighters	
SPAD 13	1152
Caudron R.11	60
Subtotal Fighters	**1,212**
Bombers	
Breguet 14 B2	225 (Day)
Voisin 10	135 (Night)
Farman F.50	45 (Night)
Caproni Ca.3	20 (Night)
Subtotal Bombers	**425**
Reconnaissance	
Breguet 14 A2	645
Salmson 2 A2	530
SPAD 11/16	305
Caudron R.11	30
Voisin 10	75
Subtotal Reconnaissance	**1,585**
Total	**3,222**

after the war. The SSW D.VI, a parasol monoplane development of the SSW D.IV, also exhibited exceptional climb and ceiling, and would certainly have replaced the D.IV biplane in production. The AEG G.IVk armoured, twin-engine ground attack aircraft with two flexible 20mm Becker cannon for tank busting was already at the Front, and the armoured Ago S.I single-engine tank buster with 20mm Becker was in flight testing. All-metal Giant bombers were also in work; the Staaken E.4/20 four-engine monoplane was clocked at 225km/h (140mph), a milestone for an airplane of its size.

In Retrospect

The airplane entered the Great War as a promising yet hazardous experiment, and soon became a vital necessity. The airplanes themselves evolved quickly, yet were still primitive and only moderately reliable by the end of World War I. Many different designs and configurations were tried, all created for a reason, but some were more practical and useful than others. The crucible of war ruthlessly sorted them out.

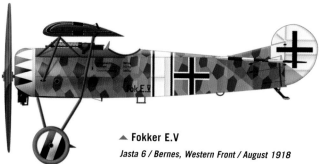

▲ **Fokker E.V**

Jasta 6 / Bernes, Western Front / August 1918

The Fokker E.V parasol monoplane reached the Front in August 1918. The wing was very strong when built as designed, but manufacturing defects soon led to wing failures in flight. It was withdrawn for wing replacement, redesignated the D.VIII and sent back to the Front a few weeks before the Armistice. This example was flown briefly by *Ltn* Richard Wenzel.

Specifications

Crew: 1

Powerplant: 1 x 82kW (110hp) Oberursel Ur.II engine

Maximum speed: 204km/h (127mph)

Endurance: About 1hr 30 mins

Service ceiling: About 6000m (19,685ft)

Dimensions: span 8.34m (27ft 4in); length 5.86m (19ft 3in); height 2.6m (8ft 6in)

Weight: 605kg (1334lb) max take-off

Armament: 2 x 7.92mm (0.313in) MGs

▲ Fokker E.V

Jasta 6 / Bernes, Western Front / August 1918

The black and white cowling, wheels and taiplane were the unit markings and the fuselage stripe was a personal marking. The E.V represented the best and worst of the German aviation industry, combining innovative, state of the art structure and aerodynamics with a 1915 vintage engine.

Specifications

Crew: 1

Powerplant: 1 x 82kW (110hp) Oberursel
 Ur.II engine

Maximum speed: 204km/h (127mph)

Endurance: About 1hr 30 mins

Service ceiling: About 6000m (19,685ft)

Dimensions: span 8.34m (27ft 4in); length
 5.86m (19ft 3in); height 2.6m (8ft 6in)

Weight: 605kg (1334lb) max take-off

Armament: 2 x 7.92mm (0.313in) MGs

Specifications

Crew: 1

Powerplant: 1 x 172kW (230hp) Bentley
 B.R.2 rotary piston engine

Maximum speed: 195km/h (121mph)

Endurance: 3 hours

Service ceiling: 5945m (19,500ft)

Dimensions: span 9.47m (31ft 1in); length
 6.05m (19ft 10in); height 2.89m (9ft 6in)

Weight: 916kg (2,020lb) max take-off

Armament: 2 x 7.7mm (0.313in) fixed
 forward-firing Vickers LMG 08/15 MGs

▲ Sopwith Snipe

No. 201 Squadron, RAF / Western Front / November 1918

The Snipe arrived at the Front in the last few weeks of the war; this example was flown by Capt William Barker in the combat for which he was awarded the Victoria Cross. Like the Fokker E.V, the Snipe represented the best and worst of the industry that produced it, a state of the art rotary engine with a structure and aerodynamics rooted in 1916 technology. Its powerful engine gave the Snipe good performance and it became the standard RAF postwar fighter despite the availability of better designs like the Dolphin II and Martinsyde Buzzard. The B.R.2 and Sh.IIIa represented the apogee of the rotary engine, a technological dead end that quickly disappeared after the war.

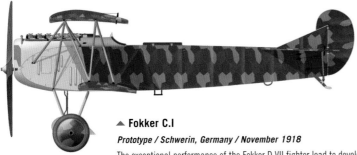

▲ Fokker C.I

Prototype / Schwerin, Germany / November 1918

The exceptional performance of the Fokker D.VII fighter lead to development of a two-seat version, the C.I. Arriving too late to see wartime service, it went on to a long postwar career in Holland and elsewhere. The prototype, the V.38, is shown here in standard factory finish without national insignia or other markings.

Specifications

Crew: 2

Powerplant: 1 x 140kW (185hp) BMW IIIa
 engine

Maximum speed: 175km/h (108.7mph)

Endurance: 4 hours

Service ceiling: About 6000m (19,685ft)

Dimensions: span 10.63m (34ft 10.5in);
 length 7.23m (23ft 8.6in); height unknown

Weight: 1180kg (2601lb) loaded

Armament: 1 x 7.92mm (.312in) fixed and 1
 x 7.92mm (.312in) flexible LMG 08/15 MGs

Specifications

Crew: 2

Powerplant: 1 x 138kW (185hp) BMW.IIIa
engine

Maximum speed: 190km/h (118mph)

Range: 700km (435 miles)

Service ceiling: n/a

Dimensions: span 11.09m (36ft 4.5in);
length 7.90m (25ft 11in) height 2.65m
(8ft 3in)

Weight: 1135kg (2502lb) max take-off

Armament: 2 x 7.92mm (0.313in) fixed MGs
and 1 x 7.92mm (0.313in) LMG 08/15 MG

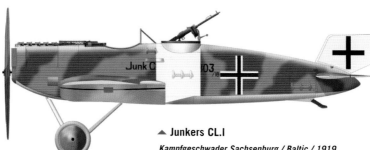

▲ Junkers CL.I

Kampfgeschwader Sachsenburg / Baltic / 1919

Junkers' innovative, all-metal structural technology was applied to a low-wing
monoplane fighter, the D.I, and the slightly larger two-seat CL-type shown here.
Arriving just too late to see combat in World War I, they served reliably with
German paramilitary units in the Baltic after the war.

Specifications

Crew: 1

Powerplant: 1 x 138kW (185hp)
BMW.IIIa engine

Maximum speed: 200km/h (124mph)

Service ceiling: 7000m (22,966ft)

Endurance: 2 hours

Dimensions: span 8.6m (28ft 2.5in); length
6.5m (21ft 3.8in); height 2.7m (8ft 10in)

Weight: 928kg (2046lb) max take-off

Armament: 2 x 7.92mm (0.312in) LMG
08/15 MGs

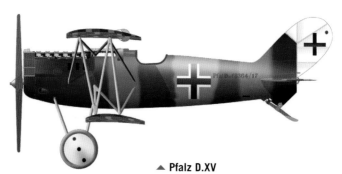

▲ Pfalz D.XV

Prototype / Germany / November 1918

The excellent Pfalz D.XV arrived at the *armeeflugparks* the last week of the war.
Considered as good as the Fokker D.VII, the Pfalz D.XV never had the opportunity
to make a reputation and is virtually unknown today. The Pfalz company did not
survive after the war and is remembered chiefly for its elegant but mediocre D.III.

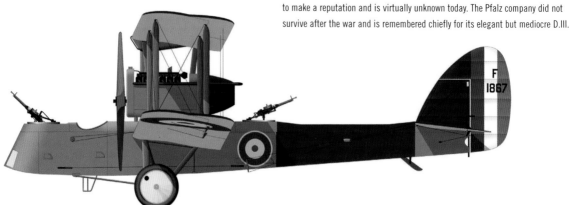

▲ De Havilland DH.10

No. 104 Squadron, RAF / Azlot, Western Front / November 1918

The DH.10 was a fine bomber that arrived in time for one bombing mission before
the Armistice. It was a typically clean, robust de Havilland design. This airplane is
the one flown by Capt E. Garland from Azlot on 10 November 1918 on the sole
DH.10 bombing mission against the German aerodrome at Sarrebourg.

Specifications

Crew: 3

Powerplant: 2x 302kW (405hp)
Liberty V-12 engines

Maximum speed: 187km/h (116.5mph)

Endurance: 5 hours 45 mins

Service ceiling: 5029m (16,500ft)

Dimensions: span 19.97m (65ft 6in);
length 12.06m (39ft 7in); height 4.44m
(14ft 7in)

Weight: 4082kg (9000lb) loaded

Armament: 4 x 7.7mm (0.303in) Lewis MGs,
6 x 104kg (230lb) bombs

RAF AT THE ARMISTICE, WESTERN FRONT		
Duty	Planes	Squadrons
Corps Reconnaissance	370	20
Fighter Reconnaissance	138	6
Day Bombing	333	19
Short-range Night Bombing	113	6
Long-range Night Bombing	80	8
Single-Seat Fighters	747	38
GHQ Communications	18	1
Of Above: Serviceable	1,576	
Unserviceable	223	
Total	**1,799**	

WWI AVIATION CASUALITES				
Casualties	British	French	American	German
Killed	6,166	2,872	681	5,853
Wounded	7,245	2,922	127	7,302
Missing	3,212	1,461	72	2,751
Total	16,623	7,255	880	15,906

▼ SPAD 20

6E Escadrille, 2nd Fighter Regiment / France / 1920

The compact SPAD 20 two-seat fighter was a completely new design that delivered the speed and manoeuvrability desired but not achieved by the SPAD XI and XVI. Too late for combat, it served in small numbers postwar. It exemplified the two-seat fighters the Allies intended to use in large numbers had the war continued into 1919.

Specifications

Crew: 2

Powerplant: 1 x 224kW (300hp) Hispano-
    Suiza 8Fb

Maximum speed: 242km/h (150mph)

Range: n/a

Service ceiling: 8900m (29,199ft)

Dimensions: span 9.8m (32ft 1.8in);
    length 7.34m (24ft 1in); height 2.87m
    (9ft 5in)

Weight: 1106kg (2438lb) loaded

Armament: 2 x 7.7mm (0.303in) Vickers
    MGs and 1 x 7.7mm (0.303in) Lewis MG

▲ Nieuport 29

Escadrille SPA 81 / France / 1920

The Nieuport 29 arrived too late for combat. The SPAD designs like the SPAD XIII had reached the end of their development potential and the all-new Nieuport 29 was chosen as the standard French postwar fighter.

Specifications

Crew: 1

Powerplant: 1 x 224kW (300hp) Hispano-Suiza
    8Fb 8-cylinder Vee piston engine

Maximum speed: 235km/h (146mph)

Range: 580km (360 miles)

Service ceiling: 8500m (27,885ft)

Dimensions: span 9.7m (31ft 10in); length
    6.49m (21ft 3in); height 2.56m (8ft 5in)

Weight: 1150kg (2535lb) loaded

Armament: 2 x 7.7mm (0.303in) fixed forward-
    firing Vickers MGs

Index

Page numbers in *italics* refer to illustrations.